Published by Molehill Books

ISBN-13 978-1-50062-261-9

Also available as a Kindle ebook
ISBN-13 978-1-84396-203-8

Cover by Bea Haut

Pre-press production
www.ebookversions.com

Acknowledgements

My warmest thanks to Asia Haut for her tireless support and many excellent suggestions; to Mimi Sanderson, a staunch and reliable reader and inexhaustible source of much-needed feedback; to Barbara Levick for her readings at various stages and steady encouragement; and to Ginger Hjelmaa and Vanessa Vie for their reassuring reception of the book. And finally, my sincere thanks to Charles Batchelor who so generously guided me through a financial crisis during the writing of this book.

In memory of Irene Smith,

my mother, and Joan Gummer, my teacher.

16 TAKES
ON A
SELF-INVENTED
WOMAN

feminism & identity

Mavis Haut

MOLEHILL BOOKS

Contents

"...how much better to have
a future in front of us, rather than
some new version of the past."
Luce Irigaray – *Sexes & Genealogies.*

"Some day there will be girls
and women whose name will no longer
signify purely an opposite of the
masculine, but something in itself ...
the feminine human being."
Rainer Maria Rilke – *Letters to a Young Poet.*

"Feminism was a passionate,
humorous, and politically rigorous movement.
Disrespectful of dominant norms, but aware
of its responsibility for the masses of women whose
rage and vision it embodied, the collective endeavour
of the women's movement is one of the most
successful political experiments of the 20th century."
Rosi Braidotti – *Nomadic Theory*.

Introduction.

Yes, We Need Another Book on Feminism

Even the most persevering and patently justified feminist demands are only implemented when they do not obstruct the purposes of the status quo. The system equivocates – a demand is unrealistic, untimely, un-affordable – and the system stays in place. Women, often angry and very vocal women, continue to protest but their perceptions of themselves and their entitlements inconvenience and annoy the system, and it clutches at clichés and straws and anything else that might preserve traditional values in a stable society. Haven't generous concessions already been made? Of course there is a place for women in male society: they are as free as men to contribute to both the public and their own household economies to the best of their ability. There is no logical reason for all this discontent. And so the familiar misogynist stereotype reappears: women are venal and grasping, they are seeking material gratifications and to ensnare future husbands, they scheme to arouse male desire.

We are all, in greater or lesser degree, entangled in this web. Feminists too. There has been a tendency for every generation of feminists to focus on the shortcomings of women's earlier initiatives, especially the most recent ones. This may provide a new momentum and direction, but it lacks the historical perspective that recognises the particular forces, conscious and less conscious, that gave shape to women's desires, needs and rights at other points in time. This book has tried to supply a simple account of some of the ideas that animated the feminist movement which had begun to ferment roughly a decade after the publication of *The Second Sex.* The inclusion of retrospective material does not make this an exercise in nostalgia . Feminist thinking always emerges from earlier struggles with the existing culture. In the beginning , it must focus on a need for basic rights, later on the failure to relate to women through their own understanding of themselves rather than through the distorting mirror of an immovably masculinist social order. For many second-wave feminists this second stage gradually hardened into a conviction that women's liberation could progress no further without radical changes to the entire culture.

A system founded on hierarchy, the accumulation of private property and power is incapable of incorporating the equity that is the inspiration of feminism. The most instinctive reaction is either to appeal to or confront governing powers. Assertive women insist that counter-actions must be more aggresive. Others take the more introspective position that only a profoundly changed perception of reality can reveal what woman could do if she could get beyond prevailing (masculinist) definitions of herself and humanity. The present text notes that women come up every day with unsubordinated interpretations of ordinary events and practical and cultural experiences. These may not have intended to be feminist or be perceived as such, but any interpretation that is able to break free of the contraints of a male-dominated context is displaying a potential for feminist transformation, an issue in which feminists are currently expressing considerable interest.

This book will not be working from within the prevailing system. It will focus on the potential of the unadulterated perceptions of women and their power to create social change. This potential has only taken on visible existence comparatively recently, but it has always existed in an undercurrent of knowledge with a long and unspoken history: women have always understood that they did not correspond with their description, were not as they were said to be, and that representations and even self-representations – often dictated purely by the need for survival – were mostly fictions. This silent undercurrent has been an essential element of female consciousness and of feminism in all its past, present and still hypothetical shapes. Whether she has done so intentionally or especially consciously, woman has lived the life of a shape-shifter, a being with no fixed identity or true likeness. In some feminist circles, it has been argued she might never see fit to take on a definitive form.

These sixteen takes are connected by the motif of a self-invented woman. This figure contains a non-exclusive invitation to perceive every experience – whether personal, political, social, legal, definitional, intellectual, aesthetic, relational, emotional, or in any other conceivable category – as potentially containing the same degree of feminine value and meaning as it currently does of acknowleged masculine content. So far, little more than half the mosaic has been assembled. A future that supported uncompromising feminine values may look utopian – true, it doesn't yet exist. But men were contemplating flight long before they had any possibility of accomplishing it. Using a miscellaneous handful of ideas, this book demonstrates ways in which concepts can shape and transform how people identify themselves and their surrounding environment. If this re-identification process appears to be endless, so too did the historical period during which no alternative to a masculinist order could even be envisaged. People who purport to be educated may have ceased to deny the fact that neither sex possesses natural or evolutionary superi- ority, but unspoken preference has still invariably been given to the male. This book asserts that if a *self-defined* and *different* woman could shape herself independently and separately from the dominant male, and – most crucially – from his definitions of her, her simple, autonomous presence would be enough to stimulate change and gradually destabilise the masculine tradition.

Of course, even though we live together regulated by theory on almost every level, to implement an idea is never simple. Innundated as we are by parings of garbled knowledge and shreds of superstition, we cling to precedents in custom and law, and often fail to think of more appropriate applications of egalitarian principles. Feminists have long since pointed out that woman has not only been defined as a substandard variety of an essentially male species, she has been constructed to complement men's imaginings and desires. If she were understood as someone who is not just an opposite in a male humanity, but is *different* in a *bi-gendered* human race, she would create a contradiction that the status quo would not be able to suppress. Her mere existence would expose the exclusionist basis on which common understanding so often rests.

The objective of this book is quite precise. It does not try to incite confrontational engagements in order to defeat monolithic masculinism (1) or to participate in a war between the sexes. Women's engagements in struggles and skirmishes have normally been fuelled more by issues in need of resolution than the desire for victory over an enemy. Feminism did not emerge out of a manly desire to conquer rival forces or to preserve a downside-up version of what is already in place. No sea-change could emerge out of this. The feminism represented here seeks to unfix the system, to expose it to itself and to others, to produce an awarenesss that leaves no rational option except to change. Change is not impossible. Women have already proved their ingenuity and the feminist experiment has moved steadily forward ever since the masculinist context first provoked it into action. (2)

Fluidity

A recurring theme here is the protean character of feminism and its apparently endless ability to find ways of applying itself in virtually any and every situation or location. Much has been said and written about the fluid character of the feminine but the longterm problem of dichotomy has been left unresolved and continues to dominate the overall organisation of our customary ways of perceiving. In the West at least, our thoughts have been conditioned by polarities which anchor fixed meanings and positions to apparently fixed oppositions. Black is opposite to white, innocent to guilty, good to evil and so on. Typically, one pole has always been preferred over its opposite, or 'other'. This opposite is produced by reflex . Dichotomous structures do not tolerate indeterminacy and we feel more comfortable when doubt does not arise. The result is a situation where a man can represent himself as the eternal standard by which being human is defined, but a woman, routinely identified as the opposite of man, can only personify the opposition (3). Thus she is often seen as hostile but, as her definition depends on his, she cannot assert her autonomy. A man is autonomous, fixed in place, because woman is his opposite or 'other'. Though this may situate him beyond change , it is not the product of self-regulation . A person in a more fluid state – she may rather more often and more easily be a woman – is harder to define.. She reconstitutes herself in accordance with inbuilt fluctuations in her bodily rhythms and her consciousness more than by rigid categories of sex and gender. While the fixed hierarchy continues to insist that social order would crumble without it, in fact fixity constricts free interplay between individual s and stunts the growth of non-exploitative relationships.

As the present text skips from one subject to another, it mimics the fluid dynamic of a feminism that can change its tack according to variations or mutations in social and cultural needs. The more patriarchal model of dogma and unbending reasoning is not appropriate when considering questions either of change or of non-discriminatory inclusiveness. A feminism which has abandoned the old model of fixed linear continuities can adapt to different others and contexts with full freedom of movement. The dedication of some third-wave feminist philosophy to free movement is demonstrated in Rosi Braidotti's term "nomadic". The word suggests a loose unity with enough elasticity to encompass an apparently scattered collection of fragments. "Nomadic" seems to have grown from sources that in many ways also produced the second wave term, "marginal", but nomadic fits better with the present age of extended spaces, uprootings and unprecedented dispersals. The nomadic also suggests a departure from mainstream attachments and ways of thinking that are based on binary splits that separate mind from body or theory from practice. Splits are invariably discriminatory and, historically, the segregative signifier which marginalised its supposed opposite was always masculine. A male monoculture is no longer sufficient to our enlarged perception of reality and the nomadic refuses to remain confined to a cramped position on the fringes. Set free to wander, it is "framed by perceptions, concepts, and imaginings that cannot be reducd to human, rational consciousness .. indexed on affirmation ..." (4). This wide and generous perception stretches out beyond the confines of the human and on into the natural world. One might perhaps claim that it is often more accessible to women. That though the longing for a world that is less brutalised by human exploitation is shared by both men and women, the endless struggle to overcome the man-made disadvantages of their own exploitation has taught women about the need for all-inclusive as well as ingenious strategies.

To persuade a society run for dominant males to accept women on terms that are fair and appropriate is obviously a gargantuan undertaking. However, most of us would concede that feminism has been a record of endurance as well as a catalogue of survival tactics. It has also supplied a picaresque narrative of a feminine self that fluctuates between being disguised and unrecognised, and steers between comic and openly heroic. But even these modes have been undergoing change. This book proposes that the best way for feminists to initiate change is through the integration of countless different contributions and expressions of female identity, never mind what their variety so long as they proceed from a self-perception that does not emerge from the fantasies of another gender that has other motivations. Authentic female autonomy is only going to be found in authentic females.

Though real social change will not happen without a profound shift in the identities of both women and men, men will have little reason to change their self-image or behaviour until they are forced to recognise that different, non-masculine, human sub-jects really do exist alongside them, and that to inherit a ready-made male superiority is no longer a mark of manliness. It is up to women to dismantle and replace the identity that a masculinist regime has imposed upon them. However tiny or uncertain the outcomes, the endless, small acts of self-construction through which women bring themselves into being are fundamental to any radical change in woman's predicament. Feminists need to be patient as well as hopeful. "...qualitative shifts will not emerge dialectically from a direct and violent confrontation with the present [but] .. as praxis from conditions that are not there yet..." (5).

These conditions are progressing in increments that are barely visible but also myriad.

Hard Realities Have Already Been Confronted

In fact, feminism has seldom had a single fixed or final objective: it has normally made specific demands in specific contexts. In their turn, many of these demands have been popularly perceived as feminism's totality. To obtain a voice in the social continuum, twentieth-century feminists had to break into entrenched masculine monopolies and force the hard-to-attain objective of rectifying the most glaring abuses of gender inequality. Equal rights have at least become a theoretical requirement, even if their practice has never been achieved. But, on becoming property-owning, voting, working, tax-paying citizens, women were swiftly recruited into an aggressive culture of male individualism. Though it may be advertised as the reward for merit or ability, power still normally rests in the hands of (selected) males, and the more evolved and collaborative social contract that would allow the mass of women to reap genuine benefits is habitually passed over. A few fortunate women may have procured at least the early stages of equality and can begin the work of self-determination, but the worldwide majority of women still have little influence in the shaping of their own lives. Modern feminism has altered the lives of many women, but it has barely brushed the surface of male society. Women in public positions have to conform to strictly masculine standards of evaluation and behaviour. 'New men' may have grown more sensitive to women's realities – some men always were – and some have recognised and accepted more 'feminine' aspects of themselves, but change has not been forced upon the male multitude. The social bedrock of long-established icons of masculine supremacy stays solidly in place. On the other hand, wherever 'masculine' aspects (*not* complete identities) of women have been developed, a flood of previously untapped potential has been released. Women have gained new perspectives and some have acquired an almost bilingual fluency in the meanings and usages of both genders. It has become much easier to imagine a future which would feel able to incorporate a different and new 'new woman'. Having proved herself competent in a man's world, she can now turn to making space in it where she can exist as a woman.

A new feminism, founded on more than demands for increased rights and concessions, would of course strike to the heart of the old male fantasy and stir up a hornet's nest of dormant misogynies and recriminations against feminists. Anti-feminist propoganda remains robust and feminists are still stereotyped as bitter, vindictive, and driven by penis envy. Feminism is portrayed as a refuge for sexually unfulfilled, unattractive women who secretly want to be men. Though this is just another chapter in an endless, repetitive conflict which has been refurbished for each new historical phase, it always generates fresh anxiety and uncertainty about the nature of 'feminine' identity. Ironically, some women become so overwhelmed by programmed opinion they increase their allegiance to sovereign masculine values. Nevertheless, some interpretations of feminism and feminine identity have also displayed an unquenchable buoyancy. One particularly memorable and lively comment captures the babel of confusion in the term 'post-feminist': "Now we're post-post-post-feminist, and you don't have to be masculine to be feminine." (6) The catchphrase 'post-feminist' suggests that, with equal rights now enshrined in law, women are free to compete with men in the open market of an open society. It implies that feminism has become obsolete and can be packed safely away in the vaults of history. But this perfunctory formula fails to note that the institutions which supposedly granted women equal rights were devised to secure perpetual advantage for the male. Equal rights in this context become a covert means of securing female collusion in sustaining male dominance.

Though equality has never been achieved through reason and altruism alone, direct action also meets obstacles. Even in modernised societies, women's struggles to acquire control over their own bodies and reproduction produce painful consequences. Fear of damaging children can block women's escape from domestic abuse and impede collective actions. Patriarchal societies meanwhile maintain punitive control of sexual unions and impregnations and justify criminal behaviour with legal or religious pretexts and talk of "honour". The male sexual organ is awarded the title of 'phallus' and a position as a symbol of moral and intellectual superiority; reason and language are famously affiliated to the masculine ; woman is summarily installed as a less rational substratum of mankind. The dominant male prototype for human excellence bars the female from ever possessing full human worth. Men and women may be bound and regulated by the same hierarchies and power structures, but the great mass of women, disadvantaged by standards applying to a sex that is not their own, are regularly to be found at the bottom of the pyramid. Aggression, repression and misogyny are unavoidable in societies where one sex dominates the other.

In hindsight, we can see that the last substantial surge of feminism did not go far enough. Modifications and improvements were agreed, where much more radical changes were, and still are, needed. If a yardstick measures nothing except masculine excellence, it empowers only the most masculine aspects of women and this disables the feminine aspect of women and reinforces male supremacy. A woman cannot establish herself as authentically female until she has disengaged from the male prototype and can start putting together her own self-invented reality. The man-made woman will always be produced to affirm a social order built on traditional positions of control and subjection.

These sixteen 'takes' visit – or revisit – a hetero-genous composite of ideas, ideologies, narratives and experiences held together by a determi-nation to find a foothold wherever it is possible.

This Book And Its Chapters

This book is episodic and may seem unsystematic. But expressions of the feminine are regularly shaped out of whatever comes to hand, and these subject materials are no different. They are miscellaneous snatches of an endless and continuing conversation about what advances, represents or goes into the making of an authentic woman, and what effects she might have in future circumstances, and what obstructs her. Some of these 'takes' on our self-generated woman-in-the-making are based on familiar subjects or on commentaries, manifestos and novels. Others focus on unconventional perceptions or rewrit-ing cultural or historical myths. Some dismantle abusive practices and institutions as they affect women. A mixed collection of feminist theories and attitudes have elbowed their way into a collective conversation. A number have French origins – Luce Irigaray's uncompromising and enriching perceptions of the strengths and unexpected uses of feminine characteristics normally seen as disabling were a special touchstone. Coming from a tightly structured culture which is well known for its enduring pre-occupation with 'reason', a French feminist is perhaps particularly well prepared for confrontations where, with irrational invariability, reason is characterised as a masculine dynamic.

Section one sets out some feminist territories.

Chapter 1 shows how 'difference' was a major issue for second wave feminists. It notes that wherever the phallus denotes power and its lack means weakness, biological and cultural issues are being confused. Because society is based on masculine norms, it is necessary to examine 'difference' in all feminist dialogues and ventures. A bona fide woman can only be articulated in an uncontaminated frame of reference. Some strands of feminism take 'atopic' (i.e. in no place) to indicate that, in a strictly masculine world, nowhere is the only unappropriated space where a woman can function without being limited by a male-based system.(7)

Chapter 2 elaborates on Michèle le Doeuff's demolition of philosophy's boast that it expresses perfect reasoning. Reason, in its pure state, with philosophy at its pinnacle, has been regularly cited as the eternal, masculine kernel of human intelligence. But in *The Philosophical Imaginary,* le Doeuff establishes that irrational/ imaginary elements must necessarily be present in reasoning and that any discourse that claims to be perfectly rational has to be suppressing non-rational elements. A feminist debate then discusses the merits and demerits of masculine-oriented logic for producing undistorted feminine meanings.

Chapter 3 explores gender-based responses to moral problems. The matter is taken up independently by both Luce Irigaray and Carol Gilligan. Each notes differences in the ethical understanding and behaviour of males and females – Gilligan includes children among her case studies – and both conclude that for optimal moral function the two understandings need, as both writers put it, to "marry".

Chapter 4 attaches itself to firm social and material realities. It re-examines the historic demand for female virginity before marriage, and reviews the crumbling of traditions about marriage as woman's destiny and therefore her foremost desire. Some of the numerous remnants of such attitudes in current western customs and practices are noted.

Chapter 5 reopens the subject of 'feminine' neuroses and examines Freud's dogmatic view that hysteria stems from repression and a woman's fear that she has been castrated. Luce Irigary explores the use of hysteria as a feminist tool and Joanna Russ plays fierce, comic games with hysteria and the feminine in her novel, *The Female Man* .

Chapter 6 discusses 'masquerade'. This hysterical and contradictory parody of femininity was seen by one of Freud's female colleagues as a response to the symbolic theft of the Father's phallus. *King Lear* is re-read as an instance of proto-masquerade and Cordelia's behaviour is represented as the natural response of a proto-feminist.

Chapter 7 considers the motives of women who prefer to perceive themselves as 'nothing' rather than conform to the projections of patriarchal definitions of woman. The text takes up this theme, once again in reference to *Lear*, and then to examples in film and the personal correspondence of three feminist novelists.

Section 2 challenges some essentially male institutions and assumptions.

Chapter 8 realigns Valerie Solanas – notorious both for her *Scum Manifesto* and for shooting Andy Warhol – as a satirist who overstepped the limits observed by her female contemporaries and how she reinvented herself in a highly theatrical inversion of masquerade.

In Chapter 9, two stereotyped notions of feminine behaviour, passive sexuality and masochism, are perceived as male fantasies arising from fear of female power. Angela Carter draws her own conclusions about Sade's sexually active women, Fatima Mernissi observes Freud's odd hostility to foreplay from a Muslim perspective, and Roberto Calasso celebrates the passive eroticism of Ancient Greece. These texts all work to reinstate a tradition that has long regarded passive pleasure as a natural aspect of love's evolution.

Chapter 10 suggests that male control over women's sexuality is the primary objective of monotheism and Abrahamic religious doctrines. Holding that women are physically unclean, spiritually inferior and a secondary part of mankind, they protect their single father-god by fiercely eliminating parallel single gods, plural, less punitive gods, and, above all, the unholy, even diabolical goddesses who represent female power.

Chapter 11 discusses the motives of contemporary pornography and asserts that it deliberately witholds satisfaction from its users with the aim of increasing consumerist desire. Early pornography was intended to amuse its readers; it did not distort or debase the female body image with physical anomalies intended to destroy women's confidence in normal female anatomy.

Section 3 reappraises some qualities traditionally associated with the feminine.

Chapter 12 examines traditions of romantic love, a passionate state, which both Freud and Lacan dismiss as fantasy-based. Two feminist philosophers discuss the links between sacred and profane love. Three novels about romantic love show some significant similarities but also quite clear variations between masculine and feminine approaches to romantic passion.

Chapter 13 considers the practice of "feminine writing" and the suggestion that it might be possible to have a feminine variant of language that could avoid masculine structures. However, interpretations of what may be meant by "feminine writing" are diverse and resonate on many levels. In this chapter the focus is on content over style and uses the work of four feminist writers to illustrate feminist diversity.

In Chapter 14, several feminist works of fiction demonstrate the expressive/ creative potential of silence and show how age-old efforts to suppress the female voice can sometimes gestate unexpected internal spaces and alternative forms of thought.

Chapter 15 focuses on the common portrayal of darkness as the feminine opposite of the enlightened masculine, then considers it as a positive force in feminine development. But a long past history that links darkness to both real and mythological women also engenders fear of the occult. The figure of the witch initially grew out of women's nocturnal cults of a fertility goddess and fear of an all-powerful mother led to violent persecution. The ordinary, human mother also seems to possess unearthly power. A locus of all its earliest experiences, she is also the mirror that reflects the infant to itself and the gateway that gives entry into the world outside. Lullabies and stories told to children at bedtime also have maternal origins and condition a child's safe entry into a primal world of dreams and darkness.

Chapter 16 revisits the works of various social anthropologists who wrote about prehistoric and matri-achal matrilineal societies. Some anthropologists con-firm the continuing existence of present-day matrilineal groups, though such views are not in favour with most scholars. Ancient Greek drama openly refers to the bloody displacement of matriarchal power. Among these, Antigone has been a particular subject of feminist and other discussions relating to moral philosophy.

And, finally, the Epilogue. As the book pursued its sixteen rather random lines of thoughts and observations, it repeatedly confirmed the need for a continuing feminism. In a few added afterthoughts, the Epilogue traces certain links between the main contents of the book and third-wave feminist theory. The thinking of second-wave feminism reflects a period of upheaval when loss of confidence in traditional political, philosophical, moral, and religious systems was causing great shifts of perspective. Some of these changes were not only absorbed by but also driven by feminism. The epilogue briefly discusses how third-wave feminist philosophers have extended problems of difference from issues related purely to feminism into questions about humankind's position in the universe. If this sounds like a problem with no possible solution, so did almost all questions before they had an answer.

Feminine/Feminist Pasts and Female Futures

Our protean and atopic feminist is both fragmentary and fantastical. But, as men presently conceive of them, women are by nature already fragmentary and fantastical. Feminist philosophers can rightly say that woman is nowhere and nothing and doesn't yet exist, but at every moment she is also everywhere, busily assembling a subjective sense of herself. Her indeterminacy has never prevented feminists from writing about her. Luce Irigaray is fearlessly positive as she urges us, "Never give up subjective experience as an element of knowledge."(8). Feminist attitudes and actions do not emerge from feminist ideologies in the way that effect emerges from cause. Nor should we assume that feminism's energies are mainly powered by formal theory. A feminist articulation is just as likely to be the less tightly knit consequence of personally conceived convictions and experiences. Any true history of feminism would need to take the personal lives of millions of women into account. Their number would have to include those numerous women who cannot afford to associate themselves with feminism, as well as an equally large number of women who might not even be consciously aware that their thoughts or actions had any feminist significance . The earlier manifestations of feminism are not diminished just because they may at a later date appear a little quaint or naive. Every time a formulation of a woman's self-perception extends beyond her role as man's opposite, it contributes towards transforming apparently personal (thus normally considered meaningless) experiences into instructive events. And it matters very little whether a formulation is ideological, cultural or activist, or even simply affirming the feminine and admonishing the forces that seek to subdue it.

Post-feminism has been acidly dismissed as "a description of something that does not yet exist and is unlikely to do so in the foreseeable future." (9) Certainly from the present standpoint, any effort to finally articulate or fix the endless fragments of an authentic feminine would inevitably end up missing the mark. If the self-inventing woman wants to reach her full potential, she must remain fluid, remain in dialogue and in process – perhaps permanently. This daunting task is fortunately not the resposibililty of any one individual but that of the collective of women everywhere.

The temptation to take refuge in familiar habits of thought and definition remains disturbingly strong, and a dominant fixed system will always try to reassure us (and itself) that it possesses some absolute, everlasting truth. But the numberless possible meanings that are waiting to burst into being cannot all be suppressed forever. A new concept of woman would inevitably disturb masculinist ways of thinking, but that does not mean that it has to be directly confrontational. It could equally well be an invitation to greater tolerance and fresh understandings. In a nutshell, "Feminism has always been a question of what concepts do, how they work and the forces any act of thinking enables." It is never just "the exposure of male bias or interests within an otherwise good reason, but ... the attempt to assess the force of concepts and to create new concepts."(10)

The connection between the second and third waves of feminism shows third-wave philosophical thinking as a natural successor to many second-wave formulations. These scattershot 'takes' reflect my own preferred readings of feminism, but at the same time they are constantly aware that every woman will have her own particular version of what a feminine identity means. She is already in possession of all that is needed for a feminist account of her own experiences, thoughts and reflections.

Footnotes

1) In this text the term 'masculinism' is not used as the inversion or opposite of 'feminism'. On the surface, the two terms may appear to be parallel, but they can never fairly or reasonably be given equivalent meanings in a culture that has rejected feminist values and been resolutely embedded in masculinist values for several thousand years .

2) The origin of feminism is very uncertain. Numerous different events claim to mark its beginning. The unitarian chapel that Mary Wollestonecraft frequented in Newington Green claims to be "The birthplace of feminism.".

3) see chapter 1 for detailed discussion of the effects of dichotomous thinking on the feminist enterprise.

4) Braidotti., Rosi. *Nomadic Theory: the Portable Rosi Braidotti.* p.3. Columbia University Press. 2011.

5) Braidotti. ibid pps 17-18.

6) The New Zealand singer, Bic Runga, interviewed in The Guardian. 07 06 06

7) "atopic feminist" is Elizabeth Grosz's usage in preference to Derrida's term "maverick feminist'. Derrida initially made the common, simplistic mistake of assuming feminists were essentially women who wanted to be men.

8) Irigaray, Luce. *Sexes & Genealogies* . p.203. Columbia University Press. 1993 (French edition,1987.)

9) *Feminist Readings Feminists Reading* p.228.Mills,Sara; Pearce, Lynne; Spaull, Sue; Millard,Elaine. Harvester.1989.

10) Buchanan, Ian & Colebrook, Claire. *Deleuze and Feminist Theory..* p.9. Edinburgh University Press. UK 2000.

PART 1

Not Quite According To His Word

1

In Tentative Praise of Difference

Feminism Has More Than One Voice

Speaking of the work of Deleuze and Guttari (1987), Claire Colebrook writes,"for the most part, there is no standard or norm for woman. If we really acknowledge that there is something like becoming-woman , then we acknowledge that there is something truly other than man: that human life is not defined by the male ideals of reason, strength, dominance and activity. 'Woman' opens the human to new possibilities. " (1) Feminism has produced many diverse interpretations of itself and of woman, it has successfully contained countless disagreements over policies and strategies, and it has been much criticised for dissension within its own borders. However, the many diverse readings of feminism are really telling us that there are multiple and very different inter-pretations of woman – what she is, what she is not, what she might become – and that no definition of feminism is set in stone or lies beyond the possibility of change. And that change contains the germ of transformation.

As new needs and objectives appear and disappear, feminism responds with an irrepressible determination. Like a blackberry, it regenerates itself underground, preparing to launch some fresh offshoot of the original stock (2). Each shoot retains an ongoing connection to the original stock and each demonstrates that the resilience of feminism lies in commonality, not dogmatic opinion. Unlike religious belief, feminist commitment does not have to carry a burden of infallible reason and unalterable understanding. Disagreements between feminists happen in a setting of their underlying connection. Feminism is, and has always been, formed of a community of different voices, each emerging out of its own different situation. Although this does not produce conformity, nevertheless, feminist initiatives, however different, all arise out of the single recognition that men, in whatever degree or manner, assert their right to power over women and the natural precedence of masculine over feminine values. The injustice of this mis-representation is always a constant, irrespective of whether a given feminist activity takes place among existing masculinist traditions and the concepts these traditions imply, or whether an incentive is dissenting or improvised and makes use of guerilla tactics and any strategies that come to hand in order to unsettle established thinking and behaviour.

Difference has long been a contentious issue. Whereas some feminists have always insisted that the disequilibrium between the sexes can only begin to right itself once woman has been understood in her *difference*, others have disagreed sharply. This book maintains that women can never be equal or independent until an identity that is now primarily an adjunct of the masculine ceases to be imposed upon her. Men's conceptions of woman either as an exotic, imaginary/ fantastic opposite to himself or as a utility-based, second class kind of male, both have to be transcended. Debates regarding difference all confirm that woman can only perform the self-denying fantasies that spring from a male imagination. The degree to which she is aware of her own dissimulation may vary, but she has displayed a remarkable talent for impersonating fantastic desires and mimicking required traits. This, however, has meant obscuring what she is, whether to herself, or to others, or to both.

Differences between expressions of feminism can usually be traced to historic causes. Many second-wave feminists perceived a very real danger in conceding innate differences between men and women. They noted that conditions for women could rapidly deteriorate if sexual difference were fore-grounded before the grip of male-defined, sexual stereotyping had been loosened. At a time when the common understanding of difference between the sexes was that women were by nature frivolous, in-competent and largely semi-rational, the most immediate need was to prove the cliché incorrect and preempt disingenuous arguments for blocking demands for equal rights and opportunities. Women of that era took care to keep the focus away from differences between males and females until widespread visible proof of female competence had been produced and more extensive changes could be set in motion. But the price was high. Even when women had fully proved their equal capability in a male-dominated world, only rarely did this mean that they were equally comfortable in it – or equally rewarded. We have all seen the most reasonable, precisely argued, and substantially supported proposals being acknowledged as valid and yet continuing to be unimplemented. It is often forgotten that the positive achievements of the women's movement reside not only in objectives that have been accomplished and implemented, but also in whatever ideas have been formulated beyond contesting. In 'democratic' societies, it is no longer acceptable to deny the validity of demands such as the inclusion of women in work previously reserved for men, or the increase to market levels of wages paid to women. Judgements have changed even where behaviour lags behind.

The time for for downplaying difference has now passed and other problems have arisen. So far, demands based on the particular needs of women have barely been defined. Though we are fully aware that women are routinely obliged to go out to work while continuing to bear central responsibility for children and others in need of care, they receive virtually no relief from double workloads during their working lives and no later compensation in terms of employment, earnings, pensions. The lack of provision for the safety of women from sexual abuse and predation or domestic violence and bullying is also widely known and just as inadequately addressed.

These are the ways in which male control of women is perpetuated in a modern context. If the modern society preaches its commitment to the betterment of women, its underlying intentions have often altered very little. Equal rights that do not incorporate the needs of the recipients, do not lead to equitable results. Equality between the sexes is, in fact, no more reliable than any other formula of words. Pre-existing foundations which have been there from antiquity ensure male supremacy. Women's struggles have to be conducted from inside a pre-fixed and prefabricated masculinist order.

As many feminists try to find a new understanding of what a woman in her 'difference' might be and to formulate a feminine that is not derived from an archaic, lopsidedly masculine prototype of humankind, it quickly emerges that the indeterminacy of this search has in itself been a source of considerable contention. The present book maintains that, in order to be anything more than a parody or a distorted figment of the male imagination, each woman has to reconstitute her own identity through her own independently conceived and therefore undetermined perception of her difference. If this difference is to do more than mirror the patriarchal order, if it is to break free from extrinsic control, then it is essential to avoid being understood as parallel or opposite to the established identity of the male. A woman's difference will always include the idea of keeping itself perpetually open to the possibility of both change and difference. It will always avoid subordinating relationship to anxiety-ridden attempts to limit and control difference. Fear of losing control may turn out to be one of the most difficult elements of male dominance to counter.

Among some earlier feminists, the defensive denial of difference between the sexes became matched by an often fierce outrage regarding its suppression. Even Simone de Beauvoir's seminal work, *The Second Sex*, has been attacked by those who viewed her rejection of difference between the sexes as a rejection of being female and a failure to oppose the masculinist foundations of the social order. She has been subjected to abuse, referred to as "a woman who aspires to be like a man and whose voice is that of a ventriloquist's dummy" (3). One feminist philosopher has commented that Beauvoir "was confined to the feminine condition," because she "accepted a ready-made philosophy."(4) Luce Irigaray gently tells us, "Not wanting to be 'second' with respect to the masculine subject, she asks as a principle of subjectivity to be man's equal, to be the same as or similar to him." (5) Even Beauvoir herself seems to be consolidating this finding when she comments: "I don't believe that when women have won equality they will develop specifically feminine values." (6)

But we have long since left behind the historical era when Simone de Beauvoir, quite possibly with a certain irony, could say that, "..woman knows and chooses herself not as she exists for herself but as man defines her. She thus has to be described first as men dream of her since her being-for-men is one of the essential factors of her concrete condition." (7) To a twenty-first-century ear, the proposition that women are defined through their "being-for-men" may sound hopelessly placatory, but, in France women only got the vote in 1944; Beauvoir was not cushioned by a large and robust women's movement against a ubiquitous hostility towards feminism. In her foreword to the 2009 translation of *The Second Sex*, Sheila Rowbotham speaks of "Beauvoir's ingenious strategy of entering male culture in order to undermine it", but then goes on to add that she "inadvertantly invests masculine culture with a depth and allure lacking in the female Other. ... Beauvoir's loathing of fixed ideals of femininity made it difficult for her to ascribe value to the lives and actualities of women." The complex character of this difficulty, which resulted in Beauvoir's apparent reluctance or inability to clothe the female Other in any form except the one imposed by the masculine imagination, simply reflects the defiitional problems that confronted any woman situated within the social and historical constructions of that period. Rowbotham also quotes Beauvoir's admission in a 1970's interview that she remained suspicious of difference because ".. it falls again into the trap of wanting to enclose us in our differences." (8) Writing in the particular era when she did, Beauvoir could not have anticipated. the extraordinary effect her book would have in changing the subsequent orientations of society. Rowbotham concludes her foreword by remarking on the book's continuing relevance despite substantial changes in women's position. If not out of gratitude, then as a simple matter of fact, we should remember that these changes owe much to the labours of Beauvoir.

Quite evidently, the meanings of woman and of equality were then still comparatively undeveloped. Certainly, if there is to be any clarity, it is essential to know what species of being, of feminine, or of difference any given speaker has in mind. Luce Irigaray would make the statement that, "sexual difference is one of the major philosophical issues, if not the issue, of our age." (9)

Different Woman, Different Strategies: the Atopic Feminist

Sexual difference was also weighing on the minds of certain male philosophers of the era. While Jacques Derrida was busy sabotaging the 'phallocratic' supremacy of the patriarchy, Jacques Lacan was gleefully asserting that the 'Law of the Father', despite the fact that it was blatantly unfair to women, was inescapable. The intervention of the Second World War meant that Freud's reception in France had been belated, and from their respective positions, each of these Frenchmen was in his own different way enjoying the novelty of introducing extended sexual metaphors in reference to the dominance of the phallus. Derrida's initial view of feminists was not approving. At first (possibly influenced by Beauvoir) he understood them to be women who wanted to be the same as men. He pointed out that to situate female equality in the context of an unchanged social order and unaltered philosophical system was actually confirming existing values and abetting an authoritarian, patriarchal establishment. When Derrida became aware of a feminism that supported difference and that was not prepared to settle for an equality that had been invalidated by immovable establishment values, he gave 'atopic' feminism his full support. Octavio Paz sums up the mistaken logic of fixity: "*permanence* ... is a metaphor for *fixity,* as *becoming* is ... a metaphor for time in all its ceaseless transformations...fixity is always momentary." (10)

Atopic (without place) is used to signify whatever or whoever does not fit in anywhere that is recognised as a 'place'. And because the atopic feminist does not belong anywhere – she has no place – she cannot have a single or fixed definition. She is culturally ambiguous, problematical and impossible to control by orthodox methods. Since her equal but different subjecthood has so far never been accomodated in a dialogue between two equal but different subjects, and her own specific female voice and identity have not been recognised, let alone authorised, the atopic feminist chooses to put herself beyond negotiation with the social order. In asserting a *different* kind of sexual *differenc*e, atopic feminism destabilises phallocentrism. Derrida feels a natural affinity with the revolutionary potential of feminist "discontinuities, a history of absolutely heterogenous pockets, irreducible particularities, of unheard of and incalculable sexual differences .. sexual idioms at a distance from the main forum of feminist activity."(11)

Inevitably, anything at the central forum for the production of meaning is going to be phallocentric. Here it should perhaps be added that, if the powerhouse of meaning were to be under the coercive control of matriarchal rather than patriarchal elements, this too would be undesirable. To have hysterocentrism or a cult of the womb replace phallocentrism is barely imaginable, but such an event would merely reverse the present positions with another misconception of what could constitute an equitable social order. Feminists are advised to move carefully here: "whenever women and the feminine are conceptualised as either the *opposites*, or identical/ similar or as *complements* of men or masculinity, some form of phallocentrism exists." (12) At this point, we appear to be mired in paradox: if women are the same as men they deserve the same rights, but, if women are the same as men, it follows that they must be castrated and defective males, and so cannot expect to receive the same treatment as men. If, however, they are *essentially* different, the simple fact of their difference in a hierarchy of dominant males immediately seems to categorise them as inferior.

Happily, the problem becomes easier to resolve when it is applied in the actual practice of feminism: "Most feminist thought grapples unavoidably with some aspect of the equality-difference problem at both the level of theory and of strategy [with] bitter disagreement about which path is more progressive, more able to change women's basic condition of subordination ... 'Difference' gained some working women protection at a time when any social legislation to regulate work was rare, while 'equality' lay behind middle-class women's demand for the vote." (13)

Popularly, feminism has often been represented as a raw desire for male power, but women need a social order that offers something more than entry into the battle to secure their share of the spoils and supremacies over which men have been fighting disastrously through the centuries. Social structures that do not disadvantage women and an equality that includes their real needs require profound changes based on the idea of *difference* (14). While practical progress derives from improved social structures, difference liberates women from the masculinist standards which make inequalities seem logical and thus permissable.

It may be obvious that a feminism that abides by masculinist rules is ill-equipped to deal with a world shaped by formulas that do not include women. But though women may recognise the nature of their difference through their reflections on their own experiences, the system in place does not. It allows no compensatory adjustments to the rules. On a practical level, women are alloted disadvantage in the guise of equality and given a stark choice between a low female status with few benefits, or the unmanageable demands of simultaneous productive and reproductive labour. On a philosophical level, a woman is defined by a similarly inappropriate choice of identity either as a creature of male fantasy or as a falsified, pseudo-male person. Fortunately, even though nothing else is officially on offer, these are not the only real alternatives. The unfixed identity of woman-in-process allows her to take on limitless different shapes. Her use – or abuse – of the same tools that have been used to subordinate her has vast possibilities. She must, however, take care to distinguish between a self in whom she can recognise her lived experiences and a self formed by a language that can only encompass a small fraction of her potential.

Taking a Position

Obviously, the full extent of phallocentrism can be more clearly perceived when feminist conceptions of female identity progress beyond the subordination, masculinisation and other negative effects of male domination. Male domination can only be fully perceived from an external and independent vantage point. However, the idea of an authentic female identity can at least provide an imaginary position from which an objective strategy for woman's emancipation can be developed. The idea of the authentic woman is also relevant to masculine evolution as without the concept of a real female subject, the male – to everyone's detriment – can continue unimpeded to be the primary model for all humankind. The patriarchy has a vested interest in ensuring that any thinking that operates from an independent position or has escaped its control is either identified as empty-headed fantasy (and so probably a woman's) or treated as dangerous subversion. In short, without claiming an authentic identity of their own, women are easily reduced to being either the creatures of male fantasy, or spurious, second-class men who are so deeply embedded in a masculine context that intimations of feminine identity are rapidly slipping from their grasp.

Real change depends on an imaginative leap into as yet unrealised spaces. Nothing genuinely new can happen until this leap is made. The atopic feminist flouts the given order of things as she separates herself from past representations of herself (from definition measured by masculine gender stereotypes), from past positionings of herself (definition in terms of classification, social status and position) and from the authority that has previously controlled her from above (hierarchy, law, the patriarchy). Her aim is to occupy a different order. For some feminists, this has also entailed political shifts, sometimes towards socialism or for some as far as left-wing anarchism. The feminist anarchist, Emma Goldman, too radical to support an "institututionalising of inequalities for women, called for the restructuring of society as a whole." (15) Or, as another feminist represents anarcho-feminism: "Feminism doesn't mean female corporate power or a woman President: it means no corporate power and no presidents. The Equal Rights Amendment will not transform society; it only gives women the "right" to plug into a hierarchical economy. Challenging sexism means challenging *all* hierarchy – economic, political, and personal." (16)

The Personal and the Political

Difference also lies beneath a much repeated feminist phrase that acted as an open-sesame for many women of the nineteen-seventies: 'the personal is the political'. Historically, the female social role has been largely restricted to the personal. The personal (especially when it is of the feminine variety) has been devalued as insignificant and, like woman, made subordinate to the Law of the Father. Sexual difference has been unable to enter history on unconditional terms, and there has never been a recognition of two different subjects of equal value. Luce Irigaray comments, "History cannot do without the existence of two human subjects, man and woman, if it is to get away from master-slave relationships." (17) The stereotypical uber-male thrives on a system that adheres to a single, inviolable standard, which is, of course, his own, while feminists wanting radical social change have often observed how a single, formalised, central ideology has always upheld the dominant order. Although many women think it would be more prudent to confront this situation with a single, comprehensive feminism, others persist in the belief that, irrespective of fears of essentialism, or separatism, or the fragmentation of the women's movement, real change is not going to happen unless it is based on difference. Even as post-feminist propaganda continues to put it about that feminism has splintered into irreconcilable factions and effectively self-destructed, the very divisions which this description denounces manifest a considerable history of mutual tolerance and support among diverse feminist groups.

The female predicament differs according to time and place, but women's needs everywhere differ from those of men and cannot be extrapolated from masculine prototypes. Masculine monism is too cumbersome to facilitate the fluid type of co-operation which seems natural or, in fact, indispensible to women in many fundamental activities such as rearing children and mutually improvising ways of surviving. To preserve itself, male dominance is obliged to prize competition and central control and to turn away from making adjustments to the constantly shifting, personal needs or the problems that relate to women and their children. Patriarchal resistence, both to the new and the other, is best countered by the greatest possible diversity of feminist strategies brought together in a united struggle for equal rights and for the establishment of woman's different subjecthood. Already sharing the aim of releasing women from confinement in masculinised values and systems, the different strands of feminism can together more readily unlock the doors to new perceptions.

Extreme variations in the situations of women around the world also emphasise the continuing importance of the personal and the need to reject a single monolithic solution to the predicament of all women. A black feminist, bell hooks, speaks candidly from mid-eighties America about problems of communication between different races and classes of women in Western cultures. She commends the enthusiasm with which women have claimed the personal as the political but is concerned that undue emphasis on the personal can block an individual's identification with the collective and that this can produce quasi-colonialist side-effects in terms of race and class. "Broader perspectives can only emerge as we examine both the personal that is political, the politics of society as a whole, and global revolutionary politics." She appeals for a feminism that will include "the diversity of women's social and political reality", but also provide the basis for a feminism able to "centralise the experiences of all women" (18).

However, though the personal has been crucial in the politics of feminism, it may seem to weaken the position of women. This anxiety is generated by the competitive context of masculinism and care is needed to avoid engendering a centralised feminine experience that is in danger of becoming as competitive as its masculine opposite. Furthermore, the means women use to counter male oppression is necessarily heterogeneous when the forms of their domination and abuse vary so greatly from culture to culture. Huge numbers of women throughout the world have been denied education, leaving them ill-equipped to challenge patriarchal control over law, reasoning and logic. In some places it must be virtually impossible to imagine any alternative to the local female predicament, or believe that anything in the accessible world could validate women's personal experiences. Private and at times even secret communication between women has been a traditional way of coping in acutely male-dominated cultures. (19) It seems futile to apply a single, centralised feminist agenda to the problems, needs or resources in all cultural contexts or expect them to be appropriate for all women. The need to include the personal is indispensible. There is a sense in which a woman's personal progress is also her real autobiography.

It is, of course, universally true that every patriarchal culture has done its best to keep women confined in a purely personal micro-space. And it is only when unashamed male domination has become politically inexpedient, that steps have been taken to subdue women through the universal application of exclusively masculine standards. A convenient refusal to acknowledge that different criteria would provide a better measure of women and their abilities has meant that traditional (masculine) structures have continued to prosper in unchanged form. In this evasionary context, women's particular needs are given nothing more than lip service, abilities traditionally regarded as 'feminine' are regularly undervalued and realistic equality can be postponed almost indefinitely. Society is founded on the property rights of men. Women "take an interest in rights having to do with the individual, and with relationships between individuals, rather than rights determined by assets – possessions, property, belongings – rights which make up the majority of masculine civil codes." (20)

Fluid, Multiple, But
Connected as a School of Fish.

Although women's efforts have exposed many facts which, if logic had prevailed, should have made change inevitable, an inflexible patriarchy still closes its mind to whatever constitutes a challenge to its primacy – or, more precisely, provides good reason to contest the entire notion of primacy. "The attitude that one approach is 'right' and the other is 'wrong' is misguided. Most if not all contributions to feminism have something to offer, and many have a great deal to contribute. ..... the range of perspectives and theoretical approaches is not in competition. The resulting diversity is a positive outcome, and indeed it would not be persuasive or acceptable for one strand to 'win out'. Such a result would only amount to the triumph of power over ideas." (21) A patriarchy is forced to suppress all opposition: it can only survive by the technique of blocking off a proper understanding of itself and its own internal dynamics. This major form of repression affects men and women alike. It makes aggression and insecurity inevitable. Although modern man's prevailing angst has been widely recognised, it seems possible that women's personal experiences may at times bring them closer to a conscious appreciation of certain of the reasons for this uneasy state. Lacanian man is a "fragmented subject of shifting and uncertain sexual identity [whose] idealogical world .. conceals this from the conscious subject who is supposed to feel whole and certain of a sexual identity." (22) Even as he seems to be celebrating male dominance, Lacan is openly recognising its fraudulent character.

The atopic feminist recognises that an authentic female subject could no longer be governed by the *Law of the Father.* She celebrates a future in which a self-created woman-subject would potentially be so resolutely alien in the midst of patriarchal structures that her mere presence could start a chain reaction capable of pulling apart an already crumbling patriarchal edifice. In the meantime, she chips away ceaselessly at small, half-forgotten, exposed parts of the patriarchy with nothing more brutal than her total disregard for its rules. She knows that canonical feathers are always going to be less ruffled by demands for concessions pertaining to the rights of women than by the intrusion of women who have already defined themselves as different and independent subjects and peaceably installed themselves in a not-male-dominated space.

Feminism is now able to suggest that women's politics, as much as the female subject, must engage in an open-ended '*becoming* ', but not in becoming grounded: "Any assertion of woman as subject must not double or simply oppose man, but must affirm itself as an event in the process of becoming." It must "demand not just to redress the wrongs *within thought* but to think differently. This is why sexual difference may be the question of our epoch."(23) (Irigaray states more flatly elsewhere that it *is* the question of our epoch.) And thinking does not have to be organised according to opposites or dichotomies. We are told that in third wave feministthinking, "the promise of 'difference' can be realised... viewed non-dichotomously, 'difference' involves much more than disagreement and the status of disagreement, in adversarial terms. It is also about recognition and rights in a context of diversity which is no longer circumscribed by dichotomous thinking." (24)

Real *difference* will unfailingly include difference of viewpoint. Irigaray points out that, not only is the recognition of a man as other "an appropriate ethical task for women, but it is also a necessary step toward affirming their autonomy... a gesture that also allows us to promote the recognition of all forms of others without hierarchy, privilege, or authority over them." (25) In a later text she tells us, "Nor does neutralis-ingthe difference serve any purpose other than a loss of human identity." (26)

A feminism taken far enough in this direction could eventually require the adapting or even the jettisoning of elements that are at present regarded as the only correct or even possible premises for thought. "If thought is not directed towards an image of good thinking but sets itself the task of thinking otherwise, then feminism might be less a task of emancipation and more a challenge of differentiation." (27) Emancipation is not yet half accomplished and at this point the need for differentiation to accompany it is more urgent than ever. If differentiation did nothing more than justify the cause of emancipation on moral and intellectual grounds, it would still be worth more than the broken promises of equal rights that have been made to women. But there is more. Difference that was more than *nominal* or imaginary, a real change in women's identity that was neither sanctioned in the Name of the Father nor done unto women According to His Word, could shift the ground on which all of us are standing.

Footnotes

1) Claire Colebrook. *Deleuze* p. 104. Routledge Critical Thinkers. 2002.

2) An image of older, unattached women "as common as blackberries" is used by Sylvia Townsend Warner.

3) Celine T. Leon, , *Feminist Interpretations of Simone de Beauvoir..* ed Simons, Margaret A. . pps 152-3. Penn State Press USA 1995.

4) Michele le Doeuff, *The Philosophical Imaginary* p119. Continuum, London & N.Y. 2002. (French ed 1989)

5) Luce Irigaray. *The Question of the Other*. P8. Yale French Studies, No 87. 1995. Yale University.

6) Interview with de Beauvoir. *New French Feminisms*, p. 149. ed. Marx and Courtivron. Harvester Press, U.K. 1981.

7) Simone de Beauvoir. *The Second Sex.* Translated by Constance Borde & Sheila Malovany-Chevalier. p.159. Vintage.2011

8) ibid pps.xvi & xviiii

9) Luce Irigaray, *An Ethics of Sexual Difference*, p.5. The Athlone Press, London, 1993. (French ed 1984)

10) Octavio Paz. *The Monkey Grammarian*. p21. Peter Owen Publishers. London 1989

11) Jacques Derrida. *Choreographies,* p69. Diacritics, Summer 1982. Derrida's *deconstruction* is based on the fact that meanings depend on

47

prior origins that stand outside meaning and are therefore unaccountable. He deconstructs texts by severing them from a fixed primary (phallocentric) ideology. This destabilises/ democratises the possibility of the single, fixed meaning. Elisabeth Grosz. introduces the more precise term *atopic* to replace Derrida's *maverick*.

12) Elisabeth Gross. in Leftwright, p.71, Intervention Publications 20, 1986, Australia:

13) Ann Snitow, A Gender Diary *Conflicts in Feminism* ed Marianne Hirsch & Evelyn Fox Keller. pps 24 & 25 Routledge, N.Y. & London. 1990.

14) 'Difference' was used for specific purposes by French feminists. It came into philosophical prominence through Jacques Derrida. Here, it is used more broadly as any particular context requires.

15) Derrida. op cit. p69.

16) Peggy Kornegger, *Quiet Rumours: an Anarcha-Feminist anthology*, p.33-4. Dark Star, London, 198?

17) Luce Irigaray. *The Other: Woman. Feminisms*. p.311. Oxford Reader. O.U.P. Oxford – New York. 1997.

18) bell hooks. *Feminisms*. Oxford Reader. O.U.P. Oxford – New York. 1997.

19) Edward Shorter in his *History of Women's Bodies* speaks of the 'sisterhood of solace', a personal grouping of women which in past times was based on mutual need, especially in matters of sex and reproduction.

20) Luce Irigaray. *The Question of the Other*. p 14. Yale French Studies 87. Yale University. 1995.

21) Raia Prokhovnik. *Rational Woman A feminist critique of dichotomy.* p178. Manchester University Press.2002.

22) Juliet Mitchell. *Jacques Lacan & the Ecole Freudienne*. p.26. The Macmillan Press. London. 1982. The phrase 'sexual identity seems to include both genders. Although some feminists might want to read it as more male-specific, the fragmented sense of identity might refer to either men or women

23) Ian Buchanan & Claire Colebrook. *Deleuze and Feminist Theory*. pps.1-3. Edinburgh University Press. 2000.

24) Prokhovnik. Ibid. p. 176

25) Luce Irigaray. *The Question of the Other*. p 18. Yale French Studies 87. Yale University. 1995.

26) Luce Irigaray. *Democracy Begins Between Two*. The Athlone Press London. 2000.
27) Buchanan & Colebrook. op cit. p.12.

2

When Speaking of the Other: Philosophy, the Imaginary, and the Feminine

What the philosophical represses

Luce Irigaray asserts that we need to understand why "sexual difference has not had its chance to develop, either empirically or transcendentally. Why it has failed to have its own ethics, aesthetic, logic, religion".. (1) Michèle le Doeuff takes a more cautious approach. She remarks edgily that, "We need not always completely reject a feminism of difference." Le Doeuff has another agenda. Her primary concern is with the behaviour of a philosophy that is essentially masculine – ".. like it or not, we are within philosophy, surrounded by masculine-feminine divisions that philosophy has helped to refine" and the escape from male domination "will necessarily involve the deciphering of the basic philosophical assumptions latent in discourses about women." (2)

As Le Doeuff conducts her business amongst the

central tenets of the notoriously male-dominated forum of philosophy, her arguments follow the exact procedures in which she has made herself proficient. She analyses texts ranging from Plato to Jacques Lacan. And with the same careful pen, she scores through philosophical self-definition and the forms of reasoning philosophy claims for itself. Despite the boast that it exemplifies pure and uncontaminated thought, it "declares its status as philosophy through a break with myth, fable, the poetic, the domain of the image .. defining itself through opposition to other types of discourse." (3) This, she points out drily, is philosophically impossible: whatever defines philosophy, or the study of knowledge, must also be a part of what it is defining.

With impeccable reasoning, Le Doeuff is attributing the exclusion of the feminine from philosophy's representation of itself to the use of false premises in its epistemology. It goes without saying that this position also clearly intends to exclude the feminine from reasoning . Philosophy has failed to know itself; it is not performing according to its own prescription. Furthermore, philosophy contends that the masculine faculty of reason is unadulterated by the irrational fantasies that belong to the feminine imaginary (a gesture Freud might have called projection). However, philosophy would be unable to perform at all if the unavoidable imaginary were not there to prop up its thinking processes. "All thought presupposes an undefined area, a certain play of structures, a certain margin of free-floating around the codified procedures. Thus shadow is within the field of light and woman is an internal enemy. For in defining itself through negation, the philosophical creates its Other: it engenders an opposite, which .. will play the role of the hostile principle, the more hostile because there is no question of dispensing with it. .. the feminine.. having been engendered by philosophy whilst being rejected by it, operates within it as an indispensible dead weight." (4) She fits all this in a nutshell with the pivotal comment, "The philosophical creates that which it represses." (5)

Taking on the role of the enemy within, Le Doeuff singles out non-rational elements that are at all times present in reason. They are necessarily present. Always dispassionate, she insists on the need to redraw the boundaries of consciousness. Philosophy must be made to acknowledge that it is using the exact elements of thought which are inadmissable according to the rules of the perfect logic it claims as its unique mode of operation. There is no question of making choices between reason and the imaginary. They are parts of a single function and never have been nor can be separated. Their representation as alternatives that exclude each other "can be seen as mythical, a connivance or complicity between forms which present themselves as opposites." (6) Once again we encounter feminism's instinctive aversion to bipolar (dichotomous) systems that thrive on opposition rather than reconciliation.

Le Doeuff also disputes the propriety of Jacques Lacan's dogmatic assertions on questions that stray beyond the boundaries of psychoanalysis and his area of expertise. Where Irigaray varies her strategies between derailing and deflating Lacan's strutting pronouncements, Le Doeuff raps him sharply across the knuckles for the slovenliness of his philosophical reasoning. Lacanians "behave as though analytical theory possessed global explanatory value and jurisdiction over a whole range of problems: metaphysical ... ethical, aesthetic, linguistic, epistemological " She would like to know "into what sector of the present-day encyclopaedia psychoanalysis has not intervened to lay down some pre-given certainty." (7) Rather than offering psychoanalysis as one possible method for interpreting certain aspects of human reality, Lacan is seeking to incorporate all human reality into psychoanalysis.

A brief (and thus simplistic) word here about Lacan. His influence should not be underestimated. As a latter-day Freudian, Lacan extends the psychological development of the child into much wider, cultural structures. He situates an irrational function, the *Imaginary*, opposite a reasoning one, the *Symbolic*. His Imaginary is an initial, unconscious phase. In this phase, the infant has no concept of itself as separate from the Mother. This un(self)conscious state, so he asserts, is only overcome when the child later becomes anchored in the masculine Symbolic and its corresponding context of definition and meaning which is contained in language. Lacan conflates the Imaginary, the unconscious and the feminine. All mental activity that refuses to pledge its allegiance to what he terms the *Law of the Father* is unconscious. It is also an article of faith that the Mother, or Imaginary, must always and inevitably be displaced by the Father, or Symbolic, whilst the child must submit to the symbolic authority of the Father. Masculine reasoning becomes the only possible avenue to consciousness and philosophy represents reason and true meaning in its purest form.

Le Doeuff rejects the claim that true meaning can only be attained through the pure reasoning of philosophy as rankly arrogant hubris. She scorns the assumption that there is such a thing as a single, infallible truth, able to override all other less censored, less conformist processes of human thought. The so-called 'great philosopher' is claiming "intellectual mastery of all that is in heaven and earth – and in human practice," and what he *claims to know* "gets confused with what 'is known' – indeed with what it is possible to know... the nerve of such and such a 'great philosopher' is what supports the idea of the existence of a form of knowledge." (8) Le Doeuff reiterates these radical criticisms in different forms and contexts: "philosophy is a discourse constantly asserting its own power," or, "The politics of the philosopher is the paternalism of reason," or, "The legislator/ philosopher has aspirations to colonize and become regent to a world of politics which he considers exterior to himself." (9)

Feminism's Tools

When Le Doeuff writes of the need to employ philosophy in the feminist struggle, her use of this idea may differ from Irigaray's, but the idea is just as determining for both women. In fact, as time has passed, many apparent discrepancies of opinion between the two seem to have drifted into insignificance. A later philosophical duo will make the general observation that, "Feminism has always been obliged to use the master's tools to destroy the house." (10) Philosophy has been the unquestioned birthright of the master for far too long.

Both Freudian and Lacanian equations between what are supposed to be essentially human characteristics and sexually differentiating body parts revive ancient cultural residues – residues which are seemingly still unaware of their purely figurative, primitive sources. Corporeal metaphors have continued to shape and limit human identity since history and myth, and, later, rational and irrational first began to establish themselves as mutually exclusive categories that were able to discard their original unity. However, the dependence on corporeal mataphors exposes the impossibility of segregating body and mind. It vividly preserves the image of reason with unreason at its heart. And it continues to distort language and to prejudice definitions of what it means to be a human.

It is not necessary to be a feminist to understand that these are problems a modern society ought to be addressing. Nevertheless, language is still controlled by a masculine establishment. Language is phallocentric. It polarises masculine and feminine, favours male values and excludes alternatives to the conceptual representations that a male lexicon produces. Reality has become phallocentric as if by stealth, allowing male supremacy to install itself by means of the language used to describe it in an impregnable ideological basis. Only by cutting down into the roots of phallocentric language and a "phallogocentric" (11) culture does it become possible to envisage a reality in which male and female might be able to coexist as different yet equal subjects.

Of course, not all cutting tools are the same. From a position that has some common features with that of Le Doeuff, a British feminist argues for the need to retain and re-examine Freudian concepts on the grounds that feminists need to understand the ideology that underpins the culture we inhabit and that what serves masculinist definition can also be used to expose it. An American feminist later concludes that in both psychoanalysis and feminism "Identity must be continually assumed and immediately called into question." (12) The basis for this comment is already more or less familiar: woman cannot participate as an equal subject in the creation of her own identity because masculine-dominated language and definition put her in the category of object.

The ways of responding to the problem of male-dominated language are multiple. Escape into an alternative space has been proposed. In a book-long dialogue, one French feminist describes the alter-reality of writing and claims that, "..a place exists which is not economically and politically indebted to all the vileness and compromise. That *is not obliged to reproduce the system*. That is writing." (13) Her co-author responds that, though language is certainly male-controlled and excludes the feminine, she is not prepared to renounce its constructions out of hand. These are the main avenues of thought and language that are currently available. "Even if somewhere it is true that rhetoric and vocabulary are formed by centuries of male cultural domination, to renounce the exercise of thought, to give it to them, is to perpetuate." To become a subject, she continues, "one would have to cut through all the heavy layers of ideology that have borne down since the beginnings of the family and private property: that can be done only in the imagination. And that is precisely what feminist action is all about: *to change the imaginary in order then to be able to act on the real*, to change the very forms of language which by its structure and history has been subject to a law that is patrilinear, therefore masculine." [my italics] (14) Her argument ends with one foot in either camp. This may, at present, prove to be the best position to occupy. Le Doeuff responds more tartly to all blanket repudiations of male-dominated language and definition, "We will not talk pidgin to please the colonialists." (15)

La Donna E Mobile
Even as these discussions continue, that troublesome gadfly of flexible identity, atopic feminism, has been spontaneously exemplifying the demand that identity should be "continually assumed and immediately called into question." The uncertainty created by an identity in constant flux is profoundly disturbing to the status quo. And when this instability begins to seep down into the foundations of identity and gender, it exposes the fact that meaning is never neutral. It reveals the disturbing presence of desire within meaning itself. This also makes it painfully obvious

that a single human identity which is essentially male is incapable of recognising feminine desire. "Lacanian devaluation of the imaginary [is] related to a hatred of the flesh, of woman and of pleasure." (16) Which surely must mean most especially of *her* pleasure.

Worse is to come. The void created by the negation of pleasure and the flesh quickly fills up with the desire for power. Power moves into the place that love might otherwise have occupied. Or if not love, then at least tolerance or friendship. Because it can only flourish if it is free to redefine itself at every turn, love will always be an unccertain thing. But, because power must depend on force, it too is contantly threatened by uncertainty. And, in reference to the loss of the earliest, most primal form of pleasure, several feminists – Irigaray is especially prominent among them – have reminded us that the symbolic and in fact the entire machinery of the patriarchal edifice require the sacrifice of the maternal. For a girl child, the severance from her mother is doubly painful. It not only takes her first love object from her but also her esteem and expectations for herself as a future woman. In short: "The symbolic is 'erected' only on the basis of the repression of the maternal. .. Civilisation, the symbolic order, the coherent text, then are possible only at the cost of the silencing, the phallicisation of the maternal." (17) The feminine not only is repressed, it is what the existing order must repress.

If we look at the writings of Irigaray and Le Doeuff we see two very different personalities and methods at work but their final assessments can be surprisingly close at times. In parts of her later work,

Irigiray pursues a train of thought so simple it is truly radical. She advocates "the practice of intersubjectivity .. coexistence between women and men, not only on the instinctual level – with all the forms of violence which the institution of the family modestly conceals – but on the level of civilisation." (18) She suggests that, with sufficient resolve and enough dedication to the truth of the other and discovery of the self, little is needed beyond the education of both sexes towards an unprejudiced understanding of each other. Such an understanding could achieve a union between an undistorted Mother and Father couple. Irigaray's moral position in this process is not negotiable: the feminine must never compromise itself, the integrity of its identity must never be sacrificed for any reason. We should not dismiss as impossible a means that has never been tried. Our courage only fails us because we have all spent so long buried in the shadow and even serving as the shadow of the phallic order. We are liable to forget that the patriarchal edifice is nothing more than a stone, man-made collosus.

Le Doeuff wants a collaborative philosophy to replace the autocratic pronouncements of 'the great philosopher'. Philosophy must accept that it is not definitive, that it contains a lack. She is drawn towards writings which admit the "penumbra of unknowledge .. which metaphysics has denied" and perceives herself as "a tributary to a collective discourse and knowledge, which have done more towards producing me than I shall contribute in continuing to produce them; and replace the mystery with a recognition of the necessarily incomplete character of all theorization." (19) She proposes "A new rationality, in which a relationship to the unknown and to the unthought is at every moment reintroduced." (20)

With snatches of meticulous qualification and snatches of complete abandon, both women are expressing a desire for a perpetual revolution, one that neither depends on force nor quickly reverts to the conditions that produced it. Both want a revolution that constantly recurs and evolves, and thus constantly adjusts its own findings. Irigarary repeatedly asserts the need for humility and an understanding of the other that is open-ended and perpetually-in-process. Le Doeuff anticipates "tension" because she recognises that "There is no closure of discourse, discourse only ever being a compromise .. between what it is legitimate to say, what one would like to contend or argue, and what one is forced to recognise." (21) Le Doeuff aims to force the Father to acknowledge the Mother's neverending co-presence and to accept the fact of his inevitable interdependence with the feminine. Irigaray, more concerned with desire than obligation, wants Father and Mother to come to a full knowledge of one another and for each to embrace the reality of the Other.

Footnotes

1) Luce Irigaray, *An Ethics of Sexual Difference*, p.14. The Athlone Press Ltd, London, 1993, (French ed 1984.

2) Michèle le Doeuff, *The Philosophical Imaginary* .p.101 Continuum, London & NY, 2002 (French ed. 1980)

3) ibid. p.1

4) ibid p.115.

5) ibid p.114

6) ibid. p.118.

7) ibid. p.161.

8) ibid. pps.126-7.

9) ibid. p.55.

10) Ian Buchanan & Claire Colebrook. *Deleuze and Feminist Theory*. p.4. Edinburgh University Press. 2000

11) 'Phallogocentrism' is a conflation of 'phallocentric' and 'logocentric'. In this way, the 'word' gains a power that is exclusively patriarchal.

12) The British author is Juliet Mitchell, who expresses this opinion in *Psychoanalysis and Feminism* . Her title is later inverted by Jane Gallop in *Feminism and Psychoanalysis* (see p xii.) Macmillan, London, 1982.

13) Hélène Cixous, *The Newly-Born Woman*. Theory and History of Literature, Vol 24. Manchester University Press. 1986 (French edition 1975)

14) Catherine Clément. *New French Feminisms*, ed. Elaine Marks & Isabelle de Courtivron. pps.135 & 131. Harvester Press. 1981.

15) Le Doeuff, op cit. p.116.

16) Gallop, op cit. p.149

17) Elizabeth Grosz. *Sexual Subversions*. p.49. Allen & Unwin. Australia. 1989. "Phallicisation" here indicates the identification of the Mother with the masculine.

18) Luce Irigaray, *Democracy Begins Between Two*, p 155. The Athlone Press, London 2000. (French ed. 1994.)

19) Le Doeuff op cit p.127.

20) ibid p.128

21) ibid p.19.

3

Two Feminists, One Subject:
Sexual Difference and Moral Meaning

A Feminine Ethic

At first sight the writings of Luce Irigaray can seem difficult. She is apt to take her discussions well beyond the customary boundaries observed by philosophy – which also means well beyond the limits of ideas and realities as we are accustomed to considering them. She does not attempt to be concilliatory when she remodels the fixed equations that normally shape discourse. She sometimes takes the view that they have been put there to block disturbing intrusions such as feminine difference.

Irigaray repeatedly asserts the need to reconstruct the order of things so that it incorporates a corresponding, actively engaged, *different* feminine. It is clear that she does not believe improvements made within a basically unchanged system will ever be enough to deliver an equality that is profitable or even applicable to women. She understands sexual difference as a living philosophical and psychological force and sets her sights on nothing less than an eventual transformation of perception. "Has a worldwide erosion of the gains won in women's struggles occurred because of the failure to lay foundations different from those on which the world of men is constructed?" (1) This question appears in *The Ethics of Sexual Difference,* and it is in this book that she sets out to examine the ways in which feminine difference conditions moral judgement.

Irigaray maintains that masculine moral judgement is founded on an ethic which renders the real or actual abstract. This produces impersonal and universal standards that are extracted from reality in the same way that science and objective reason are. A perfectly abstract, fully objective moral standard is only immune from attack because it supplies the proof of its own validity in purely abstract terms. This "self-proclaimed universal" is "a masculine imaginary, a sexed world" (2). It is a reductive process that represents the extreme of philosophical "Idealism" (3). It imposes "a model on the universe so as to take possession of it, an abstract, invisible, intangible model that is thrown over the universe like an encasing garment. Which amounts to clothing the universe in one's own identity." (4)

The feminine ethic, so Irigaray continues, does not adopt the same self-perpetuating perspective. It is not fixed, not closed to change, and does not seek to avoid adapting to the difference of the other. The feminine and the female libido "would perhaps fit better with ... 'dissipatory' structures, which function through exchanges with the exterior world [and] are not organised to search for equilibrium but rather to cross thresholds." (5) She suggests that the feminine is by nature concerned with questions of "the half-open, of fluid sets, of anything that analyses the problem of edges, of the passages between things, of the fluctuations taking place from one threshold to the other of defined sets." (6) This different feminine remains undefined partly because it is the disregarded part of consciousness and partly because the feminine is perpetually flowing across boundaries in its desire to meet with or accomodate the other.

The more closely and deliberately grounded – and therefore complementary – work of Carol Gilligan in her book, *In a Different Voice: Psychological Theory and Women's Development,* expresses an interestingly like-minded view of feminine difference in the field of ethics. Gilligan, however, bases and corroborates her findings in detailed sociological research rather than in philosophical constructions. Questions about whether certain characteristics are learned, innate or have simply been forced into the private domain are not pursued in her book. She quietly observes, "My research suggests that men and women may speak different languages that they assume are the same, using similar words to encode disparate experiences of self and social relationships." (7) Gilligan's book investigates the two very different constructions of the moral domain that are typically made by the two sexes and finds a deep division of both emphasis and values. An association is usually made between "masculinity and the public world of social power ... femininity and the privacy of domestic interchanges. The developmental ordering of these two points of view has been to consider the masculine as more adequate than the feminine and thus as replacing the feminine when the individual moves towards maturity. The reconcilliation of these two modes is not however clear." (8)

Working in a carefully monitored psycho-sociological context, Gilligan examines ethical responses and concommittant behaviours in relation to certain given situations. She analyses her findings in terms of the sex of the respondent and is able to demonstrate a profound bias that both fails to incorporate feminine values into the social body and absoutely denies such values any serious significance as adult objectives. It is "in their care and concern for others that women have both judged themselves and been judged ... The conflict between self and other thus constitutes the central moral problem for women, posing a dilemma whose resolution requires a reconcilliation between femininity and adulthood." (9)

Who Loves Who?

In her more experimental style, Irigaray points out that the conventional (i.e. masculine) ethic, in which judgements about truth and justice are eternally fixed, does not acknowledge that moral judgements could function just as well according to a dynamic powered by the "transcendental" coming together of different entities. Or, as she is not afraid to put it, by love. This coming together of different entities, goes beyond the normal human limits of either one in isolation.(10) Thus it also necessitates a coming together of different ethical understandings, and these divergent perceptions must in their turn find a means of reconcilliation. But even the delicate art of negotiation falls a great way short of fulfilling Irigaray's vision of how different entities might discover ways to love and encompass the other. In a chapter she entitles *Sorceror Love*, Irigaray recalls the speech made by Diotima, the only woman to appear in Plato's *Symposium:* "All love is seen as creation and potentially divine, a path between the condition of the mortal and that of the immortal." (11) Irigaray stresses that the sexual encounter must not be "a disguised or polemical form of the master-slave relationship. Nor a meeting in the shadow or orbit of a Father-God who alone lays down the law, who is the immutable spokesman of a single sex." (12) Finally, she reminds us that, in the end, even Socrates was prepared to indenture the immortalising "daimon", love, to duty, to order, family and the state, all of which are primary institutions of patriarchial governance.

But Irigaray is not content to leave these thoughts to shrivel into abstractions. She draws the experiential, the immediately human and the explicitly corporeal into her proposed alliance, bringing her roles as philosopher and psychoanalyst into play together. "I have carried out analysis of spoken discourse based on the utterances of male subjects, on the one hand, and female subjects, on the other." She tells us that, when faced with the question of whether or not they are loved, her male patients would typically speculate without taking the position of the other into account – *I tell myself that perhaps I am loved* – whilst female patients would normally ask the other a direct question that included both people – *Do you love me?* If left unmediated, she says, this split not only damages language but leads to "fossilized identities for both sexes..." (13).

Along with discarding psychoanalysis's ambitious claim that it is based on a system of impartial observation, Irigaray also points out that all science is guilty of the same original sin of false impartiality. "... the scientist, now, wants to be *in front of* the world: naming the world, making its laws, its axioms. Manipulating nature, exploiting it, but forgetting that he too is *in* nature... he progresses according to an objective method designed to shelter him from any instability, any 'mood', any feelings and affective fluctuations, from any intuition that has not been programmed in the name of science..." (14)

Similarities between the work of Irigaray and that of Gilligan become distinct. But the subjects providing Gilligan's discoveries are not patients. They vary in age from pubescent schoolchildren of both sexes to a predominantly female sampling of students, first at college , then later on as graduates. All of them are confronted with moral problems. A short narrative provides the children with a problem that requires them to make a moral decision and they are then asked to explain how they arrived at their proposed solutions. Female college students facing real choices about whether or not to go through with abortions are asked for detailed accounts of all the factors contributing to their decisions. A few years later, some of these women are also asked to reflect retrospectively on the moral and personal meanings of their choices. The moral analysis Gilligan requires is far from orthodox. She does not ask her subjects to base their answers on established formulas about rights or justice but rather to examine their own feelings in their own terms. This encourages her respondents to be unusually frank.

Gilligan's enquiries focus on the moment when young males and females start to diverge irrevocably. "In young adulthood when identity and intimacy converge in dilemmas of conflicting committment, the reationship between self and other is exposed. .. From the different dymanics of separation and attachment in their gender formation .. male and female voices typically speak of the importance of different truths, the former of the role of separation as it defines and empowers the self, the latter of the ongoing process of attachment as it creates and sustains the human community." (15)

"Attachment and separation anchor the cycle of human life," Gilligan comments. They condition development and appear in the adult sphere as "love and work." However, she warns us against "the equation of development with separation." She traces the devaluation of attachment to the phenomen of charting progress "by measuring the distance between mother and child," and adds that "the limitation of this rendition is most apparent in the absence of woman from accounts of adult development." (16) One is left to wonder who the young female can adopt as a model. If she wishes to go beyond a definition which brands her as a perpetually immature member of society, she must abandon her mother and decline to make herself in the image of the one she most loves and resembles.

For a moment, Gilligan and Irigarary stand in exactly parallel positions. Irigaray is intent on how woman is deprived of the ability to love herself. "A whole history separates her from love of herself. Freud claims ... that woman has to put her love for her mother and for herself aside in order to begin to love men. (17) She has to stop loving herself in order to love a man who would for his part be able and indeed expected to continue to love himself. He has to renounce his mother in order to love himself... She has to renounce her mother and her auto-eroticism in order not to love herself anymore. In order to love man alone." Irigaray concludes, "Women can no longer love or desire the other man if they cannot love themselves." (18) She holds that such a contract is no longer acceptable. Nor is it going to fulfil his desires any better than her own: in trying to ensure that the woman will give her undivided love to himself alone, he creates a situation in which the woman is unable to love him at all.

Gilligan sees all of this primarily as a moral question. "Women's deference is rooted not only in their social subordination but also in the substance of their moral concern... Women, attend to voices other than their own" and "include in their judgement other points of view." (19) She proceeds to detail what are the inevitable consequences of this different attitude. "The reinterpretation of women's experience in terms of their own imagery of relationships ... provides a nonhierarchical vision of human connection. Since relationships, when cast in the image of hierarchy, appear inherently unstable and morally problematic, their transposition into the image of web changes an order of inequality into a structure of interconnection." (20)

Just as each moral position typifies the response of one sex, it also exposes the shortcomings of the other. Both Gilligan and Irigaray perceive how this divide affects relationships. Gilligan tells us that each understanding "marks as dangerous the place which the other defines as safe." (21) Both women are clear about the danger of allowing unmodified male values to govern our understanding of a world in which the two sexes must live together. Gilligan writes that "where men depict annihilation, the voices of women comment on the problem of aggression that both sexes face, locating the problem in the isolation of self and in the hierarchical construction of human relationships." (22) Irigaray stretches this idea towards both of its historical horizons as she looks back into the era of the Father and of the Son and then forward again into a future of "horizontal and vertical becoming, with no murders." (23)

So what is to be done? Here again these two differently pitched voices harmonise curiously well with one another. Gilligan points out that "we know ourselves as separate only insofar as we live in connection with others .. we experience relationship only insofar as we differentiate other from self." (24) She sums up her findings: "The morality of rights is predicated on *equality* and centred on the understanding of fairness, while the ethic of responsibility relies on the concept of *equity*, the recognition of differences in need." [my italics] "The 'ethic of rights' weighs the claims of the other against those of the self, whilst the 'ethic of responsibility' rests on an understanding that gives rise to compassion and care. Thus the counterpoint of identity and intimacy ... is articulated through two different moralities whose complementarity is the discovery of maturity." (25) For some women, to abandon the ethic of responsibility may be the most painful choice of all.

Irigaray's conclusions turn upon a theme she often reiterates. She makes an urgent demand for a union that is inherently fertile, she calls for an integration through the "marriage", as she prefers to call it, between masculine and feminine values. She hopes that we might, at last, be about to enter "the era of the couple." She wants to get "beyond genealogical destiny to the era of the wedding and festival of the world." (26) At the same time we find that Gilligan is winding up her book with her own thoughts about the marriage of these two separate understandings: "A marriage between adult development as it is currently portrayed and women's development as it begins to be seen could lead to a changed understanding of human development and a more generative view of human life." (27)

There seems to be a widely held belief that the feminism which has emerged from France and that which has predominated in Anglophone countries do not have the same objectives. The juxtaposition of these two works goes some way towards unsettling this conviction. Both writers perceive that a feminine ethic has a profound need to maintain the integrity of the other as well as of the self and to preserve the relationship with that other even if this may not be in the direct interest of the self alone. And in both accounts the summit of such an endeavour is expressed by the same metaphor of the wedding of difference.

Footnotes

1) Luce Irigaray. *The Ethics of Sexual Difference*. p.6. Athlone Press, London. 1993. (French edition, Editions de Minuit 1984)

2) ibid p. 121.

3) *Idealism* is a slippery term. Here Irigaray seems to be referring an Idealism that originates in Plato's belief that reality is modeled on ideal Forms and Ideas that can only be known through abstract thought and ends in *Essentialism* that regards meaning as prefixed, absolute and immutable.

4) ibid p.121.

5) ibid p.124

6) ibid p. 123

7) Carol Gilligan, *In a Different Voice: Psychological Theory and Women's Development,* p.173. Harvard University Press. Cambridge, Mass and London. 1982.

8) ibid p. 69.

9) ibid p. 70-1.

10) I am assuming that this is the primary sense in which Irigaray is using the term 'transcendental'.

11) Irigaray. op cit. p.25

12) ibid p.17. Irigaray is here refernng to a statement made by Heidegger.

13) ibid p.134-5

14) ibid p.125

15) Gilligan. op cit. p.156. The terms 'separation" and 'attachment' come from the work of John Bowlby.

16) ibid p. 151.

17) Gilligan comments that Freud's belief that women's sexual self-repression reduced their inherent capabilities fails to understand that abstinence was often necessitated by the absence of adequate contraception. See p. 68.

18) Irigaray op cit p. 65-6

19) Gilligan op cit. p.16

20) ibid p. 62

21) ibid p.62

22) ibid p.45

23) Irigaray op cit. p. 149

24) Gilligan op cit. p63

25) ibid p 165. Feminists, including Irigaray, often portray the feminine as operating 'horizontally'. This coincides with the ethics of equity/ responsibility. It also reflects the dynamics of matriarchal structures, where both the mother and her own siblings on the maternal side are responsible for all the siblings issuing from her womb.

26) Irigaray op cit. p. 148-9

27) Gilligan op cit. p. 174

4

Virginity, Blanks, and Empty Spaces

The Valuable Virgin

The innumerable restrictions and practices that cluster round female virginity may vary with local factors, but the fundamental concern is constant. Everything stems from a single and invariable consideration: how to ensure that a small scrap of membranous tissue – the hymen – will be preserved until the most profitable moment for its disposal.

There is a "surprising consensus among Darwinians, Marxists, feminist historians, cultural ecologists, and classicists that raiding for women was a primary objective of primitive warfare." (1) Through history and almost everywhere, virginity has been a valuable commodity and the exchange of women a basic social mechanism. Female virginity was used by male relatives, to buy in or buy off other males, to avoid wars with other groups or nations, and to make strategic alliances – some of these uses are still current. Wherever men had control of social groups, the exchange of women became a stabilising force.

Women were prime property and men had custody of their most valuable assets, first their virginity, then their children. "Even when the goal is the survival of the family, maternal and paternal interests do not necessarily overlap. Patriarchal societies are those in which patrilineal interests have, over time, come to prevail over strictly maternal ones. The goal is to produce offspring – often many of them – of undisputed paternity, no matter the cost to their mothers." (2) Paternity is a big issue in the animal kingdom also. Chimpanzees regularly kill the offspring of a female's liasons with other males. Only the bonobo chimpanzee does not because "strong alliances that females forge with other females make mothers too formidable ". (3) The solidarity of sisterhood is apparently an effective force in both primate and human communities.

Failure to safeguard the virginity of female kin is equally failure to ensure patriarchal dominance, and at this point 'honour' also enters the equation. 'Honour' may not at first sound venal, but profit and security are still the central motives. Faltering control of any woman in a family would cast doubt on guarantees of virginity and therefore diminish the value of every female in its possession. Modernised societies may boast of having progressed beyond such primitive concerns, but almost all societies include religious or social groups that are deeply preoccupied with the control of female sexuality and preservation of the hymen. The state, too, generally elevates marriage above unions that are not legally secured or accompanied by attendant property rights .

From an unembellished start as a bargaining chip in male transactions, virginity was gradually converted into an abstraction. This tiny, insignificant membrane became the indispensable mark of womanly virtue. The virginal hymen metamorphosed from an ordinary body part into a cultural motif, and as it did so produced an endless stream of secular, mythological and, above all, religious narratives. The portrayal of a virgin mother, made pregnant solely by the *word* of God, stretches the contradictory iconography of virginity to its extreme limits. (4) Roman Catholicism is festooned with images of the Virgin Mary and presents children with the baffling doctrine of a virgin mother long before they are of an age even to grasp the meaning of virginity (5). The regulators and jealous guardians of female sexuality regard a woman who seeks to take control of her own virginity as a threat – as in fact, she is. A woman in control of her own sexuality achieves more than an increase of personal freedom. Beyond ceasing to be an object of exchange, she is stealing from the Father's store of property. This theft exceeds her own transactional value and contests the supreme power of the phallus by invalidating the father's claim to be the rightful proprietor of women, their body parts, and their children. (6)

Obsession with the female body has never been matched by a parallel concern with the male body. For a man, the most crucial issue was always the preservation of his name; a woman's name was anyway destined to be erased and replaced by the name of whatever man came into possession of her. Male honour, reputation and the inheritance of property all sprang from the unambiguous, lawful transmission of a name – the word of the father was passed on to his son – and this contract had to be accomplished through the medium of a female body. Then, even after a woman had diligently fulfilled all her obligations, the fact of her own and her children's financial dependency marked her as mercenary, scheming, guilty of trapping a man into marriage. Of course, patriarchal supremacy has suffered from its own problems: kings have been executed by their people and history has been bedevilled by questions of descent. But in most instances, moves towards ideals of fraternity and equality have ended in the restoration of monarchs or the installation of dictators. And the Name of the Father is hardly ever involved in nothing more than authenticating records: it has used its promises of inheritance to buy up loyalties and to traffick in women. "The society of men is built upon the possession of goods. Life itself is equated with property, with productive capital." (7) But it has not been so for women. Women have been possessions, not possessors. Well into the twentieth-century, in many western societies, women who gave birth to illegitimate children were still being diagnosed as morally insane and confined in asylums. A woman may now retain her own name in preference to that of a husband but it is still more or less customary to register their children under his name. Female virginity may shore up the fragile confidence of paternity and underpin the law and the rule of the Father safeguards the male's property, but it provides no material, psychological, or even informational gains for a woman.

Though the management of young women and their virginity varies widely according to circumstance and class, the sex of an infant is probably the most formative consideration influencing its reception into its family and social context. The traditional method among the more affluent families was to incite their daughters' cooperatiion with dreams of a cloudlessly happy future filled with security and comfort. Narcissism is a vital ingredient in this recipe. It is served up to boys also, though in their case it is a different brew. The girl-child's mixture has narcotic properties, and, after years of opiate dependency, it may take a huge effort for a competent, adult female to emerge from its addictive trance. Poor folk organise their business differently. With few resources and minimal wealth to transmit, its females will be most valued for the work they do. In folktales, which are the traditional narratives of the poor, women often outstrip men in strength and endurance. It is Gretel who is put to work and Hansel who gets locked into a cage to be fattened up to appease the appetite of a witch with a craving for boy-meat. Strong-minded, resourceful, and with no compunction about killing an old woman – appropriately by means of a domestic oven – it is Gretel who outsmarts the witch and saves her brother. She demonstrates no desire to be pleasing to anyone, no masochism, no passivity, and she rescues her brother without any thought of sacrificing herself. Gretel is not cultivated. She has never been tamed or *effeminated*.

Nevertheless, irrespective of class, culture or the

use to which any girl is destined to be put, all virgins represent potential profit. As a prostitute, a virgin can be sold much more gainfully than a woman who has had sexual intercourse. The sacred mission of keeping a potential mother virginal has often been executed with fanatical brutality Many cultures keep their female goods under such tight wraps that all available family members – brothers, mothers, aunts – must be recruited to ensure that no-one tampers with them. Although genetic profiling can now provide foolproof verification of paternity, male preoccupation with recorded genealogies has not disappeared. And even in cultures where the condition of a woman's hymen supposedly has little bearing on her marriage prospects, weddings continue to betray residues of the virginity cult. The ceremony is often solemnised in church even amongst normally secular families, where the traditional western bride still comes membrane-ously veiled and gift-wrapped. The connotations are obvious. But the great white wedding lingers on as the symbol of a happy ending and guests still dab their eyes theatrically with lace-edged handkerchiefs. Marriage clings to the remnants of its reputation as the primary aspiration for a young woman, and maintains the fiction of improbably docile daughters being given away by unnaturally dedicated fathers. The true content of the wedding, however, is male bonding and the reinforcing of patriarchal rights.

Hymens and Foreskins

Though the hymen has been as much fetishised in fiction as it is in social practice, virginity has always been an indication of absence. Virgins are ciphers, valued precisely because of the absence, the *lack* of activity, power, self-assertion, they represent. While the never-ending record of the begetting of sons by fathers drones on, women stay largely undefined, left to drift likeaimless trails of vapor in the wake of the real event. Whether categorised by the retention of the hymen or the loss of it, or by the penis that grants them identity or the penis they never had, women have consistently been perceived in terms of lack. In certain respects, the foreskin is a ritual equivalent to the hymen. Though it does not indicate lack, circumcision shares a sacrifical significance with the rites around deflowering. Some biblical narratives describe the posthumous sacrifice of the foreskins of enemies slain in battle, but that is where the parallel ends. A man does not suffer the loss of his foreskin in an unguarded moment. Neither does his honour disappear along with it, and he does not suffer social exclusion because an inessential body part has been taken from him. A similar discrimination prevails in social responses to rape. The pain and humiliation of a rape may be as traumatic for a man as for a woman, but a male victim arouses far more public horror and is not afterwards blamed for what was done to him. A woman can be 'ruined' by a rape because her destiny is shaped less by what she does than by what is done to her.

For a man, everything depends upon the word. The Word has been the distinguishing mark of the patriarchal God. According to the bible, it was there from the Beginning . This means that the Name of the Father is always at hand to confirm the dominant text

– though this favourite philosophical metaphor does not explain why the dominant text always inscribes male dominance. Meanwhile, once the text has been written on it, that virginally blank sheet ceases to signify anything at all. Once it has served to re-empower paternal authority, virginity becomes nothing more than a woman's dim memory of a former self-containment. For a man the line of descent inherited from his father is crucial. Without it he is condemned to exist outside history. He is equivalent to an animal. Or a woman. And yet, by itself, not even the Name of the Father as the guarantee of a man's personal worth is enough to make him safe. Not unless a woman has been used to supply the missing link.

Blanks

Women tend to approach the subject of blankness or gaps in the records with a more positive attitude. Isak Dinensen's story, *The Blank Page* (8), written in the late 1950s, has intrigued feminists. This narrative ignores conventions of plot and character and focuses on the inscribing or the failure to inscribe the parchment of virginity. The story takes place in a nunnery where bedlinen is produced for royalty. Framed portions of certain sheets, each one stained with blood from a defloration and labelled with the name of a princess, are exhibited on a wall. One frame, to which no name has been added, contains nothing but a blank white square. Without the evidence of the ordained sacrifice of her virginity, this woman has been anathematised, erased, made into an empty space without either a history or a personal identity. Susan

Gubar comments: "Blankness here is an act of defiance .. *Not to be written on is .. the condition of new sorts of writing for women.* .. The stained pages are therefore biographical remnants of otherwise mute existences, a result of and response to life rather than an effort at producing an independent aesthetic object." (9)

In the mid 1980s, the visual artist, Mary Kelly, took unmistakable steps to create a blank. Her work, *Corpus*, performs a visual disappearing act. Pieces of empty clothing outline the absent form of a woman. Each one of Kelly's five images is accompanied by a text or testament, but the person who formerly occupied the abandoned garments has disappeared. Only the fetishistic trappings of an identity remain behind. Kelly's subsequent book, *Imaging Desire*, explains her intentions: ".. the textual emphasis is more than an effort to create significance out of the *absence* of the woman's image as representational or iconic sign; it is an attempt to alter the implications of her *presence* in the spectacle of histories and practices." (10) Kelly's woman has clearly not been excised. She has actively absconded, gone off to become a *subject* in some alternative spectacle. The empty space, the blank, she leaves behind informs us that a story exists, even if, as with the Dinensen narrative, we are obliged to invent it for ourselves.

No empty spaces are ever truly empty. The space that in theory has no content is in reality filled with possibilities – most frequently repressed ones. The canon designates the repressed feminine either as non-existent or too grotesque to exhibit in the light of day.

Repression, however, generates huge supplies of compressed energy and fires the imagination. It is only too easy to put that chronicle of longstanding hubris and abuse, the metaphor of the parchment-hymen, to very satisfying imaginary purposes. Here's one scenario: for many millenia, the female body part that is so small yet so indispensible to the survival of the patriarchy was left lying like a doormat outside the entrance to the kingdom : one day, as usual gazing heavenwards in spellbound self-adoration, the Father tripped over it and fell to his knees...

Footnotes

1) Hrdy, Sarah Blaffer, *Mother Nature*, p.565. Vintage, 2000.

2) Hrdy, op cit, p 264.

3) Hrdy, op cit. p243..

4) The origin of the virgin mother in a translation error between Hebrew and Greek has not prevented it from being an article of faith. See: Uta Ranke-Heinemann, *Eunuchs for the Kingdom of Heaven*, p.33 and Ch 2. (1988) Penguin, 1991.

5) A joke nuns like to tell says rhere are three sexes: men, women and nuns; the obvious reference to celibacy signifies a discreet withdrawal from gender definitions which perceive women through their relationship with men and assert that women can exist outside the range of manly diktat.

6) Aristotle taught that the sperm of the male parent contained the child's totality, while the female's only function was to be a receptacle or a growing medium.

7) Luce Irigaray, *Sexes & Genealogies*, p.194. (1987.) Columbia University Press. 1993.

8) This story comes from Isaak Dinensen's *Last Tales*.

9) Susan Gubar, The Blank Page: Issues of Female Creativity. *Writing and Sexual Difference*, ed E. Abel, p.78. Harvester Press. 1982. Whereas the present text concentrates on blankness and namelessness, Gubar's critique extends to the writing-related meanings found in the story.

10) Mary Kelly, *Imaging Desire*, p.141. Massachusetts Institute of Technology. 1996. Each image in this series is titled according to one of Charcot's categories of hysteria.

5

"Why Would She Not Be Hysterical?"

Hysteria As Feminist Statement

Whatever form it chooses to take, from antiquity onwards hysteria has been associated with women. Extreme stress may produce hysterical symptoms in men, (1) but it is perceived as a prime and primarily female psychiatric disorder.

In ancient Greece, hysteria was thought to be caused by a displacement of the womb. Freud later came to regard it as a displacement of repressed sexual conflict and desire which generated symptoms that symbolised stifled fantasies. Hysteria was greatly in fashion during the period when the young Freud was in Paris and he liked to attend public displays of hysterical women patients at the Salpetriere hospital. A retrospective study of attitudes towards hysteria describes one much photographed young patient as, "an apt pupil of the atelier. All of her poses suggest the exaggerated gestures of the French classical acting style, or stills from silent movies." (2) Eventually, dressed in men's clothing, she escaped from the asylum and was not seen again. This might not strike everyone as an indication of cure, but nobody could deny the links between performance, disguise and hysteria.

For Freud, this sexually-generated neurosis invariably indicates the "symptomatic acting out of a proposition the hysteric cannot articulate." (3) He does not allow that the hysteric's inability to articulate might result either from a silence that had been enforced or from the need to repress material which, if explicit, would result in rejection or social disgrace. Nor is it only Freud's narrow representation of the genesis of hysteria that can be challenged. He has been accused of habitually invalidating the testimony of his female patients and of interpreting the accounts they gave of sexual abuse by male relatives or family intimates as neurotic fantasies. (4) This reading allies him with the dominant male establishment but, if real sexual abuse is consistently denied and if the demands of truth conflict with those of a powerful authority, surely hysteria is an entirely appropriate reaction. Hysteria provides a safe means of maintaining personal integrity and continuing to protest against repression, but in a codified form. It eliminates the need to challenge the forces of repression face to face.In this chapter, hysteria will be identified as the metaphorical or symbolic expression of material that has been repressed or suppressed for a variety of reasons.

Woman Doesn't Exist
The manipulation of facts is not generally quite so

obvious, but Freud's suppression of the testimony of his female patients provides a good example of the way in which the character of woman has been constructed by and for the benefit of men and male institutions. Luce Irigaray criticises Freud's interpretation of hysteria on precisely these grounds. She takes the unapologetically positive view that hysteria provides a woman with a means of defying the demands of the 'feminine' role that a male establishment has imposed on her. Her hysteric is no inert neurotic, involuntarily manifesting unconsciously repressed desires. She is a woman who is actively rejecting a humilating identification of herself as an inadequate (castrated) creature with neither sexual validity nor entitlement to equal treatment or respect. Irigaray has been described as understanding hysteria as "a refusal rather than a repression of heterosexuality" and the hysteric as "a proto-feminist .. who .. may locate the problem in cultural expectations of femininity rather than in femininity itself." (5)

A patriarchal heterosexuality of the kind envisaged by Freud is seeking to accomplish more than the simple repression of women. "Irigaray's audacious claim is that women are represented only on models that are masculine. We live in a resolutely homosexual culture." (6) A *heterosexuality* that recognises only masculine desire and encompasses only one of the two sexes or sexualities is by definition *homosexual*. And, when Freud represents all *heterosexual* desire in terms of the male and his sexual organ, his complaint that he did not know what women want begins to sound a little peevish to a contemporary ear. A man who perceives desire as invariably masculine and women as the objects of male desire is not in any position to understand the desires of women. Perhaps it should be asked whether the portrayal of desire as a constitutionally masculine force springs largely from fear that an admission of female desire might risk a parallel objectification of the male.

Freud assumes that a woman's overriding ideal must always be masculine and that the secret desire of the neurotic woman is to approximate herself to the male as closely as she can. When she does not, cannot, rest content with her lack, her castration, and in all seriousness acts out this sameness of sexual desire, she inevitably produces the symptoms of a 'masculinity complex' and enters into the competitive male struggle for domination. The feminist sees Freud's neurotic woman as a person who rejects a patriarchal definition of herself and refuses to be reduced to an incompleteness which lies on the margins of non-existence. Once her identity as a female has been suppressed, she is mutilated and ceases, socially, to be an independent or even real individual. The Freudian woman is in a no-win situation: she is deviant if she won't subscribe to masculinist norms, but if she does subscribe to them, ahe will have to renounce her own evaluation of herself and her desires. Irigaray's account of the Freudian family is biting, "..the child: never anything but a little boy; husband: man-father. Woman? Doesn't exist. She borrows the disguise which she is required to assume. She mimes the role imposed upon her. The only thing really expected of her is that she *maintain, without fail, the circulation of pretense by enveloping herself in femininity.*" (7)

These comments in fact describe the genesis of 'masquerade', a term coined by Freud's colleague, Joan Rivière. (This subject will be considered in greater detail in the next chapter.) Rivière clearly appreciates the element of pretence that such an envelopment in femininity requires, but possibly still views it as hysteria and a manifestation of a desire to be male rather than a desire to take control of her effemination through her own absurdly exaggerated performance of it. As Freud heedlessly continues to dress up his little doll-woman in 'feminine' characteristics, he uses the phallus to represent all sexual desire. His representation automatically pathologises all female experiences of homoerotic emotion. Female displays of love for other women must be understood as instances or imitations of male desire and therefore have to be discounted as neurotic. Crucially, Freud here includes a woman's first love, her mother. While the little boy reaches the Oedipal phase and wants to marry his mother, the little girl of the same age is expected to renounce her mother and dream of marrying her father. If she doesn't, this poorly-equipped, little girl-boy embarks on a pathetic quest to secure the mother's love for herself. It is just her bad luck that her father and his sons have already been assigned an official first claim to mother's love.

Hysteria In Practice

Hysteria has direct links with many of the issues discussed in the course of these chapters. We will soon see how effortlessly masquerade, pornography, silence, the persecution of witches all slip in beside it. Pornography produces sexual distortions that may differ in kind and meaning from the distortions of masquerade, but both incorporate fetishist elements. Mutism, often viewed as a form of hysteria, can reveal a wealth of concealed statement. "..to say nothing," and to use "her own body as disguise" is one of the main aims of hysteria as masquerade. (8) And while this man-made-up femininity can speak volumes without uttering a word, equally, a hysterical excess of feminised words may also be veiling the true, silent or silenced content of what is being said. Hysteria, taken as a psychological affliction which beyond all others typifies the feminine predicament, is a "priviledged dramatisation of feminine sexuality .. stigmatized as a place where fantasies, ghosts, and shadows fester and must be unmasked, interpreted, brought back to the reality of.. the original." (9) The perception of hysteria as something alien to both reason and reality confirms Le Doeuff's critique regarding philosophy's exclusion of the imaginary.

If hysteria is indeed as Irigaray understands it to be, and represents the only remaining option for expressing – though sometimes back to front – a different feminine, then it creates a problem to which a phallocracy can offer only a single solution: it must quickly be subjected to the proper controls. It must be forced to conform before it contaminates orthodox constructions. But Irigaray's strand of feminism does not regard hysteria as the problem. The problem perceived here is the *repression* of hysteria and the silencing-by-pathologising of hysteria's frequently wordless statements. The hysteric's protest against what a patriarchy requires of its women is highly complex: in taking on an extreme and exaggerated form, the hysteric's mime or "dramatisation" is also satirizing the ludicrous distortions produced by patriarchal expectations. Catherine Clément casts an unsparing light on Freud's frustrated attempts to 'cure' hysterics: "..the hysteric, reputed to be incurable, sometimes – and more and more often – took the role of a resistant heroine: the one whom psychoanalysis would never be able to *reduce*. The one who roused Freud's passion through the spectacle of femininity in crisis, and the one, the only one, who knew how to escape him." (10)

Woman, Irigary tells us, ".. borrows signifiers but cannot make her mark, or re-mark upon them. Which all surely keeps her deficient, empty, lacking, in a way that could be labelled "psychotic" .. for want of a practical signifying system." She concludes, *"Hysteria is all she has left."* (11)

Nevertheless, according to Irigaray, hysteria is anything but the last resort of the defeated or the mad. Whether silent or spoken, hysteria as statement shows that it has both the courage and the techniques to confront the establishment with the paradox of simultaneous expression and repression of concepts that this same establishment has excluded. It has earned a position as a form of communication able to convey a great deal more than personal pain and fantasy.

"And anyway why would she not be "hysterical"? ... the ludic mimicry, the fiction, the "make believe", the "let's pretend" – which, as we know, made the hysteric subject to all kinds of disbelief, oppression, and ridicule – are stopped short, impeded, *controlled by a master-signifier*, the Phallus, and by its representative(s)." (12)

Hysteria As Postmodern Narrative

Hysteria appears at the root of a sizeable amount of fiction. Not only can it represent the feminist understanding of "let's pretend", but it can provide an almost ready-made narrative. The meta-language used by hysteria to perform what has been repressed is invaluable to carnival, theatre, fiction and the entire panoply of pretence because less-than-manly hysterical extremes such as weeping, screaming, laughing and all uncontrollable manifestations of emotion and desire are acceptable here as a means of allowing inadmissible material to escape.

In *The Female Man*, Joanna Russ gives a virtuoso and very funny rendering of almost the entire repertoire of hysteria (13). Extracting the feminist kernel of many forms of hysteria, the book flits between multiple characters or personalities (14) and fluctuates between third person and first person narratives. With much ironic reference to the characteristics associated with hysteria and the feminine, Russ crams fistfuls of disparate narratives into an overstuffed and overheated envelope that is always at bursting point. Continuity disappears in a welter of locations and persons as separate narratives interweave and part company again. No one narrative is dominant and a structure that is equivocal, never firmly defined, always fragmentary, always on the brink of apparent disintegration makes hierarchical readings impossible.

"The Female Man "breaks all formal rules of narrative fiction. It has no beginning-middle-end, no clear relationship between text and meaning .. flagrantly flouting what can be seen as patriarchal conventions" (15) This comment reads much like a description of hysteria. In a different context, Russ herself points out that, "The actual world is constantly present in fantasy by negation .. fantasy is what *could not have happened. ..* Fantasy violates the real, contravenes it, denies it, and insists on this denial throughout." (16)

Russ is never a solemn feminist. *The Female Man* is playful, teasing, deflatory. It casually tells the stories of Janet from another planet and a trio of other J's, one of them named Joanna like the author. Sometimes Russ uses nothing weighter than epigram: "It takes a tremendous rearrangement of mental priorities for women to eat well, that is to spend money on their insides instead of their outsides," she remarks laconically, as she links eating disorders with both lack and masquerade. Sometimes, she reasons with a sophistry that transports logic straight into Wonderland: "I'm a victim of penis envy (said Laura) so I can't ever be happy or lead a normal life... I've never slept with a girl. I couldn't. I wouldn't want to. That's abnormal and I'm not, although you can't be normal unless you do what you want and you can't be normal unless you love men. To do what I wanted would be normal, unless what I wanted was abnormal, in which case it would be abnormal to please myself and normal to do what I didn't want to do, which isn't normal." Of course, by this reasoning, no space exists in which this (or any) woman can be both normal and herself. Russ's Jael "is really terrifying, for she's invisible. Against the black curtains her head and hands float in sinister disconnection... She stepped out against the white wall, a woman-shaped hole, a black cardboard cutout.." This sums up the fragmentary nature or even total void in portrayals of the feminine. Horror at the absence of body parts and the "woman-shaped hole" both suggest Freud's "castrated mother". Jael remarks, "I am .. a specialist in disguises." She is "a constantly changing contradiction" and "in turn gentle, terrifying, hateful, loving, "stupid" (or "dead") and finally indescribable."

The Hole That Exists To Be Filled

One interesting commentary on Irigaray's work says that it "suggests a close resemblance between the unconscious in its relation to consciousness and women in relation to patriarchal social relations .. if what is repressed is the feminine, [Irigaray] claims, it is possible to regard women, not as *having* an unconscious, but as *being* it (for men, for the phallic, for patriarchy)." (17) And so we have one more way in which woman is there only to serve masculine needs. Leading once more to "woman doesn't exist". Leaving one more "woman-shaped hole".

Irigaray seems to be telling us that the stability of (masculine) order and continuing control can depend on something as ostensibly absurd as female performances of hysterical excess. That the very survival of masculine identity as it understands itself can depend on always having the means (woman) at hand to contain the matters and conditions that have been repressed. That the system would collapse if she were not at all times available for this purpose. Just as Le Doeuff's Imaginary is a necessary component if philosophy is to appear immaculately rational, so the fictions of hysteria are indispensible to the maintenance of a smoothly controlled masculinist culture.

Footnotes

1) Shell shock in the first world war was eventually understood to be an example of male hysteria.

2) Elaine Showalter. *The Female Malady*. Pantheon Books. 1985.

3) Elizabeth Grosz. *Sexual Subversions*. p134. Allen & Unwin. 1989.

4) Jeffrey Masson gives a damning account of Freud's misrepresentations in cases of female hysterics in *The Assault on Truth: Freud's Suppression of the Seduction Theory*. He suggests that Freud declined to implicate their fathers as they were co-representatives of male authority – and paying for their daughters' treatment.

5) Grosz. op cit. p134-5.

6) Grosz. ibid p. 107. Irigaray is using 'homosexual' to include the meaning of 'of the same sex.

7) Luce Irigaray. *When the goods get together*. New French Feminisms, ed Elaine Marks and Isabelle de Courtivron. p108. The Harvester Press. 1984.

8) Michèle Montrelay. *Inquiry into Femininity.* p93. m/f 1. 1978.

9) Irigaray. *Speculum of the Other Woman*. p60.

10) Clément, Catherine, in *The Newly Born Woman* Hélène Cixous and Catherine Clément, *p.9.* Manchester University Press. 1986. (*La Jeune Née.* 1975, Union Génerale d'Editions, Paris.)

11) Irigaray. ibid. p71.

12) Irigaray. *ibid.* p60.

13) Joanna Russ, *The Female Man.* The Women's Press. U.K. 1985. Judith Clute's painting on the cover evokes the book it is illustrating with great precision. It portrays the arms and forehead of an otherwise undeliniated woman and suggests reading. An archway frames a woman's dress, empty except for a single hand that seems to be readying itself for some unspecified action as it emerges from a sleeve. The empty dress also shares features with Mary Kelly's empty garments as a portrayal of hysteria. (see *Corpus*, Ch 3).

14) According to Elaine Showalter in *Sexual Anarchy*, female hysteria as multiple personality was favoured by psychiatrists in fin-de-siecle America. It also appears later in film, e.g. in the 1957, *The Three Faces of Eve*.

15) Sarah Lefanu. *In the Chinks of the World Machine,* p186. The Women's Press. 1988.

16) Joanna Russ, *'The Subjunctivity of Science Fiction', Extrapolation,* 15. Quoted by Rosemary Jackson in *Fantasy: The Literature of Subversion*, p 22. Metheun, 1981.

17) Grosz. op cit. p107.

6

Masquerade as Performance:
Its Role in King Lear

Lack Engenders Masquerade

Masquerade is not an exclusively feminine phenomenon, but men do not make use of its subversive potential as commonly. (1) Joan Rivière was extending the range of Freud's masculinity complex when she applied the term masquerade to women's expression of problems about their sexuality through exaggeratedly 'feminine' kinds of dress or behaviour. Where Freud had seen 'masculine' behaviour, mannish clothing and so forth as indications of a woman's desire to possess a penis, Rivière made the more subtle observation that women could covertly express another version of this wish through an exaggeration of feminine self-presentation. However, a considerably more complicated interpretation was to follow this Freudian preamble to masquerade defined as a specific response to the shame and envy women experienced because they lacked the all-important male sexual organ. She suggested that these apparent attempts to conceal the inadequacy of the female sex were, in fact, a cover -up for a deeper layer of deception. A woman struggled to camoflage her 'castration' or lack of penis with extravagant 'femininity' in order to hide the far more forbidden fantasy that secretly she already possessed the penis Freud believed her to desire. Worse still, she had acquired it by castrating the father. Masquerade includes all the secrecy and deception which for Freud typified female sexuality. He comments, "The condition of forbiddeness in the erotic life of women is, I think, comparable to the need on the part of men to debase their sexual object." (2) He does not not take the contractual aspect of marriage that allows men to dominate their wives into consideration here, and though he provides a clear description of a male attitude that is contemptuous of women, it does not seem to occur to him that women often have the very different motivation of finding greater sexual freedom outside the constraining confines of marriage. Rivière demonstrated her theory of masquerade with the case history of a patient who, every time she gave a lecture, immediately felt compelled to make sexual advances to male members of her audience. This theatrical display of 'feminine' desire assuaged her guilt for usurping male (the father's) intellectual prerogatives and lessened her dread of retribution.

Masquerade operates on several levels. One feminist later summed it up as "a threefold construction: a woman who regards herself as a man who passes for a woman". (3) As masquerade wraps a woman in all manner of equivocation and disguise, it both hides and expresses suppressed aspects of her feminine identity. Its oblique performances broadly resemble hysterical disorders. They simultaneously obscure and transmit information, and draw attention to attributes – most typically those of the body – that are usually identified as 'feminine'. Luce Irigaray details the meaning – or lack of it – that an excess of 'femininity' produces in a system organised to suit the requirements of the patriarchy: "The cosmetics, the disguises of all kinds that women cover themselves with are intended to deceive, to promise more value than can be delivered .. Even if someday she plays to perfection the role of femininity in all its bourgeois perversity, it will in no way fill, will only deck with nothingness." Woman has no "possible representation of her value .. which could bring her into the system of exchange as something other than 'object'." (4)

In fact, masquerade is more threatening to the patriarchy and far more complex than its surface indicates. Behind a screen of 'feminine' whimsy lurks a clandestine female potency that ought by right to be 'masculine'. It is guilty of the theft of the Father's phallus and threatens its envied status as a symbol of male dominance. Above all, it tells us that his claim of containing the fullness of being human is purely illusory and the woman knows this.

The woman's masquerade appears to be emphasising her function as an 'object', but it is simply a way of disorienting the spectator. The protean forms of masquerade, like the fabrications of exaggerated or even unnatural attributes, are all intended to make certain that the real woman underneath is never seen. And the trick succeeds: these performances help to lessen the perpetual anxiety that afflicts the masculine order and those who subscribe to it. The extravaganzas of masquerade provide a theatre which allows a man to take refuge in the role of spectator and the illusion that there is nothing beyond what is visible, nothing more than an exotic performance, and no subordinated or excluded other who is bent on vengeance. The incongruity of the spectacle barely matters. The more meaningless the better, so long as it diverts attention (as it intends both to do and not to do) away from the castration of the Father. And, so long as it also hides that vertiginous, female nothingness in the appearance of being some thing – please god, something harmless – then, at least in its apparent lack and insignificance, it will not seem to be threatening phallic supremacy. And so the psychic melodrama goes on.

The subversive possibilities of masquerade can be imagined endlessly. They have stirred up a lot of feminist interest and sometimes turned Freudian doctrine back on itself by referring to lack (the Freudian woman's imaginary castration and lack of penis) as the lack of lack. This definition cuts two ways: as it refers to the Freudian notion of the woman's desire to possess a penis, at the same time it is making the very un-Freudian point that a woman is equipped with a non-pathological, non-penile potency of her own.

Beyond the many explanations for the existence of masquerade, a woman has good reason to fear she will be severely punished if she attempts to override the

Law of the Father (thus castrating him) either in her private life or in the more open terrain of society at large. The Father does not tolerate slights to his authority. This is most blatantly demonstrated wherever males have full control of female family members, but it also appears in absurdly trivial details such as length of hair acceptable for men and for women, or the colours and textures of garments, matters which can only be viewed as ideological challenges by absurdly artificial standards. However much a woman may be required (or *needed* if stability is to be maintained) to produce an ultra-feminised representation of herself, in the end the antics and divertissements of masquerade inevitably give rise to anxious suspicions of deception. An apparition that has been conjured up by the male imagination will quite obviously never provide a truthful account of woman. Despite the fact that it typically involves such innocent artifices as cosmetics, fanciful modes of dress and other manifestations of womanly flightiness, if masquerade is perceived as a strategy that intends to deceive, it will stimulate further, more severe misogyny and tighter control. As masquerade veils the feminine with excess, it also unveils the intense hostility that suffuses patriarchal fantasies of the feminine. But the flamboyant and enigmatic spectacles of masquerade have generally managed to deflect suspicions of deliberate subversion. Though often shrewd and disingenuous, masquerade still seems to complement or even verify the masculine order. In one form or another, it was doing these things since long before it acquired its present definition. Feminist interest in masquerade may be new, but this feminine strategy has ancient origins. This chapter will study its usage in a play that was written several centuries before Freud ever picked up a pen.

A Feminist Analysis of
Masquerade in King Lear

"Reading Shakespeare ought not to be a study in the history of ideas; it should allow us to re-confront the formation, genesis or creation of ideas. .. Repeating the past transforms the past, for the past is as much in production as the present." (5) When Shakespeare juxtaposes a pair of "unnatural daughters" and an imperious father in King Lear, the device that sets the plot in motion has all the identifying marks of masquerade. Old and in need of care, from the start Lear displays an ill-disguised dread of losing control of his womenfolk. But, in itself, Lear's predicament is not enough to explain his further behaviour or that of any of his daughters. If he has no serious motivation, Lear has no heroic stature, and his rage and despair are just products of encroaching senile dementia. A central moving force is needed for a unified dramatic purpose. Many attempts have been made to supply one. It has been remarked that, "despite a lifetime of strenuous defense against admitting feminine feelings and the power of feminine presence into his patriarchal world .. he learns to weep." (6) Certainly Lear represses all feminine traits in himself and represents himself as unmitigatedly male, but more is required if the intense and disastrous progress of the drama is to have meaning. We need to understand the function of Lear's oddly codified abdication ritual, to know why Cordelia refuses to speak, why her refusal drives him to fury, and what inspires the insane vindictiveness of Goneril and Regan. Without answers to these moral, psychological and political questions, Lear's behaviour is inexplicable, exhorbitant, and his daughters' reactions as excessive as his theatrical ceremony. What justifies such surpluses?

The codes of patriarchal conduct are crucial in the dynamics of this play. His heritage of power as a king has provided Lear with the lifelong identity of arch-patriarch. Staunchly masculine, Lear already mistrusts women and has no faith in their love, and the tragedy he creates out of his impossible demands on his daughters is magnified by this. Elizabethan audiences would have been keenly alert to the turmoil that could ensue if a king died without a male heir who could unequivocally claim the throne. And a modern, globally aware audience can readily appreciate the realism of his determination to retain absolute dominion over his female kin. Driven by a frantic desire for sons and heirs who would perpetuate his dynasty in accordance with the traditions of his ancestors, Lear resorts to conjuring the simulacra of ersatz sons out of the female materials of his daughters.

To become Lear's male heirs, each daughter must somehow possess a phallus, even if only a fantasy one. But Lear has an immediate problem: although he tries to make sons out of his daughters, he also needs to retain the daughterly obligations that stem from their female identities. The initial scene in which he bids his daughters to make declarations of their love for him has sometimes been brushed aside as a 'fairytale' component of the play belonging to an era when history was barely distinct from legend. However, the entire plot of the play evolves directly out of this scene. Goneril and Regan play his game, but, unfortunately, Lear seems oblivious to the fact that the exaggeration colouring his daughters' speeches suggests satire more than devotion. Almost immediately, his unnatural subtext reveals its true roots in the daughters who have agreed to accept his conditions. They swiftly become "unnatural" and manifest an alarming masculine aggressiveness. Only Cordelia refuses to be denatured – she also remains loyal to her father even after he has disowned her. Both as patriarch and parent, Lear is demanding a bad faith that inevitably destroys his daughters, himself, and, most ironically, his kingdom. As a king, he founds the continuance of his dynasty on a lie which, however symbolic, falsifies his own estate and also ruins his masculinity. The displays of excessive and submissive femininity in his daughters' verbal masquerade very obviously cover up the opposite statement that his daughters are not what they seem, but are secretly male. The stuff of which his life has until then been made starts to unravel.

In the tense encounter when Lear enjoins his daughters to make their formal professions of filial love, the overwhelming force of his desire is palpable. Desire has been defined as that which constructs fantasies in a never-ending search for a satisfying object in the real world (7). Certainly, fantasy dominates these ceremonial performances as well as the protestations of the daughters. Though Lear would have despised such effusiveness in his own sex, he does not seem to care that what his daughters have to say is totally devoid of sincerity and has no relation to reality. But of course, dissimulation is his precise purpose. Shakespeare is here producing a Lear who is producing a masquerade that will in turn produce his daughters' moral descent into an extreme and malignant masculinity.

Though in everyday life, costume and other bodily features may often play the major part in masquerade, appropriately in the context of drama, it is embodied in the dialogue. Wallowing in declarations of love that topple into parody, Goneril and Regan show a voracious desire to take possession of their father's kingdom. Yet, though their falsity is shameless, it is Lear who is guilty of inspiring their dishonesty. He may represent himself as honourable, frank and manly, but he is the begetter of their lies. To create the illusion that he has heirs, he bribes his daughters to be men, or be the same as men, and pays them off with portions of his kingdom. At the same time, he requires them to display their propriety by covering up the masculinity that is so immodest in a female. This humiliatingly public exhibition of their lack triggers their repressed lack of lack, which immediately becomes the core of their newly allocated parts as sons. They act these parts out far beyond the limits of their father's expectations, and Lear's fantasy sons become the murderous sons, who, in Freudian theory, have conspired to supplant the father ever since the dawn of civilisation. Lear's sustained falsehood perverts his daughters' sexuality to the point where they can no longer function as women. The dialogue notes their increasing dysfunction in this respect.

Cordelia's refusal to speak the part her father has ordained for her is at least as resolute as Lear's furious demands that she must speak. In telling Lear she loves him, "According to my bond, no more no less," she is affirming her identity as a woman and a daughter and repudiating the fictitious and falsifying masculinity that her father demands she must endorse.

Performances of Madness

When Cordelia disrupts Lear's hidden agenda she provokes him to such fury that he is said to be "mad." The false reality in which he so desperately needs to believe has been exposed. But he will need to become much madder before his blurring of the boundaries between his fantasy re-gendering of his daughters and his far from imaginary division of his kingdom finally forces him to a radical reshaping of his understanding of himself. He is going to learn that reality does not bow to imagination – neither that of a father nor a king. Balance is only restored to the kingdom, and to Lear's troubled mind, when Cordelia returns.

The older sisters openly lay claim to masculine prerogatives. Goneril remarks, "I must .. give the distaff/ Into my husband's hands." Lear struggles to reverse the dangerous maleness he has enjoined upon them, "I should be false persuaded I had daughters." "Thy sister's naught," (8) he tells Regan, as if, once again by only the power of words, he can cut Goneril back to her former ineffectual female size. Lear's speeches show how completely they have become masculinised for him. They "are not men of their words." He perceives his aged friend Gloucester as "Goneril with a white beard." But if he now regards them as "unnatural hags", it is Lear himself who has pitted them against the laws of nature. (9)

Soon he is seeking revenge on his daughters' very femaleness. He calls on Nature to turn against Goneril and "dry up in her the organs of increase." His preoccupation with sexual abberation and dysfunction is feverish. "Down from the waist they [women] are centaurs .. all the fiend's – There's hell, (10) there's darkness, there is the sulphurous pit.." His sexual insecurity increases in proportion to her unnatural masculinity. But it is too late; Lear has already stirred the cauldron, already disrupted the natural order.

Lear's madness is less an illness than a refuge, a disguise, a form of masquerade that serves to cover his own castration and lack. He addresses Tom o'Bedlam as "philosopher" and "sapient sir", and begs this fellow madman, who is even deeper in disguise, to "tutor" him. Lear wildly declares that a madman is, "A king, a king!" He has begun to abandon dreams of worldly power for unperverted Nature. "Expose thyself to feel what wretches feel," he advises. "Thou art the thing itself," he tells mad Tom. Soon Lear is acknowledging the universal sexuality of nature – ".. let copulation thrive" – and, as he begins to appreciate the folly of trying to subvert the natural order, he agonises, "Oh let me not be mad". Undeniably, he still fears the dishonour of a feminised condition – "let not woman's weapons, water drops, stain my man's cheeks", but his feminine aspect becomes clearly visible when he crowns himself with flowers, taking on the appearance of an ancient, crumbling Ophelia more than a virile king. By the end of the play, he finally abandons his hopeless desire to force the real world to enact his fantasies, lets go his lifelong male defences, and unashamedly weeps over Cordelia's body. Tragedy records the struggle to transmute the fantasies created by desire into realities. Lear's progress from the installation of his daughters as sons spirals into his own lack, hysteria, masquerade, madness and the bitter taste of fantasy. "Give me an ounce of civet," he begs, "sweeten my imagination."

Putting Penis Envy Where It Belongs

Happily, masquerade is often more comic than tragic and the histrionic Freudian concoction of the 'castrated' woman who is contorted with penis-envy has been unexpectedly stimulating for feminists. At moments, it has become a rallying point in the struggle to formulate a realistic feminine identity. The Freudian female is composed of contradictions. In her divided sexual identity she is both the enfeebled, mutilated male and the empty and untrustworthy fantasy female. This division produces instant and insoluble conflicts. In discussing male fear of the feminine, Michele Montrelay refers directly back to the Freudian construction of woman: "femininity experienced as real and immediate is the blind spot of the symbolic process analysed by Freud. Two incompatible, heterogenous territories coexist inside the feminine unconscious: that of representation and that which remains 'the dark continent'."(11) A woman who is represented as a castrated man must either openly exhibit her lack or disappear behind a screen of fantasy. Or can she perhaps do both?

What started life as a clinical neurosis turns out to be busy about more than the simple veiling of a "dark continent". Masquerade is free to invent and reinvent itself. In spite of the distracting intrusions of commercial exploitation, it provides an unfettered space in which otherwise problematic activities can take place. The simple fact that it exists confirms that there is something which needs to be hidden, and something that has been hidden always creates a threat of exposure. Masquerade simultaneously serves two opposite aims. It is innately paradoxical as it seeks to hide and reveal what it is really up to. As a form of both exhibitionism and discretion, while it is hiding the insufficiency of a masculine order which excludes the reality of women, it is also exposing masculine weakness.

And as masquerade takes its parody of the feminine ever further into the baroque domain of artifice, its excesses stress the sheer fictivenesss of the gender roles society imposes. Penis-envy begins to look like a wilful absurdity and even the supreme phallus seems to be wilting beneath its own inept and cumbersome embarrassment. Not so masquerade. It has always understood itself to be a fiction.

Footnotes

1) Male masquerade appears in transvestism and cross-dressing and is fully accepted in carnivals and pantomimes.

2) Freud, volume 7 On Sexuality. Taboo of Virginity. P.255)

3) Catherine Millot, The Feminine Superego, from The Woman in Question, p.302, ed Parveen Adams & Elizabeth Cowie, Verso, London, 1990. For Rivière's account see Womanliness as Masquerade. IJP X (1929)

4) Luce Irigaray. Speculum of the Other Woman. p.114. Cornell University Press. 1985. (French Edition 1974.)

5) Claire Colebrook, *Gilles Deleuze*. P. 73-4. Routledge. London & New York. 2002

6) Coppelia Kahn, "Excavating those Dim Minoan Regions: Maternal Subtexts in Patriarchal Literature." p.41 Diacritics, Summer 1982.

7) Jacques Lacan. Ecrits, A Selection. Tavistock Publications Ltd. 1977. (Editions du Seuil 1966.)

8) As well as being a synonym for "nothfing" in Shakesperean English, "naught" meant "sinful", as did "naughty".

9) 'Unnatural' referring to female inheritance of the kingdom (not according to patriarchal law) contrasts with the unnatural maleness of Goneril and Regan (not according to natural law). Natural, meaning illegitimate, applies to Edmund, the son whom Gloucester acknowledges despite the patriarchal disapproval that attaches to illegitimacy, but, like

Goneril and Regan, Edmund treats his father with unnatural cruelty.

10) 'Hell' was used to mean female genitalia in demotic Elizabethan English.

11) Montrelay. op cit. p.263.

7

On Being Nothing

Is Cordelia Neurotic, Psychotic, or a Crypto-Feminist?

In the last chapter, we saw the disruption resulting from Cordelia's refusal to speak according to her father's formula. The one word – "nothing" – that she offers to her father snatches control over herself away from him. Rather than collude with the illusion that will regenerate the supremacy of his royal line, she leaves him empty handed. The refusal to exhibit or enunciate an illusory feminine self concerns many contemporary feminists. Of the modern writer, Marguerite Duras, it has been remarked that "... nonspeech .. exhibits the fascinating dimension of feminine lack.," and "wants to make this lack 'speak' as cry." (1)

Certainly, "nothing" is the most conspicuous word in *King Lear*. (2) The word might seem opaque or have no special meaning to a modern audience, but to Shakespeare's contemporaries the bawdy Elizabethan use of the word 'nothing' to mean female genitalia (3) would have been instantly clear. Cordelia's ruinous "nothing" unhesitatingly states that as a woman she rejects spurious masculine empowerment. She refuses to misrepresent, betray or deny the feminine, even on an entirely symbolic plane. If woman is held to be nothing, then that is how she too prefers to be known. Her unconditional loyalty to her own proper sexual identity and her shameless use of the nakedly female "nothing" are a repudiation of the entire patriarchal order. This 'nothing' asserts the truth that shatters Lear's dream of creating heirs to perpetuate his line. And even as she exposes the one fact that is intolerable to him, she is also committing a second offence: her open disobedience to her father changes her role as a subordinate female object through which the patriarchy can demonstrate its dominance. Her refusal to serve, to impersonate the creature he desires – son and heir as well as dutiful daughter – and her insistence on her lowly female status both oppose the very thing he needs for his drama to proceed. Not only does her disobedience challenge his supremacy, her refusal to accept the crowning symbol of patriarchal authority, the phallus-sceptre, adds to his public shame. She exposes as charade what Irigaray, in a quite unrelated context, has described as a "circulation of pretense" (4). Her actions not only bring down Lear's fantasy but his sanity along with it. At this point, if he is to shore up the wreckage of his elaborate pretence, his only option is to exclude her and disown her as his child.

This retrospective reading of the plot shapes Cordelia as a tragic heroine who is prepared to sacrifice everything in order to authenticate the true value of her identity as a woman. She prefers to define herself as a lowly "nothing" rather than become a puppet of the patriarchal system. Shakespeare has given us a Cordelia who reconstructs herself before our eyes. Her "nothing" produces the precise opposite of masquerade. "Nothing" becomes the instrument which unmasks masquerade – including Lear's own performance. To be 'no thing' is to be not-an-object. It is to be one who is not produced by the desires of others. 'Nothing' rejects the performance required to enact the part of woman in a man's world. Why stoop to steal the father's phallus when female reproductive organs have their own equal potency? None of the facts are changed merely because male-dominated language forces the feminine to express itself in negative form. This "nothing" clearly identifies Cordelia with her female descent and maternal inheritance.(5) Though the play barely mentions the mother with whom Cordelia's silence unites her and Cordelia's own physical presence in *King Lear* is also slight, the audience is constantly reminded of her absence – her nothingness – by the eruptions of violence and barbarism that inevitably follow the denial of the feminine and the untempered ascendancy of masculinism .

This same insistent "nothing" is also Lear's undoing. It is used repeatedly to emphasise his impotence. The fool tells him, "I am better than thou art now; I am a fool; thou art nothing." He asks, "Can you make no use of nothing, nuncle?" But Lear only reiterates his contempt for women: "Nothing can be made out of nothing," he replies, revealing the depth of his needy despair beneath these words. The "nothing shall come of nothing" with which Lear disinherits Cordelia and his frantic attempts to force her to speak both echo Freud's stated wish to have women speak their desires. It is patently obvious that the patriarchy only wishes to believe every woman's desires will passively complement its own. However, "attempts to 'make' femininity 'speak' would surely jeopardise the very repression that Freud had known how to achieve." (6) *King Lear* reveals the risk to patriarchal authority whenever the female tongue is urged to speak. Even in a long past era, even when it has nothing to say beyond a blank "nothing", unwanted truths are likely to escape.

Being Nothing: Some
More Modern Perspectives

Though the forms of interpretation may have altered, modern women may prefer to avoid the aggressive visibility and illusory artifices of masquerade. However this may be expressed in the different context of the modern world, its meaning remains in many ways continuous. The search for escape from a spurious identity returns persistently to the idea of being nothing. In two films, Federico Fellini's *Juliet of the Spirits,* and Maria Luisa Bemberg's *I, the Worst of All* , this feminine and (perhaps unexpected in the case of Fellini) feminist "nothing" plays a leading role.

Fellini's film makes considerable reference to his marriage with Guilietta Massina.

It portrays the reactions of a woman whose sense of living in an unreality has become personally overwhelming. It has been emphasised that Juliet's difficulties are magnified by an inconsiderate and unsupportive husband who is having an affair with another woman. But other factors are also involved. "Juliet is caught in a hall of mirrors reflecting conflicting cultural representations of Woman.... – images that are 'incessantly held up, suggested or exhibited to her by her culture, her family, her religion, and her fantasies.' " (7)

Juliet has been taken over by 'spirits', many of which are besieging her in the shape of disembodied whispers and hallucinations. These invasive alien forces seek her attention, demand her submission and threaten her own sense of identity. As they seem to thrust themselves upon her from the outside we are led towards the sources of her problems and anxieties. She is beset by flashbacks from a school play in which nuns had cast her in the role of a martyr. Her impeccably groomed mother reproaches her for failing to maintain the properly cosmeticised artifices of feminine presentation. Her sister bullies her into hiring an obsequiously insolent detective who tracks the movements of her husband and captures his infidelties on film. The husband in turn requires her to pretend to ignorance of his affairs with other women. Her social class expects her to consume beyond both her needs and desires. Her neighbour does her best to entice her into taking part in the heartless pleasures of sexual licence and the empty spectacles of masquerade. (8) Mediums and astrologers claim to have knowledge of her that she does not herself possess and thrust their predictions and advice upon her . Pervasive hallucinations intrude into her everyday reality, making her confusion of the two appear not only inevitable but seamlessly integral. A female psychotherapist perhaps comes slightly closer to providing the help Juliet needs when she speaks of the benefits of depending on herself, not others, in her search for a solution. Significantly, this scene takes place in the woods that lead towards the beach which has been a central stage for dreams and hallucinations. But it is only when Juliet starts to understand herself as someone who has "lost everything" that she can begin to abjure the forces that have been tormenting her. In the final scene we see her standing in an empty landscape outside the garden fence that surrounds her house. Her husband has left, the maids have been dismissed. The haunting spirits have also been sent away. Nothing is left. Emptied of all the projections that others have forced upon her, Juliet is at last at peace.

Maria Luisa Bemberg's film, *I the Worst of All,* (9) also takes up the subject of becoming nothing, this time as a deliberately adopted condition. The seventeenth-century Mexican nun shares certain traits with Cordelia, but this modern depiction of Sor Inez is more psychologically complicated and her response to her situation is much more detailed. The film is a homage to a woman of outstanding intellectual and creative ability who is persecuted by conservative elements in the Catholic Church. Inez enters a convent under the guidance of a priest who persuades her that this way she can pursue her studies without opposition or distraction. She does her best to teach the young girls who are being educated in the convent that the mind and knowledge have no sex and that they should never suppress their inborn curiosity or the impulse to question anything. She is certain that a woman's intelligence, even if not specifically feminine, is not masculine either. Modern feminism's much discussed contention that a women has to think like a man if she hopes to be heard is not then relevant, so she feels no sense that she must be male in any way in order to express herself.

Though Inez, now Sor Juana, describes herself as someone who is not very pious, she also says she has always acted in the belief that, by making use of the gifts God had given her, she was following his will . However, her self-definition is seriously unacceptable to the Inquisition-ridden Church of seventeenth-century Mexico. Bemberg shows us the intense and jealous misogyny of the priestly caste of that time and place. Denying that it was possible for a woman to possess intellectual powers or have a mind equal to that of a man, the fanatical archbishop only grudgingly admits the existence of a female soul – and he only goes that far in order to ensure that the Church has full spiritual jurisdiction over women. In the name of the Church, he decrees that learning, philosophy and theology are the exclusive preserves of males and priests and, with all her hopes crushed, Inez is forced to abandon her writings and her studies. Even the priest who originally encouraged her to become a nun, when he sees his own position threatened by increasing Church hostility towards Inez, betrays and abandons her to save himself from censure. She also has to forego the intense female friendship and the protection of the Vicerine after the Viceroy is recalled to Spain.

When the Inquisition prohibits the exercise of her studies and writings and makes it impossible for her to continue to use these gifts, she takes the path into which she has been forced into her own keeping. The orthodox view is that women and nuns are made to serve others and she enacts her defeat in an admixture of determination, desperation and something that, in its consciousness of the absurdity of her enforced self-denial, is close to parody. Rather than be forced into submitting to beliefs she does not hold, she will act of her own accord and within her own personal understanding of reducing herself to nothing and in an extreme symbolical gesture, she signs a vow of submission to the will of god in her own blood. Yet even when her defeat seems absolute, she does not relinquish either her integrity or her autonomy – perhaps it is not possible for her to do so. Rather than yeild to a misogynist authority, she embraces unavoidable submission as her own and offers it directly to her own god. In making a deliberate decision to renounce all expression of herself as a remarkable woman, she is not only internalising her own proper identity but expanding her definition of female identity to embrace all the ordinary, suffering women in the Mexico of her time.

Of course the need for women to use 'masculine' structures in order to be heard does not always stem

124

from an external source. A discussion of this need appears in an interesting correspondence which started up in the1970's between the pseudonymous James Tiptree Jr, who was in reality a woman by the name of Alice Sheldon, Joanna Russ, author of the appropriately titled *The Female Man,* and Ursula Le Guin, a notable writer of science fiction. (10) Sheldon and Russ both speak about their need to pretend to be men in order to be able to write. Tiptree's dependence on this pretence was even more extreme and she suffered acute anxiety after she had been exposed as a woman. Russ, at first believing Tiptree to be sensitive and unusual but nevertheless a man, speaks of how difficult it is for a woman to have intellectual authority and confides that, "To learn to write at all, I had to begin by thinking of myself as a sort of fake man, something that only ended with feminism." (11)

Tiptree could not adapt so easily. After the years spent hidden behind a false identity and masquerading as a man, she found her private self so seriously threatened that it became very difficult for her to write at all once she had been publically exposed as Sheldon. She describes this newly vulnerable existence as a "kind of animated puppet show, with its own validity to be sure .... but those 8 years in sf was the first time I could be *really* real." (12) Then, "In a burst of inspiration she wrote five stories and part of a novel, 'some of it old 'Tiptree'-ish , some of it starting to show the new thing. But the 'real' stuff was to follow.'" Instead, on impulse, she burnt all this new work. "And so, she told Le Guin, 'I *am trying to become nothing.'* " (13) (my italics.)   This episode provides an insight into Sheldon's struggle to locate the blank canvas on which she could begin to inscribe her female identity and reinvent herself as a woman. In Alice Sheldon's later self-inflicted death there are unmistakable echoes of the decision taken by Sor Juana to eliminate herself rather than concede her true identity.

Where Russ is the more demanding and dominant of Sheldon's two epistolary friends, Le Guin is the correspondent who freely offers her affection and support. But Le Guin is experiencing her own struggles with identity. She reacts fiercely to Russ's stance in *The Female Man,* protesting that it is "Womanhood as power, sex as power, violence as power. And it's all power-over [rather than power-to]. It's a total role reversal, but exactly the same game. ... I reject it utterly." Le Guin nevertheless continues to admire Russ's work even if not her belligerent position and she does not deny that she herself also experiences anger . Later Le Guin would add,"I had lost confidence in the kind of writing I had been doing, because I was (mostly unconsciously) struggling to learn how to write as a woman, not as an 'honorary man' as before, and with a freedom that scared me." (14) Here, Le Guin is frankly admitting to her fear of the freedom that accompanies any struggle for a state of being that has not yet been formulated or sanctioned. Her struggles evoke her intense need for a transformative "affirmative ethics" of the sort that Rosi Braidotti describes in formulating the idea that, "Affirmation is about freedom from the burden of negativity, freedom through the understanding of our bondage." (15) Insofar as Russ is playing "exactly the same game", she has engaged in a traditional conflict and is using traditional means to do it. Unlike both Sheldon and Le Guin, she does not have to confront fear of an unborn self. In one way or another, all of Le Guin's books are preoccupied with questions relating to true names, true identities, true realities. Her work has a fluidity which suggests that every thing and person has many complex meanings and is capable of being both more and different from the aspect it is presenting to view at each given moment. The quest for a true self may be in such flux it is always slipping from the hand, but it remains a valid one.

Each in her own way, these writers are struggling to abandon some aspect of the false identity that has been thrust upon them without consultation, to cast off what has been made of her, or made-up about her, or to make up her own version of herself, in order to be free to find or retrieve a truer self than the one which society portrays. Russ is a warrior who fights to establish that woman is not impaired by 'lack' and has neither been castrated nor emasculated. Le Guin never abandons the hope that woman may find her own conscious perception of what it is to be herself.(16) When the defence of the male persona of James Tiptree was wrenched away from the more fragile Sheldon, she found it almost impossible to settle for a half-life spent watching "the vanishing shreds of Tiptree whirling through the suburban air, evaporating under the impact of a chatty, if erratic McLean matron" (17) and eventually chose to kill herself.

To be 'no thing', includes the determination to be

not-an-object, not in essence produced by the desires of others. " Nothing" rejects the performance required to enact the part of woman of male fantasy. ï Being nothing is not in essence a form of renunciation or of capitulation. It can be a struggle which may threaten sanity and even survival as it labours to find a way out of an enveloping fog of looming illusion and false representation. (18) But the fact that its final ghostly goal is an unknown and unseen condition which makes no promises to provide an easier life does not seem to diminish the desire some women feel to attain it.

Footnotes

1) Michele Montrelay. *Inquiry into Femininity. The Woman in Question.* p.264. m/f. ed Parveen Adams & Elizabeth Cowie. Verso. 1990.

2) Even the subplot reverberates with "nothing" as Edmund, Gloucester's bastard son, draws deliberate attention to a forged letter by appearing to conceal it. The ambiguity that typifies masquerade appears here in the message that the spectator must see and yet must not see. Gloucester, lured by concealment, responds with unconscious irony, "The quality of nothing hath not such need to hide itself."

3) E.A.M. Coleman. The Dramatic Use of Bawdy in Shakespeare. Longman. London. 1974.

4) See previous chapter, *Why Would She Not Be Hysterical/*

5) In this, she shares certain properties with Antigone, whose loyalty to her female descent will be discussed in the last chapter of this book.

6) Montrelay. op cit p.267.

7) Shohini Chaudhiri. Feminist film theorists – Laura Mulvey, Kaja Silverman, Theresa de Laurentis. p.63

8) Montrelay comments that the aim of the elements of masquerade in this film "is to say nothing. Absolutely nothing.". op cit p.264.

9) Bemberg's film is scripted from a novel by Octavio Paz.

10) All details of this correspondence have been provided in the

excellent biography of Sheldon byJulie Phillips. See *James Tiptree, Jr. The Double Life of Alice B. Sheldon*. St.Martin's Press, N.Y. 2006.

11) ibid. p.223.

12) ibid. p.367

13) ibid p.375

14) ibid p. 332.

15) Rosi Braidotti. *Nomadic Theory*. P. 294. Columbia University Press. 2011.

16) This hope is reflected in what is probably her least understood work, *Always Coming Home*. Le Guin is clearly experimenting with feminine *forms* of writing in this unusual novel . For further detail see chapter 14.

17) Tiptree, as quoted by Julie Phillip. p 166.

18) This chapter has not included discussion of eating disoeders or self harm, but these also achieve the goal of becoming nothing to the point of self-destruction in preference to submitting to a false identity. It is interesting to note that both eating disorders and self-harming are particular prevalent at the time when girls are making their transition into womanhood.

PART 2

Breaching Barriers

8

A Salty Tongue: Satire, Comedy and Polemic in the *Scum Manifesto.*

Using the Master's Tools to Destroy the House

Satire bypasses the proper procedures of direct confrontation or the attempt to reason judiciously with the patriarchal system. It makes use of a particular form of subversion which provokes ridicule by taking up an *unreasonable* position – one that deviates from the norms of convention and common sense but that simultaneously also reflects the position of the status quo and at times may parody even the sacrosanct assumptions that lie at the root of its reasoning. Historically dominated by men, satire was held to be inappropriately aggressive for female use. "Satire, ancient and probably modern too, is a male, or rather a masculine mode of discourse." (1) Reactions to female ventures into this traditionally male-dominated genre have tended to be extremely negative.

More than forty years after its first publication in 1968, some reassessment of the *Scum Manifesto* (2) is long overdue. This work by Valerie Solanas merits fresh consideration, not only in the light of satire and gender, but as an extreme example of 'atopic' feminist writing. *Scum* exposes the terror that grips the patriarchal heart when a woman scorns male authority in openly confrontational ridicule. Solanas does not bargain or concede. As if claiming a birthright, she takes possession of a form that had until then, at least outside the less immediately direct and milder confines of fiction, been considered a male preserve.

By any standards, *Scum Manifesto*, is a turbulent text. It fuses a rough, demotic style of satire with an unexpectedly subtle polemical content. When it first appeared, its unapologetic vitriol far exceeded that of any previous text associated with feminism. Though much has changed since that time, *Scum* has never fully settled into the main corpus of feminist expression and continues to be perceived as an oddity or slightly deranged anomaly. And *Scum* is odd. It firmly resists "normalisation". In cultural and political terms it sides with "the strange, the risky, the minoritarian, the excessive, the outlawed, and the alien." (3) Solanas's manifesto highlights the exact distinction between the *reactive* feminist, who struggles "to be *like* men, to have a fixed identity", and the *atopic* feminist who prefers to "*differ from* rather than act as the opposite of the masculine" and who will "abandon the.. demand for a stable identity". (4). The rebellious disorder of this feminism sabotages "the foundations or anchorings of Western rationality" and "notion of male firstness." (5)

Scum's initial reception and interpretation, and the subsequent, prolonged failure to enjoy its satirical or darkly comedic content deserve renewed attention. *Scum* has certain properties in common with Swift's enduring satire, *A Modest Proposal*. This eighteenth-century pamphlet recommends that the Irish poor avoid starvation by marketing their babies as meat for the tables of the English settlers who had commandeered their land. With an equally pertinent view of world governance, Solanas proposes ways of avoiding global disaster. She suggests this be done by eliminating the male sex and all those who sustain a masculinist regime of repression, devastation and warfare. Both satirists make their cases in matter-of-fact tones that match the ruthless character of the forces producing these situations. Both aim to expose posturing, lies and moral/ political corruption. Swift commented that satire ought to be an expression of "a *publick Spirit*, prompting Men of *Genius* and Virtue to mend the World as far as they are able." (6) *Scum* surely meets this standard.

But this was not the judgement made when *Scum* first appeared. It amused very few to see a woman writing such savage and inflammatory satire. Predictably, the breadth of attack in *Scum* provoked disgust and misunderstanding. Taking the view that virtually all social and political institutions are male-dominated, *Scum* 's denunciations are almost as ubiquitous as they are merciless. Her far-reaching programme provided Solanas with a rare opportunity to give offence on every side at once, both to male and female readers, and even to many of the feminists among them .

Solanas and the Destructive Father

Solanas meshes together rage and derision, in a style that is probably best described as *carnivalesque*. This "marketplace" form of expression combines an indiscriminate mixture of humour, chaos, and high and low cultural elements and aims to unravel traditional standards. A carnival brings "temporary liberation from the prevailing truth and from the established order." (7) The order Solanas wishes to topple is of course the one that has operated historically in the *Name of the Father*. However, she refuses to honour her own authoritarian autocrat with the title of Father and refers to him as *Daddy*. "Daddy only wants what's best for Daddy, that is peace and quiet, pandering to his delusion of dignity ("respect"), a good reflection on himself (status), and the opportunity to control and manipulate." (p.42)

The immediate outrage aroused by *Scum* suggests that the public had grasped that something which was refusing to be disposed of as mere feminine hysteria had entered the picture. Solanas is demanding swingeing action. She is rejecting the offer of a share in the same old, unchanged, male-dominated society and will not be satisfied with anything less than the total abolition of a social body that makes no effort to accomodate feminine difference. *Scum*'s much quoted opening sentence, which exhorts women to "overthrow the government, eliminate the money system, institute complete automation and destroy the male sex" (p.35), also tramples on safely moderate ambitions of increasing women's rights. To negotiate would be to condone and thus reinforce the existing condition of male dominance. Solanas makes herself perfectly clear: patriarchal society and all of the structures that have sustained it over the centuries are so steeped in blindness and corruption that the only solution which remains is the total destruction of the entire ensemble. "If SCUM ever marches it will be over the President's stupid, sickening face; if SCUM ever strikes, it will be in the dark with a six-inch blade." And, she continues, "SCUM will always operate on a criminal as opposed to a civil disobedience basis... SCUM is against the entire system, the very idea of law and government. *SCUM is out to destroy the system, not attain certain rights within it.*" [My italics.] (p.76)

Though these sweeping threats of violence to come encompass the full socio-political spectrum, it soon becomes apparent that she particularly loathes the spirit of the bourgeoisie. This group receives her special contempt on the grounds of its incurable, closed élitism. Inequity is not tolerable, no matter where it appears or which class or gender may be guilty of it, and she refuses to accept that it is in any way outside the proper business of a woman to criticise the system. Perhaps her ambivalent use of gender is more difficult to follow. She intermittently uses "men" to refer to persons of either sex, depending on their behaviour, and her criticisms of women who are *masculinised*, or of those who collude submissively with male dominance and "cast their lot with the swine", are unsparing. In the end, however, her main attack remains firmly trained on a society that has organised itself in the sole interest of advancing masculinist power and control.

It follows that Solanas will also refuse to restrict herself to issues that specifically concern women. Her harsh and abraisive style has clear features in common with certain politically-inclined, male stand-up comedians. A male comedian who attacks the behaviour of his own sex will, if only grudgingly, be tolerated, but a woman who pours contempt and ridicule upon the masculine will not be so readily excused. Avoiding the self-deprecating kind of humour that so often provided a refuge for the embattled woman comedian, Solanas made no concessions as she ruthlessly assaulted male self-esteem, dignity and privilege and satirized maleness itself. The verdict was automatic: this woman's attacks were far too savage to be a joke; Solanas must therefore be mad, not funny. At the time when *Scum* was written, Solanas stood alone. No established tradition of extreme feminist satire on which she could have fallen back existed at that point.

**Theatrics, Masquerade
and the Rejection of Artifice**

The colloquial immediacy of *Scum* puts it close to theatre or performance. The only surviving play by Solanas was lost for over thirty years, but her brief manifesto is shot through with dramatic devices such as abrupt breaks, rapid shifts and short sections that function like scenes from a play. The staccato urgency of Solanas's voice gives dramatic priority to the urgency of speech over the careful finish of the written word. But, despite her bent for the theatrical, she refuses to have any part in the typecast spectacles of masquerade – she has no intention of concealing her desire to destroy the power of the Father. For better or worse, masquerade represents a male fantasy. The male establishment accepts a degree of decency in the classic disguise of exaggerated 'femininity' , if only because it does not openly expose the mutilated father's shame, and even if in itself it does not explicitly consolidate existing power structures, it is more admissable than the unveiled face of feminine challenge. Solanas never stoops to muffle her hostility in an indirect attack. The introduction to the most recent English language reprint of *Scum* comments, "Certain diseases become a woman .. poor Valerie refuses the prestige and license of hysteria or any of the neighbouring neurotic dialects that might be understood in feminist precincts." (p. 16) Where are these "feminist precincts" and why is their understanding so limited? Though right about the writer's refusal to shelter behind effeminised subterfuge, this remark takes a safely patronising position on the inside of that from which "*poor Valerie*" might not have not been excluded if she had only displayed a little more feminine modesty and a little less immoderate aggression.

Normally – and masquerade is accepted as comparatively normal in a never entirely normal female sex – if the performer appears to be attributing the escape of repressed material to the hysterical folly of her gender, her performance can be condoned. Until comparatively recently, much female comedy was based on exactly such performances, though now women comedians seem to feel less need to offer themselves up "as objects of ridicule."(8) Solanas makes her stand in the precise opposite of masquerade and incites laughter without a trace of apology or self-dismissiveness. Rather than cover up the father's castration, she wishes to proclaim it, to exhibit it in a boisterous parody of what is usually seen as 'male' behaviour. She revels in immoderation, anger generates the energy for her apparently irrational and ludicrous spectacle. Though Freud would undoubtedly have diagnosed a severe masculinity complex, Solanas deserves to be understood as a person of serious purpose and as more than a neurotic male impersonator. Female rage is always alarming and threatening. "Angry women .. are dangerous .. because their anger unsettles ideologies about gender." (9) Solanas attributes fear of female strength to male dependency: "The male is, by his very nature, a leech, an emotional parasite" who "can live only through the female." (p.67) He "wants Mama in charge, wants to abandon himself to her care." (p.70)

Solanas's foul-mouthed, caustic, defamatory satire came closest in style to stand-up comedy coming from men who largely belonged to minority groups. She has a special resemblance to the acerbic and anarchic Lenny Bruce. But, where Bruce emerged from a long tradition of Jewish humour, Solanas seemed to come out of nowhere. Bruce's fierce, satirical comedy has since passed through several further incarnations, and for a while surfaced in the dark comedy of black American satire, where it was used to define a brotherhood of abused outsiders. (10) As a woman satirist, Solanas was equally an oppressed outsider, but this did not mean that she was going to be admitted into the male preserve of political satire.

The *Scum Manifesto* never adopts defensive measures. It does not trifle with ironic reflections on the female sex. Solanas writes without a trace of self-depreciation – sardonic or otherwise – or of self-mutilation – symbolic or otherwise. Either concession would have rendered her a little more conventionally female, but she refuses evasions – 'feminine' or otherwise – and does nothing to placate the bourgeois sensibilities which she so despises. Though it is both anarchic and Bacchantean, her text homes in on a fully recognisable world. It takes on real corruption and real despotism in the political and social institutions of the patriarchy. In an unprecedently open offensive, Solanas challenges her oppressors to take her on, no holds barred on either side, and in full view of everyone.

Anarchy, Madness and Rejection of the Social Order

Scum's dizzying broadsides on the status quo are constantly on the brink of toppling into absurdity. Scum is a chiaroscuro of high and low culture, great and small significances and contrasting categories of vocabulary: "maleness is a deficiency disease", or, "To call a man an animal is to flatter him: he's a machine, a walking dildo." (p.37) "The male has a vested interest in ignorance," she writes, and then, with melancholy poetic echoes, (11) where the female "wants the company of equals .. the male and the sick, insecure, unself-confident male-female crave the company of worms." (p.54)

Solanas tells us, "... the most obnoxious or harmful types are: rapists, politicians; lousy singers and musicians; Chairmen of Boards; Breadwinners; landlords; owners of greasy spoons and restaurants that play Musak; "Great Artists"; cheap pikers and welchers; cops, tycoons; scientists working on death and destruction programs or for private industry; .. liars and phonies, disc jockeys; .. real estate men; stock brokers; .. psychiatrists.." (p.73) This endless and indiscriminate cast list assembles members of wildly different social classes and treats offences that range from the unequivocally criminal to the mere lapse of taste with the same degree of condemnation. Here, it is the absence of all distinction between categories that produces laughter. Along with law, ethics and orderly procedure, Solanas is tearing apart the concept of hierarchy itself.

In his preface to Solanas's text, Maurice Girodias, her original publisher, expresses appreciation of her humour and her "iconoclastic disposition". (12) He claims to agree with the idea that men have reduced women "to a sexual and child-rearing function .. love to sex, and refused to apprehend, cultivate and liberate the hidden wealth of the feminine nature. Because they are frightened, uncertain and jealous of their prerogatives."(p.11) However, his intentions seem a lot less sympathetic when he changes the word *Scum* into S.C.U.M., which he claimed was an acronym for Society For Cutting Up Men. One later edition firmly asserts that Girodias was responsible for the change.

Its sensationalising effect almost certainly increased the sales of her book, but this small alteration has caused widespread agitation and misunderstanding. Solanas distributed streetcorner handouts which flatly denied any such significance in SCUM.

Scum Manifesto is in fact a highly appropriate title. Not only do "the thematics of carnival" include "mess" and "dirt", (13) but "dirt" covers "all events which blur, smudge, contradict or otherwise confuse accepted classifications .. a system of values .. a given arrangement of things has been violated." Furthermore, "the idea of dirt implies a structure of idea."(14) The abusive use of *dirty* is probably more often symbolical than literal, with 'dirty whores', 'dirty foreigners', 'dirty communists', 'dirty Jews', and so on. And on. Solanas's "scum" resonates on many levels and encompasses many different affiliations.

Yet, although Girodias's S.C.U.M. seems to have stuck quite widely and has been translated as such into several languages, it conflicts with Solanas's well delineated reinterpretation of gender – both male and female – as flexible and largely symbolic. "It is most tempting to pick off the female "Great Artists", liars and phonies; etc. along with the men, but that would be inexpedient, as it would not be clear to most of the public that *the female killed was a male*." (My italics.) While this non-literal usage of gender casts aside biological differences, it nevertheless continues to assert *difference* and, through it, the possibility of *change*. Solanas's long list of offenders concludes with the intriguing remark that, for "a man whose *behaviou*r falls into both good and bad categories, an overall subjective evaluation of him will be made..." (p.74) And even here, in full, jubilant swing, Solanas keeps her political objectives firmly and precisely in mind: it is not men per se, but the manufacturers and the deliverers – *most frequently* men – of patriarchal institutions in a repressive and masculinist society whom she is proposing to eliminate .

Of course, the most decisive factor in establishing the myth of the madwoman is Solanas's apparently unprovoked shooting in 1968 of the artist, Andy Warhol. (One should note that Girodias undertook the publication of *Scum* only *after* the shooting.) Much has been made of the event, including a film, but no conclusive explanation has been offered. Solanas was never a person to plead that she was the innocent victim of fantasies or that sexual abuse or paranoia had engulfed her in uncontrollable hysterical disorders. Solanas never pleads. Instead, she takes a step the society she deplores considers unforgivable, especially in a woman. Whether or not the notorious shooting of Warhol was 'hysterical' or 'psychotic', it totally repudiated the palliative, socially redeeming qualities of 'femininity' and avoided any taint of masquerade. However, as a profoundly symbolic manifestation, it is linked with hysteria. Hysteria always represents something beyond what it appears to have enacted. Warhol's shooting, even if pointless in itself, clearly represents something beyond the literal, and, when Solanas applies a real solution to a symbolic problem, her action has the dramatic force of being utterly unexpected. Stepping out way beyond the limits of satire, she enters into a dadaist (15) realpolitik performance in which the gun becomes a central and even stereotypical symbol of male aggression. And with it Solanas asserts her right to an attribute that sums up masculine power. The shooting has been described as an "aestheticised event". (16) It is "the pivotal gesture in a radically subversive project aimed at recalibrating the American avantgarde." (17) If this perhaps emphasises the element of cool control unduly, it dismisses the idea of a meaningless and undeliberated act and bridges the apparent lacuna between words and deeds.

However, the question that is less often asked is why, of all people, Warhol? Solanas was obviously angered by his casual loss of the manuscript of her play and further enraged by his insults and offhand rejection. (18) *Up your Ass* was a "satirical play about a woman shooting a man." Loss of the manuscript became the precipitating force of an *aestheticized event* . Solanas's "confrontational guerilla theatre tactics" in *Scum,* in the play, and in the shooting "erased the artificial boundaries that bourgeois theatre erected to separate actors and audience." And, "Solanas .. simultaneously acted to bring about a radical change of theatrical practice and a revolutionary shift in social politics, and to create a common forum for both." (19) Her action has also been described as a "form of avantgarde performance" which "revolts against exclusion from avantgarde history." (20) In brief, when Solanas shot Warhol, she was erasing the distinction between life and art.

In a sociopolitical sense, Warhol was deeply elitist. He was also a prime producer of unreal or virtual women. His depersonalised female icons approached the extreme limits of masquerade. And so Solanas, who was so fatally attracted to iconoclastic gestures, flung a spanner into the works of The Factory – an appropriately named studio where, amongst his other mass-produced art works, Warhol produced his special line of women, some of whom in reality were men, as factitious art objects. The shooting had obvious parallels with the manifesto: it was urgent, abrupt, oblique, inappropriate. It was also the ultimate proof of its author's serious intent. *Scum* was never meant to be a purely verbal exercise. Solanas desired to have her vision take root in the real world. That is not an indication of madness.

This book has already referred to the paradoxical difficulties feminists have encountered in writing or speaking as women: to write or speak as a woman, necessitates maintaining a position that is both inside and outside the available (i.e. masculine) framework for expression. Ronell's preface to the Verso edition of *Scum* appreciates the extent to which Solanas "borrowed the language and .. complicities of urgent philosophical concerns" (p.8) and makes the point that it is not possible to "take on the declared enemy without entering the war machine". (p.14) However, the desire to take effect in the 'real' world conflicts with the desire to see that world abolished. By its nature, masculinist culture distorts both female desire and the words that express it. The preface comments that Solanas was bound to meet serious difficulties as she pierced "through to the real with a series of highly calibrated psychotic intensities", then adds breeziy, and as if from a purely personal perspective, that *Scum* may not be "a psychotic text." It mentions the "steady psychotisation of women" (p.16) yet does not note that Solanas's supposed 'insanity' derives from her perception of the *mass* psychosis of a society that is run on exclusively patriarchal principles. One must ask if this omission also assumes that a person who questions the sanity of the patriarchy must be mad.

Solanas views male sexuality with a ruthlessly clinical eye. Rather than embrace an object of desire, it turns sollipsistically back on itself: "Relieving sexual tension isn't the answer, as masturbation suffices for that. It's not ego satisfaction: that doesn't explain screwing corpses and babies." (p.37) She then proceeds to reason that a masculine desire to dominate sexual congress is due to a male sense of being incomplete and worthless – "men have pussy envy" – and she arrives through this argument at the unexpected conclusion (the punch line) that, "Screwing is for a man, a defense against his desire to be female." (p.38)

But *Scum Manifesto* has more serious political purpose than it is generally given credit for: when Solanas proposes eliminating "the government", she is aiming at the institution of *Government*, pinnacle of authoritarian patriarchal dominance; when she recommends "complete automation", it is as a means to human happiness over monetary value and towards the symbolic redressing of the gross imbalance between male and female stakes in reproduction. Her final reference to the destruction of "the male sex" – is not directed at "men who, regardless of their motives, do good, men who are playing ball with SCUM". (p.72)

She is clearly speaking of what she perceives as the incurably negative morals, standards and effects of an unbridled patriarchy and all those who condone it.

On the subject of society, the manifesto lays the blame for the disasters of human civilisation on patriarchal constructs rather than on human nature – "They label the male condition the human condition." (p.53) Unfortunately,"No genuine social revolution can be accomplished by the male, as the male on top wants the status quo, and all the male on the bottom wants is to be the male on top. The male 'rebel' is a farce: this is the male's 'society', made by *him* to satisfy *his* needs... Ultimately what the male is rebelling against is being male." (p.54) She denounces hierarchy, class, the father, the family, male sexuality and men's inability to communicate – one section is titled "Prevention of Conversation" – and also law, capitalism, work, the govermnent and the patriarchal and religious or philosophical justifications for imposing all these institutions that promote human misery. "Happiness being for him impossible on this earth, he invented Heaven," (p.52) she remarks. Her view of human nature as redeemable and human civilisation as retrievable is probably the taproot of her thinking and the source of her summation that, "If women don't get their asses in gear fast, we may very well all die." (p.55)

Solanas, however, points out that the work has already begun of its own accord. The male "is gradually eliminating himself." (p.67) She is therefore proposing a long-term resolution when she writes, "The conflict is not between males and females, but between SCUM and the feminized, bourgeoisified

female who can only have value in a male 'society' ".
She tells us a little sadly that, "*All* women have a fink
streak in them, to a great or lesser degree, but it stems
from a lifetime of living among men." Solanas is
firmly of the opinion that, "Women are improvable ..
Eliminate men, and women will shape up." (p.37) By
now, it is undeniably obvious that by 'men' she means
the patriarchal body politic.

Perhaps Solanas could be best described as a
woman masquerading as a man who is both concealing
and displaying the fact that sexual categories have
broken free from the confinement of segregation in
their former ghettos.

Nor does Solanas succumb to the cultivation of
self. "Looking inside yourself for salvation," she tells
us in one of her rarer, quiet moments, "is not the
answer.... Self-forgetfulness should be the goal, not
self-absorption." (p.75) This has a ring of vocation
about it. Solanas scorns even the briefest association
with the cult of the great individual. Her work is
misread if framed "within the hierarchical order of
greatness that the SCUM *Manifesto* critiques and
rejects." She is intent on "undoing the logic of
canonization." (21) For herself, she claims no following or status – "SCUM doesn't yet prevail" – and never
requires or even imagines an accepting public-
"SCUM's still in the gutter of our society." (p.62) It
keeps company with the everyday expression of
ordinary men that is honoured by the carnivalesque.
Jokes that depend on the collusion of an in-group
reinstall the élitist habits of masculinist discourse.
There is nothing radical about reversing privilege

rather than eradicating it. And neither did Solanas ever see political sense in withdrawal: "Dropping out is not the answer: fucking-up is .. Dropping out gives control to those few who don't drop out .. it plays into the hands of the enemy; it strengthens the system instead of undermining it, since it is based entirely on the non-participation, passivity, apathy and non-involvement of women." (p.75)

Solanas is too often relegated to the realms of notoriety, scandal and madness, while the full extent of her contribution goes unremarked. She was too intent on the crucial importance of her vision of impending disaster to interest herself in ratings formulated in a bourgeois scheme of evaluation. One particularly evocative and poignant comment points out that Valerie Solanas wrote ".. in order to become something else than a great writer .. from a place far beyond the construction-sites of 'theory' or the dressings up of analytical practice." (22) This description properly observes both Solanas's essential political aims and her linguistic transgressions. And yet, though her script is resolutely other-referenced, the self-constructed, dramatic persona of her performance is still pointing directly at herself as the female abberation best guaranteed to exacerbate patriarchal sensitivities. She is not only defying the male establishment, she is also performing a highly dangerous stunt that few comedians of either sex attempt. She is daring the enemy to attack her in her own, unprotected person. The essence of her satire lies in her refusal to collude with *any* existing social order.

Solanas has still not received the recognition she

deserves. It would be futile to deny her the pain and anger she so clearly experienced on a personal level, but, whatever else we may think, we cannot fail to admire her unflinching integrity and the courageously independent stance which she takes to represent herself. Neither should we overlook the complexity of her writing, or the frequently alarming intensity of her humour. Not all of those who read *Scum* when it was first published appeared to be ready for a woman to produce such forthright satire. Solanas has been called many names; it is time for satirist to be included among them. She undoubtedly knew that, "As long as satire exists there remains the possibility of democratic politics, and it is the great debunker of the phallocratic myth." (23) So far as I am aware, no subsequent female comedian has castigated the social order from quite as vulnerable a position as Solanas occupied.

Footnotes

1) S.H. Braund, 'A Woman's Voice? Laronia's role in Juvenal's Satire 2.' p.207 *Women in Antiquity*. ed Richard Hawley & Barbara Levick. Routledge. London. 1995. Italian satirist and comedian, Sabina Guzzanti, ("revolution is possible") was instantly attacked by right-wing politicians who refused to recognise her television series as "satire" and had it terminated after the first episode.

2) Quotations from the *Scum Manifesto*, including those from Avita Ronell's introduction, unless otherwise specified all come from Verso's 2004 edition and are referenced in that text as they appear. All other editions are specified.

3) Mary Russo. *The Female Grotesque: Risk, Excess and Modernity*, p.vii. Routledge. 1994

4) Elizabeth Grosz. *Sexual Subversions*, pps 33-4.Allen & Unwin. 1989.

5) Jacques Derrida. *Choreographies*. Diacritics, p. 68-9Summer 1982.

6) *A Vindication of the Beggar's Opera*. Jonathan Swift (1975. p.241)

7) Peter Stallybrass and Allon White. *The Poetics and Politics of Transgression*, p.10. Metheun. London. 1986. The term *carnivalesque* comes from the writings of Mikhail Bakhtin.

8) Jane Arthurs, *Revolting Women: The Body in Comic Performance*.p151, ed Jane Arthurs and Jean Grimshaw. Cassell, London, 1999. Lizbeth Goodman, 'Gender and Humour and Comic Subversions.' *Imagining Women: Cultural Representations and Gender*, Polity Press, 1992. likewise asserts that "self deprecation is now largely

outdated" (p.290) Like other oppressed groups, women have always been convenient objects for ridicule. The female comedian is able to exploit this fact by representing herself as a person who fails to achieve male cultural norms or who embodies men's expectations of women with such excessive fervour that their full absurdity is revealed. Such performances indict patriarchal misogyny through their transparent awareness of the mechanics of sexism as it relates to themselves.

9) Kathleen Rowe. *The Unruly Woman: Gender and the Genres of Laughter*. p.42. University of Texas. 1995

10) E.g., Richard Pryor or early Chris Rock. Interesting gender and race overlaps have appeared more recently in the work of Eddie Izzard, Julian Clary and Ali G.

11) See *The Sick Rose*, W. Blake, *Songs of Experience*.

12) The first edition of Scum Manifesto was published by Olympia Press, Paris (introduction by Maurice Girodias) 1968. It was subsequently reprinted by the Matriarchy Study Group in 1983, Mille et une Nuits (introduction by Michel Houellebecq) in 1998 andVerso (introduction by Avita Ronell.) in 2004. The same (deliberate?) misrendering appears in Michel Houellebecq's introduction to the 1998 French edition. James M. Harding's paper in *The Simplest Surrealist Act: Valerie Solanas and the (re)Assertion of Avantgarde Priorities.* The Drama Review 45. Winter 2001. describes the title as "one of the first instances of .. publicly embracing and appropriating an offensive characterization of a political agenda.." p.148.

13) Stallybrass ibid, p.182

14) Mary Douglas. *Implicit Meanings*, p.51. Routledge & Kegan Paul. 1975

15) "Warhol himself .. cited 'the paternal signifiers lurking in both *pop* and *dada*." Because "dada had its own patriarchal baggage" Solanas does not acknowledge "her dada predecessors." Harding ibid.p.150

.16) Harding, ibid, p.154.

17) Harding, ibid, p.143.

18) Ronell's introduction to Scum (p. 26) describes the insults jointly directed at Solanas by Warhol and Viva.

19) Harding, op cit. pps.154-155 Footnotes.

20) Harding, ibid, p.156

21) Dana Heller. *Shooting Solanas*. Feminist Studies, p.187. Vol 27. Issue 1, 2001.

22) Meaghan Morris. *The Pirate's Fiancée.* p 69. Verso. 1988

23) Sharon Wood. *Italian Women's Writing – 1860 – 1994* p. 208 re the work of Carla Rame. Athlone. London & Atlantic Highlands. 1995.

9

Sadeian Women Revisited:
Masochists and Passive Pleasures

The Sadeian Woman

Popular assumptions relating to human sexuality are not just surprisingly enduring, it is also commonplace for them to ignore the social construction of gender. For this reason it can seem perfectly logical to designate traits such as passivity and masochism as 'feminine' . This then allows chauvinistic attitudes and behaviour to affect the perception and treatment of women. (1) Meanwhile, the sexual axioms of psychoanalysis provide a conveniently supportive ideology. Freud's male-centred assumptions provide a water-tight rationale for the patriarchal subordination of women.

Angela Carter's 1979 text, *The Sadeian Woman*, reaches back further than Freud to reassess the influence of aspects of a cultural past which has been crucial in shaping a modern understanding of sexuality. (2) Extrapolating from the eighteenth-century writings of the Marquis de Sade, Carter enlarges on the many ways in which contemporary interpretations of female sexuality are still fixated on a biased understanding of human sexuality. She notes how, in the interpretations of both Sade and Freud, sexual desire is automatically assumed to have a fundamentally masculine character. Sometimes, however, the positions she takes have been understood over-literally, leading to a description of her book as a "pseudofeminist literary essay"(3). This criticism seems to be based largely on Carter's representation of Rose Keller as something more than a victim. When this abused servant had to be paid off not to take Sade to court, Carter refers to her as a blackmailer, "and who can blame her? .. The affair enchants me .. A woman of the third estate, a beggar, the poorest of the poor, turns the very vices of the rich into weapons to wound them with." (4) Carter does not baulk at praising a feminist-socialist triumph merely because the injured woman is shown to have had her own share of cupidity. But Carter's writings have never permitted over-simplified, black or white, villain or hero solutions.

This chapter will reconsider certain aspects of feminist sexual politics that have been longtime subjects of debate. It will attempt to analyse the chronically male-dominated understanding of what *erotic* means, and to reassess and redeem the meaning of 'passive' .

Carter comments bluntly on "the ambivalence of the word 'to fuck', and on its twinned meanings of sexual intercourse and despoilation: 'a fuck up', 'to fuck something up', 'he's fucked'. "(5) She highlights a key cultural difficulty for feminists during two decades of social change that were described as a sexual revolution. During this period, although numerous sexual freedoms came to be more fully realised, in many instances the longterm cultural rewards have not been what was promised and some of the consequences have been undeniably deleterious. And although most feminists believed, and many probably still believe, that greater sexual freedom was an essential component in the liberation of women, some also recognised that the sexuality being held up as the standard for progress was still serving exactly the same interests which had sustained the old, familiar model of the dominant and unshakeably patriarchal, male.

Carter sets forth Sade's view that "male means tyrannous and female means martyrised, no matter what the official genders." (6) However, Sade also maintains that women are not *necessarily* the sex that must be fucked, and she outlines his objections to the engrained belief that female sexuality is inherently and incurably passive. As Carter comments: "Women do not normally fuck in the active sense. They are fucked in the passive tense and hence automatically fucked-up, done over, undone. Whatever else he says or does not say, Sade declares himself unequivocallly for the right of women to fuck .. he urges women to fuck as actively as they are able so that, powered by their enormous and hitherto untapped sexual energy, they will then be able to fuck their way into history and, in doing so, change it." (7) But although this Sadeian woman has virile properties – she does not fear to fuck and is able to assert an active sexuality and to make sexual demands without hesitation or self-disgust – Carter is well aware that this apparent advance still does not address the complex question of the woman's own sexual desire or identity. Continuing with the Sadeian motif, she examines the patriarchal controls that keep this question from being addressed. Sadeian women have "acceded, as women, to the world of men .. their mastery of that world reveals its monomaniac inhumanity .. Their liberation from the limitations of femininity is a personal one .. they gratify themselves fully but it is a liberation without enlightenment." (8) Carter is here forcing us to reconsider what, in feminist terms, would be needed for a sexual ideology that was genuinely revolutionary. Although she is coming from an altogether different place, she emerges somewhere not so far from the Valerie Solanas who urges women "to get their asses in gear fast." While the masculine remains ensnared in a web of privilege and inherited authority, the feminine, with nothing to lose, must become the agency of social change. To imitate male power and privilege is to reinforce it: "The Sadeian woman, then, subverts only her own socially conditioned role in the world of god, the king and the law. She does not subvert her society."(9)

Even if Sade 's characters gain powerful mastery of the world of men, their achievements will always be limited because of their female actuality. For the Sadeian heroine, Clairwil, the prime object of loathing may be the male, but her prime object of desire nevertheless continues to be the "depersonalised prick, the sublime penis," She is "dedicated to sexual warfare", but a post-mortem dissection would reveal "a penis growing in her brain". Carter concludes, "Sade's female libertines .. ingest but do not integrate within themselves the signs of maleness."(10) They are damaged as women and haunted by an alien masculinity,

The question of why it is inevitably so demeaning to *be* fucked remains unanswered. Until recently the word was categorised as obscene, but 'fuck' has lost the power to shock. Sexual intercourse is largely portrayed as a reflex biological function that produces strongly pleasurable bodily sensations which can be enhanced by using drugs that increase male potency. Its potential as a shared emotional experience is either forgotten or regarded with scepticism or contempt. 'To fuck' is the most widely used term for sexual congress; it is also *what a man does*. Apart from the penis, sexual organs possess little validity. A woman does "not *normally* fuck" because she has already been defined as the object to be acted upon. If 'fuck' sometimes refers indiscriminately to either sex, it reveals the extent to which women have "acceded, as women, to the world of men". On a linguistic level, 'making love', 'copulating' or having 'sexual intercourse' all suggest that women could be participating in the event. But 'fuck' remains dominant. Beside it, other terms seem effeminate – prudish, evasive, too feeble to speak out in forthright, *manly* terms. Too like a woman.

An American feminist who engages closely with

gender issues in the field of language discusses the claims made by standard language to be a 'neutral' form of expression that is neither biased towards the masculine nor prejudiced against the feminine. She finds two very disparate attitudes at work here: "Americans .. want women – who have been segregated into a special 'women's language' – to accede to the use of 'neutral language'. French feminists, on the other hand, see 'neutral language' as itself an 'area of oppression, the alienation of difference in the order of the same of the phallus'." (11) With Sade in mind, she comments that Luce Irigaray, "impertinently" exposes "the phallic religion masked as libertinism". (12) This reference to religion is highly appropriate: libertinism and religion often both manifest a primitive need for a sacrificial object. The object of sacrifice may not necessarily be a woman, but it must still behave with a properly 'feminine' passivity and fulfil its purpose of being subjugated to the phallic power that has taken over control of life and death. Carter's thorough interrogation of 'to fuck' also has European leanings. It reveals how a term that generally manages to pass itself off as neutral is in fact *censoring meaning*.

The idea that women must either fuck their way into history or be excluded from it invokes a bizarre logic. A simple question of active or passive parties does not constitute a signpost marking the divide between being and non-being. We cannot be expected to accept that, to have any meaningful identity, women must either imitate a theoretically 'masculine' sadism or fill the void of their lacking identity with whatever 'feminine' follies the masculine happens to dream up for them. Sexual intercourse that is taken to mean the performance of an active male upon a passive female, does not even begin to take note of woman's many other and equally vital sexual properties. When reproduction and nurturing are omitted so also are indispensable biological functions. One has to wonder if 'fucking' has come to be the dominant term because the male is unwilling to recognise that a female might enjoy forms of sexuality unconnected with himself. Where he is not the sole initiator and dispenser of a woman's pleasure, her activities must seem dangerously close to infidelity.

The Roots of Masochism

One particularly outspoken feminist lawyer asserts that, "Men's power over women means that the way men see women defines who women can be." And, when exclusively masculine assumptions control the understanding of human sexuality, "misrepresentation .. institutionalises the sexuality of male supremacy, fusing the erotization of dominance and submission with the social construction of male and female." (13) An understanding of this sort suppresses knowledge of the identity and character of one of the participants, and so sexuality itself soon begins to appear inherentely sadistic. Carter puts the idea more directly: "Sexuality stripped of the idea of free exchange .. is nothing but pure cruelty." (14) Lying beneath Sadeian fantasies of torture, the desire for eroticized power can always be discovered. This seems to be unavoidable where the allegedly mono-sexual character of desire is encouraged to function according to a male-only template. In a sollipsistic denial of all desires other than its own, male sexuality succumbs to the belief that nothing has real significance outside itself. Then this belief presumes a complementary masochism which licenses, justifies or even welcomes sadism. An apparent polarity provides a spurious authenticity and also condones sexual sadism, coercion such as rape, and other violent kinds of behaviour that aim to disregard or destroy the individual humanity of a woman.

A masochism which parallels the virile vice of sadism appears to fit into a space as preordained as the carefully prepared niche awaiting the murderer in crime fiction. The improbability of such a convenient fit already makes it slightly suspect, but its reputation as a primary *feminine* attribute persists and it is regularly invoked to explain 'womanly' compliance, even when submission has been enforced. The more loudly a woman denies her desire for pain, the stronger that desire for pain is presumed to be. Masochism may be regarded as unadmitted or unconscious, but remains by all accounts inbuilt. Paradoxical ly, a masochistic man is seen as an aberration from his sex, but it is considered *normal* for a woman to be masochistic. It's as normal as her penis envy, isn't it? And so this perverse symptom of a distorting and alienating society goes uncontested and continues to serve a similarly uncontested masculine desire. In everyday life, this double-bind is mirrored by the advice that for their own safety women should not actively resist sexual violence, even though they will be accused of complicity in it if they do not.

The Freudian formula that defines masochism as an inverted form of aggression which the female turns against herself might seem plausible at first sight. Social censure has sternly repressed aggressivity in women, and Freud's labyrinth of interpretation has entangled observation with speculation and insight with cultural prejudice. His repellent stereotype of the envious woman who is seething with inward-turning anger is not taken as seriously as it once was, but suggestions of perversity still infiltrate every aspect of female sexuality. While the active male organ obligingly fulfils its single, unequivocal role in the foreground, the desires of women remain tortuous and incomprehensible, unwilling or simply too unformed to reveal what they are. But Freud's real problem arises from the fact that these desires are visibly not-masculine and thus not accessible to masculine definition. Male desire continues to be the accepted norm, and women remain enfeebled by masochism. A normal woman's desire is never more than an adjunct to a man's wholesomely robust eroticism. A 'normal' feminine passive produces the desire to submit to (male) sexual domination in whatever form the powerful male may desire and passivity becomes inseperable from masochism. 'Normal' feminine sexuality must always be perverse and the 'normal' woman must always be always an anomaly. Even if a woman of outstanding stature does manage "to fuck her way into history", she will be guilty of gender-inappropriate behaviour and of usurping the prerogative of the male sex. Damned if she does and damned if she doesn't, whether sexually active or sexually passive, woman is forever guilty of perversity.

There is a widespread myth that females are helplessly attracted to powerul, often called 'alpha' males. The idea presumably rests on the assumption that phallic power is what women lack and therefore must desire. But power or domination, whether in a sexual or any other context, always entails dispossessing the other. The eroticising of phallic power not only adds yet another 'feminine' characteristic to the already burdened female, more pertinently, it endorses the dominance of the most actively aggressive males and reasserts hierarchies among both males and females. Female sexuality that obediently echos the male's loses the means to express itself. Freud repeatedly complained that women would not tell him what they wanted, but the heterogeneous elements of female desire are beyond inspection if sexual passivity is shackled by a 'feminine' masochism. An unprejudiced understanding of a sexual passivity that does not distinguish between genders and does not suppose any innate female masochism would greatly enrich the catalogue of human wishes. It would also extend the scope of male desire .

Beyond Repression and Envy

Used as a virtual synonym for masochism,'sexual passivity' becomes a pretext for male force and abuse. But what would the term mean if this connection were severed? As a form of desire, sexual passivity suggests an unfocused immersion in the erotic that makes little distinction between subject and other. Undifferentiated, unregulated, increasingly fluid as the demarcations between self and other dissolve, as it forgets about active performance, this sexuality would leave behind self-awareness. The exercise of power would no longer be relevant. Power not only precludes the freedom of the other, it can neither play nor relax and certainly it cannot become self-forgetful. It must remain alert, it must be in control, but it will also be perpetually exiled from dreams of a non-conflictual utopia. Eroticised phallic power inherits a legacy of sadism. Its existence depends on a presumed opposition of female and male traits. However, passive sexuality is not in essence either a masculine or a feminine attribute. It is fluid enough to wash over such rigid divisions. It has no agenda.

It is not a surprise to see that even the most marginal hints of purposeless and playful sexuality can meet with patriarchal disapproval. Foreplay, which the majority of women seem to consider the minimum, or sometimes even the only requirement for their pleasure, is regarded as a prelude to rather than an integral part of the sexual act. When Freud expresses a strong distaste for foreplay, he fails to explain his reasons and only advises that it should be expedited as swiftly and clinically as possible. Foreplay is what comes beforehand; it does not have meaning in the serious business of giving the woman what she needs (never mind what she wants) in order to be normal. And Freudian normality requires vagina-centred sex, which is just another way of saying penis-centred sex.

Less respectful sources of pleasure are immature and perverse. The Moroccan feminist writer, Fatima Mernissi, points out that Freud's view of foreplay as a perversion "which should normally be rapidly passed on the way to sexual union" is not universally shared by Muslims and that Muslim perceptions of female sexuality contain irreconcilable contradictions. Aqqad, like Freud, believes women enjoy suffering and "experience pleasure only in their subjugation, their defeat by males." But, unlike the "passive, frigid Freudian female, the sexual demands of Imam Ghazali's female appear truly overwhelming, and the necessity for the male to satisfy them becomes a compelling social duty .. Ghazali recommends foreplay, primarily in the interest of the woman, as a duty for the believer." Mernissi concludes that, "Women are considered not only outside of humanity but a threat to it as well .. The entire Muslim social structure can be seen as an attack on, and a defence against, the disruptive power of female sexuality." (15).

In practice, foreplay may possess little of the spontaneity of play. It can amount to no more than a set of manipulative techniques a man should master if he wants a female to behave compliantly. And, though the prevailing force in sexual intercourse may either be dominance or uncensored play that is enjoyed freely by both parties, linguistically speaking, feminine pleasure is routinely marginalised. The word, 'foreplay' does not suggest that it is an integral part of intercourse – it suggests a curtain-raiser, an optional means of warming up the audience before the real event, which only begins when foreplay is over and done with. This view only gives genuine significance to phallic sexuality; any other reading is in error, and probably offensive too.

Roberto Calasso's study of Greek myth offers a frank analysis of the ethos of (pederastic) eroticism amongst the ancient Greeks:"For the Greeks, the unnameable aspect of eros was passivity during coitus .. it is not simply because of the indignity attached to whoever accepts the woman's part, thus debasing his own sexual status. Rather it is the very pleasure of the woman, the pleasure of passivity, that is suspect and perhaps conceals a profound malignancy. This treacherous pleasure incites the Greek man to rage .. precisely because he senses that this grossness might conceal a mocking power that eludes male control .. women might have their own indecipherable erotic self-sufficiency ." Tiresias was blinded because he revealed that "if the pleasure were divided into ten parts, the woman enjoyed nine and the man only one." (16) Disentangling a significant part of this notoriously indecipherable eroticism, Calasso-Tiresias pinpoints both the specifically feminine "pleasure of passivity" and the depth of male suspicion and hostility towards such female sexual pleasures. But there he stops. He offers no further insights into the nature or genesis of passive pleasure.

What Sade and Freud Forgot

It is possible that the origins of passive pleasure are to be found in the most primal of human needs. It would run counter to the interests of human survival for women to be as sexually one-dimensional or as uni-directional as the male's ideal stereotype wants to paint her. Women's sexuality, massively complicated by her complex reproductive functions, has many more components. Significant differences in male and female sexualities emerge in the woman's relationship to the infant. The need to accomodate the baby gives female sexuality its flexibility and even an infantile aspect that corresponds to the passive dependancy in which everyone begins life. Infantile sexual pleasure, known as polymorphous perversity, has no fixed location and can surface in any region of the body. (17) But polymorphous pleasures are not only considered childish, they are degenerate and unmanly. They do not fit either the canonical norms of male sexuality or the criteria of active and strictly genital sex. However, if children are to receive the care they need in order to reach maturity, it is essential that women should find pleasure in an extended range of biological responses that do not relate to men. The nurturing aspect of female sexuality depends on this. Physical vestiges of female sexual characteristics in men tell us the male is also fully capable of experiencing the same pleasures as woman. These will not of course number among the masculine traits that the patriarchy would admit to or wish to see encouraged.

Then there is the question of the child. A desire to have possession of the child has been a longterm source of conflict in heterosexual relations. It appears in early Greek tragedy and is the overt subject of *The Eumenides*. But that is only where it starts. It is over possession of the little Indian boy that Oberon and Titania quarrel in *A Midsummer Night's Dream*, and it is still often the pivotal issue in the contemporary courtroom drama of divorce. Possession of the child – and often enough also of the woman who gave birth to it – has always been a prime patriarchal concern. Children of both sexes must be weaned away from the mother in order to secure a sufficiently strong allegiance to the father. Michele Montrelay analyses the accomplishing of this process in terms of a substitution of "the unconscious representative" (the mother) so that, "Masculine, phallic representatives ... law and the paternal ideals of the father .. constitute the new representatives ... Femininity is forgotten, indeed repressed and this loss constitutes the symbolic castration of woman."(18)

Baptismal initiation is almost impossible to interpret except as a ritual cleansing of the taint left by the embryo's proximity to the female body; the waters of baptism wash away the animal impurity of amniotic fluids. Christianity maintains that an infant must be baptised – named and registered as the offspring of a heavenly father – before it can qualify for salvation. Ritual immersion in water not only symbolises the washing away of original sin (which, of course, was originally Eve's sin) and the defilment of maternal origins, it allows the child to be born again in the spiritual medium of the Father's amniotic fluids. The stain of female blood is also washed away by 'the blood of the lamb'. Even beyond religion, secular societies medicalise and control female reproduction through the male-dominated practice of obstetrics. Sexuality is studied "separately from *maternity*, as if sex has nothing to do with maternity or keeping infants alive." (19) This segregation again displays a desire for the control of maternal functions and female reproduction: if women's maternal powers were let loose in the midst of a patriarchy dedicated to preserving the supreme value of masculine sexuality, they could set off an uncontainable chain reaction.

But endless representations of the mother have failed to resolve her mysteries. Freud seemed to regard this early phase as inaccessible and possibly preferred to have it stay that way. Portrayals of the mother oscillate between madonna and gorgon. Perhaps this original wellspring of love is too deeply steeped in primal emotions to foster only pleasure. Among inevitable negative readings, special attention has been given to the infant's envy of the breast and, by extension, the mother. Melanie Klein regarded envy as central in infant life. Freud, however, often left it to female colleagues to speculate on the inconvenient subject of pre-oedipal psychological processes. With an untypically ingenuous air, he admitted he was puzzled to find that women tend to marry men who resemble their mothers rather than their fathers. He did not, however, care to venture too far into territory that might erode the advantage of the Father. Certainly his claim that a woman desires above all to have a male child because it represents the penis she lacks would quickly wither in a more feminised context. In the preverbal, pre-genital, pre-oedipal phase, the phase which creates such a close union between mother and baby, the infant's sex, whatever Freud might say, is not usually of overriding importance to its mother. Patriarchs crave sons; maternal preferences for sons are more often precipitated by punitive male-initiated reactions to the birth of girls.

But not all Freud's contemporaries take such a strict view of what is properly male or female. Freud's less well known colleague, Georg Groddeck, does not feel any need to segregate sexual behaviour into categories of normal and perverse. He barely separates mature from infantile, masculine from feminine, or love from sexuality. For him, the love between mother and child is not the origin of later conflicts, complexes or pathologies. He sees no reason why this first love should not develop naturally into the emotional life of adults of both sexes. "All love is love between mother and child," he writes, ".. everything else in love is merely a game and as such inessential." (20) Groddeck is paying homage to the indestructible character of the early mother-child union and to a remembered bliss which, if all goes well, will continue to resonate throughout adult life. He perceives mother-child love as fluid, unobstructedly erotic, a space where pleasure can exist without fixed boundaries, specific identities or temporal limits. With Freud, no: "With Freud the pimple never goes away .. and will become part of the human being, pimply forever, indelibly marked, forever. You're the one I love, Groddeck, all you past and present Groddecks .. you thought it was possible to be cured." (21)

The insights of child analyst, Donald Winnicott, are surprisingly close to Groddeck's. He comments that, ".. the pure distilled uncontaminated female element leads us to BEING, and this forms the only basis for self-discovery and a sense of existing (and then on to the capacity to develop an inside.)" (22) He regards this element as essential, even as the basis of good maternal relations. In mutual acceptance of one another, a mother and child couple can be passive yet simultaneously communicative. An erotics of *being* has no goal, no need to discharge itself, no need to assert its power or reproduce. A profound longing for romantic passion weaves its way through many centuries and cultures, valued as a source of mystical experience as well as of eroticism. Romantic adult love is always at least partly shaped by nostalgia for a return to a lost condition when two beings could, for more than a brief moment, be one inseparable flesh. An early twentieth century anthropologist paid homage to the mother: "At the lowest, darkest stages of human existence the love between the mother and her offspring is the bright spot in life, the only light in the moral darkness, the only joy amid profound misery... Woman at this stage is the repository of all culture, of all benevolence, of all devotion, of all concern for the living and grief for the dead." (23)

Whereas sexual passivity does not exile the memory of early nurture and its accompanying dependency, sexuality that regards itself as a vigorous signifier of masculine power is forced in the opposite direction, forced to turn away from the memory of original unity and the sharing of consciousness. This chapter has not attempted to analyse the masculine plight or examined how the eroticising of masculine power may be experienced as repressive by many members of the sex it is seeking to glorify. The son may not invariably prefer to be so remorselessly dominating. Nor so sadistic. Signs of sexual passivity may be brutally or covertly suppressed when they appear in the male, but to regard passive pleasure as an improper feature of male sexuality is to severely limit the lives of men.

Perhaps rashly, Freud himself recommended us to turn our attention to literature. John Donne's poem, *The Ecstasie*, describes the species of erotic love that Groddeck in his later century identified in the mother and child. The poem describes an intense, passive communion in the linked adult consciousnesses of a man and a woman. In this poem, a mutual and total passivity becomes the insignia of consuming passion. While the lovers lie still as "sepulchrall statues", their "soules negotiate". Free of material pressures such as time and space, the lovers enter their own microcosmic infinity: "All day, the same our postures were/ And wee said nothing, all the day."

Angela Carter's novel, *Nights at the Circus*, concludes with a pellucidly fluid and unstructured incarnation of love. On a note of infectious laughter that spills out beyond the boundaries of the narrative, she celebrates love's playfulness. Such playfulness is rarely perceived as germane to feminism, but in fact *The Sadeian Woman* also concludes with an unmistakeable assertion of sexual pleasures to which Sadeian understanding will be forever blind. If some readers have had ideological problems with Carter's study of Sade, (24) her final statement is unambiguous: ".. only the possibility of love could awaken the libertine to perfect immaculate terror. It is in this holy terror that we find, in both men and women

173

themselves, the source of all opposition to the emancipation of women."(25)

Footnotes

1) Male masochism and its theoretical relationship to the father, will not be discussed here. For a discussion of these issues see Deleuze, *Masochism: An Interpretation of Coldness and Cruelty*. Barbara Levick drew my attention to the role of the dominatrix. Statements made at a prostitutes convention in the 1970s suggested that this was a way of avoiding both male domination and physical contact. For the men it apparently repeated a remanant of infant powerlessness that their adult status forbade them. Freud would have called it neurosis.

2) Angela Carter, *The Sadeian Woman*, Virago. London. 1979. Simone de Beauvoir had already raised the subject of Sade and modern feminism in her article, *Must We Burn de Sade?* Grove Press. 1966.

3) Andrea Dworkin, *Pornography. p. 84-5.* The Women's Press, London, 1981.

4) Carter, op cit. p. 29.

5) Carter. ibid. p.27

6) ibid. p.24

7) ibid. p27

8) ibid. p.89

9) ibid. p.133

10) ibid. p.90

11) Jane Gallop. *Feminism and Psychoanalysis: The Daughter's Seduction.* p.46. The Macmillan Press. 1982. London. Gallop is referring to Stephen Heath's text, *Notes on Suture, Screen,* vol 19.

12) ibid. p.87

13) Catharine MacKinnon, *Feminism Unmodified,* p.172 Harvard. 1987.

14) Carter. op.cit. p.141.

15) Fatima Mernissi. *Beyond the Veil: Male-Female Dynamics in Muslim Society.* revised ed. p.45. Al Saqui Books. London. 1985. Freud's opinions on foreplay appear in In *Three Contributions to the Theory of Sex.*

16) Roberto Calasso, *The Marriage of Cadmus and Harmony,* p80. Jonathan Cape, 1988.

17) See, for example, N.O. Brown. *Love's Body.*

18) Michele Montrelay. *Inquiry into Femininity. The Woman in Question.* p.266. m/f. ed Parveen Adams & Elizabeth Cowie. Verso. London. 1990.

19) Sarah Blaffer Hrdy. *Mother Nature.* p.xiv. Vintage. 2000.

20) Georg Groddeck, *Exploring the Unconscious:* Unconscious Symbolism in Language and Art, p.143. 1927. Vision Press. London. 1949.

21) Catherine Clément. *The Weary Sons of Freud.* p109-10. Verso. 1987.

22) D.W. Winnicott, *Playing and Reality*, p.97. Penguin Books. 1974.

23) J.J. Bachofen, *Mother Right,* An Investigation of the Religious and Juridical Character of Matriarchy in the Ancient World, 1926. *Myth, Religion and Mother Right, Selected writings of J.J. Bachofen*, p. 79. Routledge & Kegan Paul, London, 1967.

24) Susanne Kappeler in *The Pornography of Representatio*n (Polity Press, 1986) expresses the opinion that, in *The Sadeian Woman,* "Besides falling into the trap of "literary sanctuary", Carter lapses into the fallacy of equal opportunities."

25} Carter. op cit. p.150

10

Monotheism, Misogyny, and Multiplicity

Monotheism Makes No Concessions

The gynophobia underlying the ritual of baptism has already been discussed. This chapter will consider some ways in which a religious doctrine – that there is only one, true, absolute, and invariably male god – justifies a deeply negative attitude towards women and provides a screen behind which misogyny can shelter from reasoned criticism

Whenever a religion claims to worship the only true god, it is also simultaneously falsifying all other systems of belief. The dominant position of a monotheistic god can only be maintained if he is absolutely inviolable. Therefore, to verify its own absolute truth and preserve itself from idolatry and heathen infiltration, a monotheistic faith needs to eradicate rival gods, alien creeds and anything else that might erode its spiritual supremacy. To remain above all others, this god must preside over a pyramidal hierarchy – even the angels of monotheism are kept in hierarchical order. Most churches that worship one single god have long histories in which the need to exclude all change, religious error, contamination (heresy) or even difference has justified inquisitions, colonialism, slavery, and slaughter. Heresy is the enemy within. Able to corrupt the truth with unorthodox or foreign perspectives, it has been exterminated with particular ruthlessness.(1) But monotheistic religions have reserved their most organised antagonism for religions devoted to other unique deities. All the three bible-based or Abrahamic religions (Judaism, Christianity and Islamism) feel especially beleaguered when rival beliefs approximate closely to their own. Though no material threat exists, their histories are pock-marked with religious wars waged to ensure the survival of true belief.

Where Sexual and Religious Politics Meet

Secular and religious institutions are not, however, as dissimilar as they are usually assumed to be. The massing together of large groups of people under one flag or one set of political and economic interests has much the same characteristics as the congregating of members of a faith. But, though governments and political groups may claim to accept that women have the same entitlements as men, they usually fail to provide women with an equal stake and status and it is generally accepted that religions may exclude women without the least gesture towards rational justification. The three monotheisms all maintain that man was made by a Father-God in his own (male) image and likeness. The maleness of this god requires the installation of patriarchal institutions which will reflect and glorify the godhead . Women cannot be inserted into this heavenly tautology. Even where church and state are formally separated or a society disallows religious practice altogether, vestiges of the same divinely endowed heritage of male primacy continue to exert their influence and changeless prejudices from a religious past slumber on in the foundations of contemporary political practice. Religion and state continue to reinforce each other below the observable surface.

Unsurprisingly, the domination of women and control of female sexuality are especially crucial in creeds that centre round the single Father-God, whether he is of Judaic, Christian or Islamic origin. God in his maleness must be kept entirely separate from the female. All three faiths adhere resolutely to this doctrine. The male's spiritual purity must also be safeguarded from female taint at all times. The Catholic church not only regulates all sexual liasons, it requires its priests to be celibate. The dynamics of this whole operation is less overt: it is thanks to unredeemed womankind, the sons of god have been able to separate themselves from brute materiality, and thanks to the devil, the world and the flesh that so conveniently embody evil and unredeemed nature, god is able to exist in his pure and perfect holiness, protected from the obvious imperfections of humankind. Male domination installs itself automatically wherever religious conviction and faith have separated man's 'spiritual' aspect or 'soul' from the body and the natural world.

Feminist theologians have written comprehensively about the effects of monotheistic religions on women's lives. (2) Feminist philosophers also have insisted on the need for "images and representations, which were appropriate to them [women]: on a cultural, and also on a religious, level, since 'God' has always been an important accomplice of the philosophical subject." (3) The precise style of divine collaboration with male supremacy will, of course, vary according to location, while perceptions of the philosophical subject will be shaped by regional conventions.

"The dominant element in Western religious traditions .. tends to be institutional, historical, and dogmatic in its orientations. This is true for normative Judaism, for Islam in its Sunni and Shi'ite branches, and for Christianity, whether Roman Catholic, Eastern Orthodox or mainline Protestant. In all of these God essentially is regarded as external to the self." (4) And when the externalised character of a religious tradition has caused it to be firmly fixed into the material world, it will at the same time become fixed into a highly paradoxical category of *spiritual fact*. Unfortunately, the attempt to legitimise and secure 'real' but also 'spiritual' facts and to install them in a real, material world has too often segued into the appropriation of material possessions. The installation of the one true Father-God and the acquistion of the non-believer's property have appeared together with infamous regularlity as state powers have routinely defended colonial atrocities in the name of of the one supreme god.

Religions that are not modelled round the unique

Father-God may celebrate many gods. Polytheistic divinities do not conform to a single pattern, either in their features or behaviour. They can take almost any form, including female and animal shapes and the stories told about them are equally varied. Hinduism provides a useful template here. Not only have the philosophical implications of its never-ending pantheon been precisely formulated, but its ideology contrasts revealingly with monotheistic creeds. Gandhi gives a meticulous explanation of the pluralism of Hindu gods. The ".. one thousand names of God were by no means exhaustive. .. God has as many names as there are creatures. Therefore we also say that God is nameless, and since God has many forms we consider Him formless, and since he speaks in many tongues we consider Him to be speechless and so on." (5) Gods and goddesses, and the oceans of stories relating to them, all manifest belief in a divinity present in everything and everyone of either sex. And with God personified in so many forms, "it is not doctrinal agreement that provides the unity of Hinduism." (6) Foreign cults and differences mix naturally into this context and other religious narratives can be embraced without effort or need for conflict. Polytheism is able to incorporate one or another supreme god alongside its endless other gods without experiencing anxiety – a claim to absolute supremacy is absorbed as just another facet or quirk in the infinite variety of divine expression. Religion "becomes many as it passes through the human medium .. Whose interpretation is to be held to be the right one? .. True knowledge of religion breaks down the barriers between faith and faith." (7)

The subjection of women has flourished in almost every culture. Women are oppressed in both monotheistic and polytheistic cultures, in those which are secular as in those where religious doctrines or iconographies deny female equality. However, though cultures that are polytheistic may often abuse women in relation to personal autonomy or human rights, they do not lock women out from the ideal of divinity. This difference is essential. "The (male) ideal other has been imposed upon women by men. Man is supposedly woman's more perfect other, her model, her essence. If she is to become a woman, if she is to accomplish her female subjectivity, woman needs a god who is a figure for the perfection of *her* subjectivity .. deprived of God, they (women) are forced to comply with models that do not match them, that .. cut them off from themselves and from one another." (8)

Fluidity and Fixity

Pluralism is by its nature fluid rather than fixed. It encourages unification through immersion in accepted difference rather than division by otherness and in this respect is able to provide a model appropriate to woman. The remaining question is what sort of figure might be needed to represent to woman "the perfection of her subjectivity". Luce Irigaray repeatedly reminds us that the feminine is both fluid and multiple by nature. In various texts and contexts, she replaces the Freudian model of a singular (masculine/ Judaic) sexuality with the fluid plurality of woman's sexuality:

"... the woman who doesn't have *one* sex organ cannot subsume it/ herself under *one* generic or specific term." (9) Woman's sexuality is not only multiple when it is contrasted with the masculine, it is also multiple without reference to the male. This is most apparent in the maternal sphere. Freud took the very narrow view that a woman feels a profound need to bear a son who could serve as her surrogate penis. But in a female reality, a woman is concerned with all her offspring, male or female, first born or last born, all her children require care and nurture. It should be self-evident that in a male reality, *patriarchal* has a very different meaning from *parental*, and that patterns of patriarchal ideology should not be confused with nurturing, fatherly behaviour. However, the differences between the fluid, all-mothering (matriarchal) ideal and the fixed, automatic (patriarchal) ideal which favours the eldest son are equally self-evident.

The one true god must be adored as eternal, unchanging and forever exclusively resident in the one true religion. Man can "orient his finiteness by reference to infinity .. man has sought out a unique *male* God. God has been created out of man's gender", and, "nothing should be added to that revelation .. the incarnate, manifest sign is masculine, and nothing must go beyond it." (10) This leaves the patriarchal god in a strange and quite depressingly solitary position. If he is to be the only one of his kind, he must be set apart and kept in isolation from everything except himself. And so, without consort or anything resembling human feeling, his libido has no object beyond his own unimpeachable selfhood. In place of co-creating, he has to create alone, create all that exists through the power of his solitary will. To contest this conception of god is to challenge the patriarchy.

Irigary has steadily implemented her invalidation of this divine singularity. She speaks of the necessity of "suspending the authority of the One: of man, of the father, of the leader, of the one god, of the unique truth.." A woman must refuse "to be reduced to the other of the same, to an other (male) or another (female) of the one.." She must constitute herself "as an autonomous and different subject." The next step is simple: "If we are to get away from the omnipotent model of the one and the many, we have to move on to the two.. The paradigm of this two is to be found in sexual difference." (11)

Man annexes woman in the same way that the solitary god is presumed to have annexed his creatures: he models her on himself. Also in the manner of his god, man separates himself from woman, placing himself above her. The Christian singularity has been modified by the inclusion of a triple (male) person in a single god. It has been still further adapted by the presence of a dual Christ and the incorporation of the human along with the divine. Christ's human mother was almost certainly added in deference to the deep attachment to the mother found in earlier, non-Christian faiths. This mother-of-god is often made the conduit for intercourse between the divine will and human desire. But, though Catholics pray to God's mother, in principle, the Christian God-the-Father remains aloof and in modern form tolerates even less intimacy than the Judaic god, who was apt to express dynamic reactions to human behaviour by means of floods, plagues, burning bushes and other similarly extreme manifestations. As the Christian god did not engage in the sexual congress with mortal women which was enjoyed by most pagan gods, angelic and spirit intervention were required for Mary to conceive his son. This allowed Mary to remain a virgin and thus be effectively desexualised. The asexual or male forms in which angels are normally represented are doubtless intended to make them less repulsive to god. (12) Female angels would have carried destabilising feminine impurities into the divine realm.

Religious Side Effects

Monotheism has cast a long shadow over determinedly secular institutions and some oddly similar effects also appear in psychoanalysis. Its fervid preoccupation with issues of sexual repression produces undertones of quasi-religious concern, and Freud himself termed psychoanalysis the "science of the soul".(13) While acknowledging that Freudian thought is far more complex than popular accounts suggest (present account included), psychoanalytic doctrine frequently shows signs of being enmeshed in the Judaic origins of the founding father. Certainly Freud believes in the universal wish of both men and women not to occupy "the feminine place, which is the only, and ever-present, alternative to where anyone really wants to be – in the male position, within the patriarchal human order." (14)

Whether or not Freud's representations of the desires and attitudes of women found echoes in bourgeois, late nineteenth and early twentieth-century Vienna, they clearly have not described the unalterable condition of women everywhere. In addition to a limited view, Freud has also been accused of professional dishonesty in routinely attributing lies, deviancy and neuroses to his female patients in preference to accepting that his patients' (fee-paying) fathers or his other male relatives or friends might be guilty of incest and sexual abuse.(15) He may have resisted the urge to sentimentalise children, but he succumbed to the temptation to whitewash fathers and preserve paternal purity at the expense of women. Putting the blame on women when men give way to moral lapses conforms with the biblical depiction of Eve.

Among present day patriarchal religions, Islam possibly expresses the idea of female blame the most forcefully. Fatima Mernissi comments that sexual inequality is the basis of both the Muslim and Christian systems. (16) Fusing broad Christian, Judaic and Freudian positions, she ennumerates the effects of these systems on the perception of women: "In the Western Christian experience sexuality itself was attacked, degraded as animality and condemned as anti-civilization. Freud viewed civilization as a war against sexuality. Civilization is sexual energy 'turned aside from its sexual goal and diverted towards other ends, no longer sexual and socially more valuable.' " Islam takes a different view: "What is attacked and debased is not sexuality but women, as the embodiment of destruction, the symbol of disorder. The woman is *fitna*, the epitome of the uncontrollable, a living representative of the dangers of sexuality and its rampant disruptive potential." (17) Mernissi further tells us that the Islamic sage, Ghazali, believes that, "the Muslim message .. considers humanity to be constituted by males only. Women are considered not only outside of humanity but a threat to it as well." (18) For this branch of Islam, the control of the female and her sexuality is essential to maintaining civilised life.

More Than One Voice

Malinowski's studies of matrilineal communities strongly suggest that patriarchal religions are an ideological means of suppressing matriarchal social structures. He was fully aware of "the difficulty of teaching a patriarchal religion to aborigines whose true kinsmen were their mothers' brothers." He says, 'We must realize that the cardinal dogma of God the Father and God the Son .. would completely misfire in a matrilineal society, where all personal unity between them is denied, and where all family obligations are associated with mother-line. We cannot wonder that Paternity must be among the principal truths to be inculcated by proselytising Christians." (19) In the widely Christian context of the early twentieth century in the West, Malinowski, along with a number of other anthropologists, (20) were drawn willy-nilly into the conflict between firmly established religious groups and the wave of assertive feminist politics that was emerging at the time.

Feminist politics have moved on since the less

honed and confident confrontations of that period. Also since then, the context in both the East and the West has become less universally Christian so that the political agenda of religion is more exposed to view. In their different ways, some to more aggressive effect than others, all three monotheisms have been affected by similar changes. Feminism continues to play an important role in the shifting understanding of what is meant by 'man.' Irigaray writes, "We have to rethink the model of subjectivity which has served us for centuries, not in order to add a little bit here or a little bit there, but so that we can abandon the model of a single and singular subject altogether .. the subject is at least two, man and woman, a two in relations that are not biunivocal." (21) (The word 'biunivocal' seems to mean 'a single signification repeated in two voices'.) Nor can the model of the divine be exempted from this same process of rethinking.

Irigaray also speaks of trying "to find a way of making an alliance between these two natures possible without one being subordinated to the other" and of how to "rethink our tradition, particularly the religious one, in order to be able to love each other here below, making of each other a horizontal transcendence..." .(22) She says, "The patriarchy has separated the human from the divine but it has also deprived women of their goddesses or their divinity. Before patriarchy, both men and women were potentially divine, which perhaps means that they were both *social*." Religion has become "an all men affair, and it often accuses the religious spirit of women of being the devil's work." (23) It is Irigaray's opinion that a love between the sexes that recognises the alterity of the other and exists on all levels is the necessary basis for realising the feminist ideal of equality.

We should welcome the containing phrase "not biunivocal". It has taken a long time to imagine a voice that neither subsumes the second voice into itself nor represses its otherness. Perhaps we will not have to wait equally long before (feminine) difference will have no further need to phrase itself in negatives or to mark itself out as "nothing" or as 'that which is not' and can begin to acquire a place for itself and a name that will be recognised even in the highly charged political arena of religious culture.

Footnotes

1) Even so, here and there, some pagan figure, name or custom has been discreetly incorporated. Easter, for example, is a version of the Saxon fertility goddess, Eostre, who is herself a version of Astarte. Many holy wells have enjoyed prior sacred status in pagan times.

2) See Uta Ranke-Heinemann's excellent and thorough account of the treatment of women by the Catholic Church. She chronicles its reconcilliation of persecution and misogyny with religious doctrine. (*Eunuchs for the Kingdom of Heaven*. Penguin Books. 1990.) Fatima Mernissi (*Beyond the Veil*) gives an account of Islamic misogyny, and Eva Figes (*Patriarchal Attitudes*) touches on Judaic prejudices.

3) Luce Irigaray. *Democracy Begins Between Two*, p.131. The Athlone Press. London. 2000. (Fr. ed.1994)

4) Harold Bloom. *Omens of the Millenium*, p.1. Fourth Estate. London. 1996.

5) *All Men Are Brothers. Life and Thoughts of Mahatma Gandhi as told In His Own Words*, p.91. Navajivan Publishing House. Ahmedabad. 1960.

6) K.M.Sen. *Hinduism*, p.19. Penguin. 1961.

7) Gandhi. op cit, p.88.

8) Luce Irigaray. *Sexes and Genealogies*, p.64. Columbia University Press. 1993. (Fr ed.1987)

9) Irigaray. *Speculum of the Other Woman*, p.233. Cornell University Press. 1985. (Fr ed.1974) Ideas relating to fluidity/ multiplicity appear in many of Irigaray's texts, such as This Sex Which Is Not One, The Mechanics of Fluids etc.

10) Luce Irigary. *Sexes and Genealogies*, p.61.

11) Irigaray. *Democracy Begins Between Two*, p.129

12) Harold Bloom observes that Milton replaces the male angels of orthodox Judaism, Christianity and Muslimism with angels that are "alternately male and female, exchanging genders with their sexual partners." His Adam and Eve and his angels "exalt again the image of the human" and "celebrate the divine possibilities implicit in human sexuality." Bloom. op cit. p.39. Milton's risky presentation is a rare exception. Catherine Clément constitutes another exception in her irreverant novel, *Jesus au Bucher.* (2000, Editions du Seuil.) The angel, Iblis, clutches a one-eyed, female angel, Lilith, to his bosom as together they devise their own version of religious history. According to Lilith, Jesus will have to remain fatherless as "the fathers of God's people were [only] made to transmit God's commandments." (p.59)

13) Bruno Bettleheim discusses Freud's use of 'soul' in *Freud and Man's Soul* (First Vintage Books 1984) pointing out that he uses the term "seele" very freely. Freud wanted to see "secular ministers of souls, who don't have to be physicians and must not be priests."

14) Juliet Mitchell. *Psychoanalysis and Feminism*. Allen Lane. 1974.

15) See Geoffrey Masson.

16) Fatima Mernissi. *Beyond the Veil*. Al Saqi Books. (revised edition) London. 1985.

17) Mernissi. ibid p.44.

18) Mernissi. ibid p.45.

19) Evelyn Reed. *Woman's Evolution*, p.362. Pathfinder. USA. 1974. Her quote from Malinowski appears in *The Sexual Life of Savages in North-Western Melanesia.*

20) Bachofen and Briffault were two founder members of an anthropology that foregrounded the role that women played in the formation of society and saw it as crucial to an understanding of the human species and societies, including matriarchies.

21) Irigaray. *Democracy Begins Between Two*, p.6.

22) ibid. p.47

23) Irigaray. *Sexes and Genealogies*, p.190.

11

Pornography As Endless Dissatisfaction

A Little Bit of Background

Pornography has not merely come into the open, it has saturated the total context in which we live. We don't seem to know quite how we got to be in this pornographised world and we don't know how to get out of it. There seems to be no escape. Nor do all of us want to escape. What happened?

Over the course of recorded history, cultures changed and the sexual frankness which characterises most ancient civilizations disappeared. Pornography became a clandestine activity comparatively recently. In mid-twentieth-century Britain, it was still a shady enough business to provoke attempted prosecutions of books for circulating pornographic material.(1). Since then, both the visibility and accessi-bility of pornography have increased enormously, but it remains an undecided issue in both definition and law.

How are we to decide what is or is not porno-graphic? Initially it appeared to be a moral question or at least one of public decency. Often now it seems to be judged according to whether it is 'normal' or 'pathological'. But these categories are also unclear. Some feminists see this lack of clarity as seriously problematic. The feminist lawyer, Catharine Mac-Kinnon, regards "*indefinability*" as "central to pornography's *definition* ... because the fought-over invisible in this .. obscures the fact that the fight over a definition of obscenity is a fight among men over the best means to guarantee male power as a system." (2) This may seem extreme to some people, but it is certainly true that indefinability has led to case-by-case decisions over the exact status of possible instances of pornography, ranging through high art all the way down to unequivocally hard core pornography that exists solely to produce sexual arousal by any possible means. Thus the questions asked are mainly about style and degree, or on rare occasions about issues of actual harm suffered in the process of production. However, any argument that is based only on the *degree* to which it is proper to represent women as sexual objects which are available for any sort of use is already assuming that sexual objectification, per se, is acceptable. The present discussion will restrict itself to historical and political attitudes and bypass distinctions between pornographic and erotic.

Already, in the post war period, materials such as the Kinsey Report were circulating sensational accounts of sexual fantasies and behaviours. Supposedly serving disinterested scientific research, this unprecedented flood of intimate data began to gain influence. At the same time, more surreptitiously but more far-reachingly, a new pornography was becoming unprecendentedly exploitable as a resource for commerce. Primarily women, but children and men too, could be bought and sold in virtual form along with the material products they accompanied. More explicit sales of humans were still covert, but in product-related form they were a magic lubricant which could dissolve resistance to the sale of other objects.

For many in the western world, the 1960s represented a spell of hopeful experiment that was often referred to as a sexual revolution. Sexual candour appeared to be promising a change for the better. The young believed that secrecy and hypocrisy were the enemies and, if a strong enough light could pierce through the fog of obscurity that surrounded sex, an age of honesty would come to pass. But they were too busy asserting their new-found right to sexual freedom to notice that they had themselves become objects of scrutiny. Although in relation to the instinctual urges of people there was a genuine new openness, greater sexual explicitness did not come without cost. As sexuality lost the right to privacy, it was first studied, then reshaped into a manipulable biological function. Passion, meanwhile, fell under the control of reason and became mere fantasy and slightly absurd. Doubt arose regarding whether instinct and human sensibility could coexist. As the emotional content of sexual love was either trivialised or pushed aside, a gap appeared. Pornography quickly seized its opportunity as objectified sexuality opened the way to new kinds of exploitation. It invaded social life at epidemic speed (3) and, as if by prearrangement, new, fully formed models of sexual pleasure and habits were slotted into place. Disguised as permissiveness, these were just as crudely insensitive to private feelings and vulnerabilities as the moral and religious standards controlling sexual conduct had been before them. Morality had anyway lost much of its power of social control, displaced by a new conformity that now represented itself as *normality*. Details of sexual performance – its duration, frequency and the all important achievement of the orgasm – could all be evaluated according to how well they matched the norm. Sex had moved into line with mass production. These new objective standards, allowed the body and its imperfections to be measured with unvarying precision and to become unprecedently open to improvments and alterations promising to enhance it as a desirable object. The need to rectify physical imperfections had opened up yet another, almost limitless potential as a 'perfect' body was made saleable in the abstract.

Acutely violent male fantasies of the sexual uses to which women's bodies might be put were being normalised in public contexts. Feminists responded with prolific commentaries. These excited responses, polarised opinions and inflamed divisions, and anomalies appeared. Pornography was examined in its political, historical, economic, legal, sociological, and recreational aspects. Andrea Dworkin, Catharine MacKinnon, Susanne Kaeppeler and a host of others too numerous to name took positions that strongly opposed it; women such as Kathy Acker advocated producing a pornography that women would enjoy in the same way that men did. Dworkin emphasises that traditional political struggles have never seriously incorporated the aim of freedom for women. Certainly, it has never been seriously implemented by either the left or the right. At times feminists have adopted positions that do not correspond with any existing political formulations. It is central to Dworkin's critiism of pornography that, although in normal circumstances the left opposes censorship, it does not follow that a woman who opposes pornography must be holding rightwing views. Neither can leftwing sympathies be inferred from the fact that a woman condones pornography. Sexual politics are complicated by problems that are frequently absent from state agendas.

In her seminal work, *Sexual Politics*, Kate Millett remarks that lessened censorship has led to an increase of "frankness in expressing [masculine] hostility in specifically sexual contexts" and to the "freedom to express what was once forbidden outside of pornography." (4) Millett engages with the wider issues of sexual politics rather than the specifics of pornography, but her expositions of entrenched misogyny in certain admired works of literature encouraged feminist opposition to pornography on the reasonable grounds that it incites hatred and violence against women. Dworkin focuses on the operation of this hatred and violence in more explicitly hostile and outspoken terms: "The celebration of rape .. is the paradigmatic articulation of male sexual power as a cultural absolute," or, "In adoring violence .. men seek to adore themselves" (5). At the same time, however, she also endorses a feminism which embraces numerous objectives and alliances and expresses an unequivocal desire for tolerance when she says: "I'm not saying that everybody should be thinking about this in the same way. I have a really strong belief that any movement needs both radicals and liberals." (6) Dworkin was commemorated as someone who would not be tolerated in a lukewarm climate where "postmodernism" has removed "all politics from feminism". (7)

Every bit as uncompromising as Dworkin, Catharine MacKinnon slices bluntly through political, social and class divides: "pornography institutionalises the sexuality of male supremacy, which fuses the erotization of dominance and submission with the social construction of male and female .. the liberal defence of pornography as human sexual liberation, as derepression – whether by feminists, lawyers, or neo-Freudians – is a defence not only of force and sexual terrorism, but of the subordination of women." (8) She has also suggested that perhaps the greatest damage done by the institutional sexualising of male supremacy has been to indoctrinate both sexes with the idea that the exercise of power over women is an intrinsic feature of male sexuality and so, by extension, of male attractiveness to women – in a nutshell: "Pornography makes sexism sexy." (9)

Meanwhile, legislative and commercial forces have continued to bicker about what is permissible and what is not, what is pornographic and what not. Broadly speaking the rubric runs: erotica – allowed; obscenity – occasionally not – may require scrutiny;

child pornography – definitively not; that which involves adult females – generally that's pretty much alright. The context becomes all important, implying that, in the hands of appropriate users, the production and the consumption of pornography need do no harm to anyone, although some regulation is required when it affects under-age people or trafficked women. 'Ordinary' pornography might as well be regarded as a legitimate part of the leisure industry.

The dynamics of pornography have been interpreted in many different ways, but its unfaltering misogyny is always obvious. Though the motives of individuals are less accessible, institutionalised misogyny has been quite widely understood in terms of male domination that seeks self-justification by pornographising women and pre-emptively defending itself against female responses to its abuse. This is a description of paranoid aggression. It explains many crimes against women – gang rape, for example, demonstrates collective misogyny as a means of male bonding and of subordinating male disputes over the possession of women to the overall principle of male dominance.

MacKinnon is as succinct as always when she contends that pornography "creates an accessible sexual object, the possession and consumption of which *is* male sexuality, to be consumed and possessed by which *is* female sexuality." (10) There may be many shades of opinion among women who are opposed to pornography, but a belief that pornography is a form of male violence is always an underlying constant.

Economic Interests

Sexual candour is not the cause of misogyny. The switch that sets misogyny in motion is sexual objectification, just as the sexual object is pornography's required tool. Early male-controlled societies used marketable or exchangeable women to defend themselves and their territories. Women were the currency which made it possible to buy off aggressive male rivals and acquire allies. Where more modern circumstances prevail, the use of women as a medium of exchange is shrouded in obfuscation. Sexual liberation might perhaps promise an antidote, but this does not mean that in practice it would discontinue using women as property. Dworkin describes the "old pornography industry" as secretive, devoted to the "secret buying and selling of women .. The new pornography industry .. promoted especially by the boys of the sixties .. [had] the whore brought out of the bourgeois home into the streets for the democratic consumption of all men .. The dirty little secret is not sex but commerce." (11) Dworkin's analysis was echoed later by Susanne Kappeler, who regards prostitution as the crucial symbol for the assertion of power in sex – "The dirty secret at the heart of our culture is not sex but money." (12) The same familiar hypocrisy is being observed here. Ironically, although its commercial motives cause words like "dirty" and "secret" to be levelled at pornography, it is with precisely such words that pornography has so successfully marketed itself.

Meanwhile, pornography and commerce stroll hand in hand in broad daylight. Represented as innocuous, even as able to offer borderline social benefits, pornography is in reality, "a huge profit-making industry masked as a social service for those left out of the national orgasm. It not only aids the economy, but takes people's minds off their discontents."(13) Most women cannot afford such luxuries as a national orgasm. Nor can they afford the shopping sprees that are so shrilly proclaimed as the remedy for boredom, depression and emptiness. Only too many women have very little to bargain with beyond their own bodies. Finally, the effects of pornography are not confined to a female ghetto: mechanisms seeking to pervert the sexuality of women are also deeply damaging to men's sexuality and men's self-understanding.

The Uses of Addiction

The responses that pornography exploits are not complicated. To maintain a steady level of commercially exploitable stimulation, it is necessary to withold sexual satisfaction and to do so on a routine basis. Regular increments of sexual excitation and a constant bombardment of the senses are routinely allied with sexual frustration, desensitisation and turmoil.

A person's memories of original desires are ground to dust, replaced by mechanical and increasingly empty cravings. These can be readily directed into the acquisition of more material goods which also fail to satisfy. And so a spiral is installed. Commerce insists that well-regulated pornography does little damage, yet, by patterning itself closely on addiction, pornography becomes a fuel that powers the market.

Rooting out child pornography is now an international crusade, but, although women are often as lacking in power as children, they are offered no protection against this form of exploitation. And, in spite of legal prohibitions, child pornography is increasingly big business. Perhaps this suggests that pornography only achieves its final goal when it succeeds in despoiling innocence, and if women are now too besmirched to be icons of innocence, then children must serve in their place. Finally, differences of opinion amongst women provide yet another pretext for allowing pornography to prolong the debate until everyone has forgotten what the original issues were. A convenient amnesia, looking oddly like a further symptom of addiction, promotes the fiction that we have entered a post-feminist era. Once again we see the historical feminist difficulty of challenging "institutions that were designed without women in mind, and social practices that subordinate women .. a feminist agenda must address all women." (14)

But pornography is not containable in neat categories. Its long, undisturbed tenancy in the public imagination has granted it the power to take possession of images and objects that in themselves have no pornographic or even sexual content. Once displaced from its original location, desire can be freely transferred into almost any receptacle. Shoes, knives, cars, money, guns, political dictators and entire ideologies from fascism to consumerism can all be fetishised. Newspaper magnates can sell their political whims in images of naked breasts. It is all but impossible to distinguish pornography from propaganda or advertising when all three modes rely on illusion to create a reflex response and control the viewer's reactions, ideally without his or her conscious consent. While pornography is promising to grant its consumer a sense of taking full control through converting a fictively represented other into a manipulable object, it is also slyly concealing the fact that its depersonalising sexual imagery is controlling, manipulating, and so objectifying the consumer too.

With typical subversiveness, advertising is also furtively exploiting the female consumer's perceptions of herself. Already the distorted *object of desire*, woman is also being solicited to buy into her own reconstruction. Advertising exhorts her to purchase whatever will help her to meet standards of beauty that are unachievable in reality. It tells her that she needs to compensate for her miserable inadequacy, and so seeks to inspire her with an insatiable craving for shopping. If she does not have the money to finance this shopping addiction, she may be reduced to shoplifting. Appropriately, a favourite device in pornographic films and literature is the young, inexperienced, female shoplifter who is led off to a back room to be intimately searched and punished. (15)

As the goods on sale are converted into replacement erotica, sexual desire becomes indistinguishable from them. In this flux of illusion it is small wonder that the shopper, especially if she is a woman, may sometimes be hard pressed to appear stable. In any case, the myth of the needy, semi-hysterical woman shopper has huge commercial value.

Whether she pays, steals, or suffers from a "female malady', in every case the remedy – more and more shopping – remains the same. She is a model consumer and a mainstay of commerce. (16) But the need to fill her emptiness is a better remedy for flagging sales than for flagging desire or self-esteem. Both advertising and pornography do more than displace the natural wellsprings of desire, both make those they have manipulated appear to be intrinsically perverse. The central activity of pornography is to dehumanise the body and reduce it to a dismembered collection of hyper-sexualised body parts. It provides a falsified, no longer quite human stock onto which inanimate articles of merchandise can be grafted. Adept packaging may draw the eye away from the bald fact that all these bodies have lost their personal identity, leaving only a sexualised assemblage of body parts to take the place of an integrated body.

Susanne Kappeler sums up the effects all of this in a few chilling sentences: "The remorseless diffusion of gender stereotypes, of ready-made and imperative life-styles, of regulated uniform 'relationships' – the ideological diffusion of 'mind-images' of humans – through the remorseless diffusion of their material basis – consumer goods – renders human subjects increasingly marginal." She points out that women "kill their own experiences in an attempt to conform to existences imaged for them." (17) It may not need to be added that any such objectifying imagery, whether it represents children, women or men, also distorts men's self images. Pornography has never respected either men, women or boundaries.

Historical Perceptions
of Sexuality and Pornography

A coterie of unreflective popular opinion may view pornography as progressive and forward-looking and express some disdain for women who regard it as offensive. But pornography has not always had the same motives as it does today. The sixteenth-century author, Aretino (18), sometimes referred to as Europe's first pornographer, wrote only for simple entertainment. Though money openly occupies the foreground, he takes no interest in the promotion of commerce. As a mother instructs her daughter in the arts of successful prostitution, she enumerates the sexual foibles of many clients and explains in ribald detail how to satisfy them with minimum effort and maximum profit. This early pornographic text is holding the mirror up to male desire and above all to its comic eagerness to be deceived, but it does not exploit or objectify women. There is no place for patronising representations of female sexuality or desire, because, in full consciousness of the illusions they are producing, these women are self-governing and neither passive nor masochistic. Aretino relishes their lively and calculating characters in a celebration of the sheer artfulness of (female) wit over (male) folly. Nobody is hurt in this contest, and even the pockets of the rich are only mildly abused. Conversations between a neophyte and a more experienced prostitute were to become a convention in pornographic works, including Sade's *Philosophy in the Boudoir*, though in this text the social and philosophical construction of gender is much altered .

Aretino is perfectly candid about illusion – the self-elaborated female, her pretended sexual response, and the man's delusory pleasure, behind which real people are playing a game, laughing at a joke. The same joke appears even earlier in the work of Chaucer. (19) Sade's women are obliged to choose between 'masculine' sadism and 'feminine' masochistic submission. *Justine* and its companion novel, *Juliette*, are both grounded in a deeply sombre conception of human desire.

Though it is now quite acceptable for women to record their own perceptions of female sexuality, to gain broad approval these must be framed within the accepted (masculinist) limits. The 'woman's novel' and, above all, 'romantic' fiction frequently excite sociological rather than literary analysis. But the situation changes when women's erotic writings endorse a sado-masochistic or masculinist sexual politics. The work of Anias Nin is widely praised alongside the work of her friend, Henry Miller, to which it provides a natural complement. In general, accounts of female sexuality seem to wield greater authority if they are the product of a man's pen. The Story of O, published under a female pseudonym, sparked heated and protracted arguments over whether this sado-masochistic novel was the work of a female or a male author. (20) It seems that where the sex of the writer is not known the literary value of a text cannot be gauged. Literary merit does not, however, guarantee either the authenticity or the politics of sexual writing. Of the distinction between pornography and erotica, Kappeler remarks that, "The implicit assumption is still that some of it – the non-violent sexual material, the art, the legitimate fiction – has to be 'rescued', rescued it seems from abolition, but in fact from analysis and critique themselves." (21)

Difference and Definition

Each successive age rephrases sexual difference in its own cultural dialect. Freud's culturally-determining, 'scientific' vision of the vital role of sexuality in the interpretation of the human mind and heart re-enforced the traditional motif of humanity as a primarily male species. Woman remained in a sub-category labelled substandard and had to be cajoled into once again accepting her unhappy lack. In Freudian terms, sexual equality could never be achieved unless women could somehow become the same as men. In Freud's bourgeois milieu, a woman's life began in the bedroom, and bedroom practices were a microcosmic version of society. The struggle for a sexual identity that differs from the masculine model has come into focus more slowly than women's struggle for equal rights, but, Freud's judgement that society is modelled on male sexuality would not lead us to expect to see social equity unless we had first reconstituted an authentic sexual counterpart to the male. To deny a specifically female sexuality is not only to subsume feminine difference into the masculine, it is to oppress one sexuality with the other. The erasure of difference (22) inevitably leads to the desire of one sex to *erase* the other. Women's sexuality has not been liberated. The need for another (and this time quite different) sexual revolution is indicated.

As long as a masculine prototype shapes the common understanding of all human desire, female desire will be prevented from taking its natural form. In Freudian terms, it will be *repressed*. Freud's quest to know what women want will not be successful and it is absolutely certain that pornography will not enlighten anyone about the real desires of real women. Pornography intended for the use of women is equally useless since a model of misandry based on the pattern of the old misogyny can only serve to reinforce resistance to social change. An inverted power structure merely reaffirms rule by force and justifies the patriarchal order which it mimics. Feminism is not advanced by reflecting the masculine.

Collected evidence strongly suggests that pornographic representations of women precipitate abuse and violence. Of course it does: pornography manipulates both male and female sexuality. There is nothing progressive or liberal about the promotion of commerce through the sacrifice of sexual satisfaction and of real engagement with another human person.

Unreal Body, Unreal Self

The distorting machinery of pornography does not reveal bodies stripped back to a natural or animal condition. In fact, pornography bears no resemblance to nature. There is no pornographic biosphere. Pornography's only connection with the biosphere consists in wiping out symbiotic alliances: as it destroys communication and the interdependence of two different subjects, whatever their sex, it replaces them with a mechanically produced illusion made for solitary consumption. The perpetual disappointment of engineered desire, the perpetuation of an insatiable craving for more, the promise of power over another, followed by the delivery of nothing, can precipitate nothing but anger, loathing and sadism. By suppressing or *de-realising* the female body, pornography too often allies itself with a male supremacy that glories in triumphal politics and a fascism that basks in machismo and misogyny. It also amputates the male self-image both by excluding its secondary female characteristics and by erasing possible empathy with otherness.

The effects of pornography on women's self-appraisal stretch outside the immediate confines of sexuality. Unreal representations of women mainly focus on the external body, but their effects are nevertheless internalised. A woman may deny that she is 'feminine' with an intensity that rivals the most extreme male rejection of all feminine characteristics, but she is destined to be disappointed if she hopes by this to escape humiliation through a masculine identity – her spurious masculinity asserts that a woman in herself is worthless. The woman who tries, however painfully, to survive as herself is at least retaining the possibility that she might eventually find her real identity. But directly or indirectly, women are constantly being pornographised and hampered by feelings of personal shame. 'Womanly shame' is an edgy, phantom presence. It has the power to afflict even the most enlightened woman. Echoes of its condemnatory resonances still linger on. However, over a comparatively short historical period, what once was called 'shamelessness' in women has to some extent ceased to brand them as social outcasts. Even so, substantial problems remain and the temptation to avoid the emotional content of sexual relations still casts its malignant shadow. Admittedly, there are risks in emotionally charged sexual liasons – they do not promise to provide a joy that is exempt from sorrow. But neither do they validate pornography's promises of instant gratification that is guaranteed to be effortless, ego-bolstering, and free of any lasting effect on the purchaser's life.

Angela Carter has made the thought provoking comment that, "when pornography serves – as with very rare exceptions it always does – to reinforce the prevailing system of values and ideas in a given society, it is tolerated; and when it does not, it is banned." (23) After Kate Millett has reproduced Henry Miller's dictum, "THE GREAT ARTIST IS HE WHO CONQUERS THE ROMANTIC IN HIMSELF," in resounding capitals, (24) she rephrases his idea less rhetorically as a man's desire to make himself ultra virile by destroying 'feminine' emotion in himself. Emotional satisfaction found with another individual might have its own hazards, but at least it is not deliberately calculated to produce frustration. And though they may have what is taken to be a 'feminine' character, such emotions are open to members of either sex. But where profit is the central and sole motive, attachments that are personal and imbued with feeling will inevitably be discarded as 'feminine' and weak.

Women who describe their experiences of themselves often speak of the sense of shame that can infect the mere idea of being female. A woman in a consciousness-raising group of the seventies is quoted as saying, "Now I can be a woman; it's no longer so humiliating. I can stop fantasising that secretly I am a man.. Now I can value what was once my shame." Another woman, referring to the same humiliation, concludes, "Now I don't have to be a woman anymore... Now the very idea 'woman' is up for grabs... feminism will give me the freedom to seek some other identity altogether." (25) Despite a few surface discrepancies, an identical sense of shame is evident in both summations. Each of these women feels that a change of sexual identity, over and above a change of her external situation, lies at the core of her experience. Each is asserting that she has become someone other than a pornographised, male-defined female because of changes in her perception of her own sexual identity.

The invasion of depersonalising pornographic imagery will undoubtedly continue. Women will have to struggle on against the sense that there is something entirely too personal about their excessively real bodies and shamefully emotional sexuality. Even so, the future of this struggle is not hopeless. The brutalising activities of commerce are being unveiled to increasingly wide audiences. And though the old, patriarchal order will not readily renounce its power over the sexual lives of men and women, a feminine desire for love has already shown endless stamina in its determination to realise itself.

Footnotes

1) E.g. the trials of *Lady Chatterley's Lover and Fanny Hill* in the early 1960s or the case relating to Linda Marchiano (Lovelace) of *Deep Throat,* brought in 1986, in which Catharine MacKinnon was involved.

2) Catharine A. MacKinnon, *Feminism Unmodified*, p. 153. Harvard University Press. 1987.

3) The demand for physical perfection has already been moved on into the medicalised body, where the idea of a standardised healthy body sustains industries from drugs to surgery and diets to anorexia.

4) Kate Millett, *Sexual Politic*s,p. 46-7. Abacus, London, 1972.

5) Andrea Dworkin, *Pornography*. Perigee Books. New York. 1981. The Women's Press edition, pps 23 and 53. London. 1981.

6) The Guardian 12-04-05. Dworkin is quoted in Katharine Viner's profile. An obituary of Dworkin by Julie Blindel appeared on the same day.

7) Katha Pollet on Dworkin in The Nation, May 2, 2005. Pollet adds that she will miss Dworkin, and "even more I miss the movement that had room for her."

8) Catharine MacKinnon. op cit. p. 148. Mackinnon is not often given credit for her quirky humour. A footnote in this book remarks, "An erection is not a thought unless one thinks with one's penis."

9) MacKinnon. ibid. p. 200.

10) Mackinnon. ibid. p 150. MacKinnon's position is attacked by Laurie Shrage (The fallacies of anti-porn feminism. Feminist Theory, Volume 6, Number 1) who argues that male sexual behaviour cannot be accused of having an objectifying effect when "it is obviously possible for a man to be sexually objectified by a man, a woman or himself" and that "suppressing pornography" does not "protect women's freedom and equality". But the sexual objectification or exploitation of men does not cancel the reading that the sexual exploitation of either sex can be traced back to patriarchal ideology. The

"objectifying" of a man "by himself" appears to refer to masturbation, but, if non-abusive sexual satisfaction is possible with another, why should it be defined as self-abusive in the absence of another?

11) Andrea Dworkin. op cit. p.208.

12) Susanne Kappeler. *The Pornography of Representation*, p.203. Polity Press. 1986.

13) Women's Report Collective: *Pornography. No Turning Back*, Edited by Feminist Anthology Collective, p.226. The Women's Press, London, 1981.

14) *Conflicts in Feminism*, ed Marianne Hirsch & Evelyn Fox Keller, p.160. *Adjudicating Differences*, Martha Minow. Routledge. 1990.

15) In reality, penalties for shoplifting vary according to class. Women with no financial motive for shoplifting can usually escape punishment with the excuse of an exonerating *female malady*. See Elaine Showalter's book, *The Female Malady*.

16) Nineteenth-century department stores were designed to entice women shoppers. The economist, J.K. Galbraith, once cited housewives

as major contributors to the economy in their role as primary consumers.

17) Kappeler. op cit. p.79.

18) Pietro Aretino. *The School of Whoredom*. Hesperus Press Ltd., London, 2003.

19) See Angela Carter's essay titled "Alison's Giggle" in *Shaking a Leg* .

20) Published under the name of Pauline Reage, the book was quite widely assumed to be of male authorship. Later it was established as the work of a female academician, one Dominique Aury. A recent reprint of the text includes an essay by Jean Paulhan, who praised the book for its 'virility'.

21) Kappeler. op cit. p.39.

22) Science and philosophy have separately emphasised he need for difference. Reflecting on how the exclusion of *difference* from any complex process results in stultifying oversimplifications, Gregory Bateson considers difference to be "of the nature of relationship", and asserts that, "the interaction of parts of mind is triggered by difference." Gregory Bateson. *Mind and Nature*, p.94. Wildwood House, London, 1979.

23) Angela Carter, The Sadeian Woman p. 18.

24) Kate Millett. *op cit. p.9.*

25) Ann Snitow, A Gender Diary, Conflicts in Feminism, p.9.

PART 3

She Reads and Writes Between the Lines

12

A Defence of Romantic Love

'Rosy Apple, Lemon, Tart,
Tell Me the Name of Your Sweetheart
The old, playground skipping rhyme goes through the alphabet letter by letter until, when the (girl) child stumbles on the rope, the initial of her destined lover is foretold. Many traditional games involve childish rituals of romantic prediction, reminding us that a woman's position in the world was, and very frequently still is, defined by her relationships with men. As practised among the wealthier classes, marriage has been the longstanding bedrock of social and economic order. A male head of family has provided money and protection (especially from the intrusions of rival males), while his wife has provided unequivocal heirs (preferably male) and a motley array of personal and domestic services. Until women finally became entitled to their own money, property, and personal status, the stereotype remained unaltered. Yet the past lingers on, as, despite gaining these basic concessions, even fully independent women with no

need for the support of their menfolk have continued to have the ideal of a secure, hetereosexual marriage impressed upon them from their earliest years.

There has also been a long and persistent history of hostility towards marriage. A stubborn adherence to an opposing ideal that has disconnected itself from issues of social order produces fierce animosity to the boundaries and duties created by marriage. This ideal finds its most complete expression in the quest for an irresistible, unconditional and 'romantic' love. And even though, as a legal institution, marriage excludes chaotic and unrealistic desires that threaten to disrupt a contract formulated to regulate the reproductive lives of women and the property rights of men, the belief persists that females are incurably romantic and possessed by a blind craving for love. Inevitably, marriage is then advertised as a natural continuation of love and therefore the ideal and goal of all women. But representations of marriage, like those of love, contain their own paradoxes and conflicts of meaning. Women or men, as also libertines or lovers, may perceive marriage as an intolerable restriction. Some cults of romantic love may put experiences of engulfing emotion before sexual satisfaction – this ideal appears in yogic and other spiritual practices – and an obsessive desire for total immersion in love can become an asetic, quasi-spiritual and boundless quest. In both life and literature, total and unconditional love has refused to submit to reason or regulation and can exercise an overwhelming fascination . The desire to experience romantic love is the mortal enemy of confinement, whether to the limitation of reason or on a purely material plane.

Few words produce quite so many blurred or contradictory responses as *romantic*. Its applications are by no means limited to sexual relationships. Ranging from meaning visionary and marked by heights of passion to sentimental, delusory and unrealistic, it can be used to refer to entire historical periods and cultures or to the private desires and proclivities of single individuals. It can be applied indiscriminately to philosophies, aesthetic or ascetic movements and styles in the arts, as much as to emotional tendencies. Manifestations of the desire for the romantic abound, but adequate definitions of it are rare. Despite a widely held persuasion that reason should exclude anything which defies cogent definition, or the fact that romantic inclinations can so often be regarded as credulous, mawkish, perhaps even a tedious source of embarrassment, the desire for the romantic shows no signs of becoming extinct.

Some Past Assessments
of Romantic and Courtly Love

This chapter will consider various historical interpretations of romantic love, followed by an analysis of some representations in more modern thought and fiction. The fictions all portray a romantic love that oscillates between two disjoined locations or realities and suggest that romantic love is at once ethereal and corporeal, and that the need to represent it in dual form reveals inadequacies in the present cultural framework.

The stream of songs, poems, operas and so forth

celebrating romantic love seems inexhaustible. It has flowed on down through the centuries, while love, its 'madness' and its vicissitudes have been regular subjects in the novel. Whether sacred, profane, or an amalgam of both, love has been a magnet for very different kinds of writers, and in the context of fiction, the protagonists, encrazed by passion, may be represented as anything from tragic or heroic to pathological. Most naturally expressed in sighs and silences, love that is over-articulate may appear absurd or insincere. The condition is never simple to portray and efforts to express it have been seen as dangerous. The emergence of romantic love as an explicit ideal in western culture in the Middle Ages soon attracted attacks, some of them extremely violent. Though the justification for such aggression was ostensibly religious, the romantic celebration of the feminine was probably an equally great offence. Science may sometimes seem to be claiming that objective analysis will eventually abolish all the mysteries of human nature and behaviour, and Freud's belief that he could subordinate the passions (pre-eminently sexual desire) to what he regarded as the requirements of a rational civilisation now also seems self-deceiving. Love, however, remains incoherent yet eloquent, painful yet desirable, and apparently deeply committed to retaining its final core of mystery.

Roughly two centuries ago, Stendhal was already anticipating a problematic response to his intimate and wonderfully relaxed treatise on love. "The power of convention," so he tells us, ".. has turned the word (love) .. into something which people do not care to pronounce alone, and which may even seem offensive." Though he speaks of his fear of "relapsing into *unintelligibles*", he holds fast to his intentions and explains that, in his eyes, women only become ridiculous when they engage in social affectations, absolutely never when they are sincerely in love – this is the central theme in *Le Rouge et le Noir*. Stendhal anticipates a sympathetic response from the sincere woman, and unashamedly establishes himself in a conventionally *feminine* territory when he remarks, "Love has always been the biggest thing in my life – or rather the *only* thing in my life." However, he expects many male readers to react with hostility to his analysis of love. Analytical, often ironical, but never cynical, Stendhal believes that it is precisely these men who are "ridiculous" if they have "the double vanity to pretend they were always above such foibles of the heart, and yet still had enough insight to pronounce *a priori* on the exactness attained in this philosophic treatise." (1)

And Stendhal's fears have bloody historical antecedents. Romantic love, with its exaltation of the feminine, provoked savage responses in a more distant past. Denis de Rougemont examines earlier forms of romantic love and, in particular, "the cultivation of passionate love." He considers it to be a reaction to Christianity and especially to marriage, "by people whose spirit, whether naturally or by inheritance, was still pagan." (2) Establishing striking parallels between Courtly Love – it was also known as the Religion of Love – as expressed in the songs and poems of the troubadours (3) and in certain practices of the heretical

Cathars in their Church of Love, (4) he traces them both back to common eastern roots. Cathars and troubadours elevated love to a quasi-sacred, ethereal plane – the kiss was a Cathar sacrament, while a knight of Courtly Love unquestioningly served and at times literally worshipped his lady. For Arab and Languedoc poets of the twelfth-century, she was the Lady of Thoughts, the Form of Light, the Feminine Saviour. According to Rougemont, courtly love expressed "the Feminine Principle of *Shakti*, the worship of Woman..." He writes, "from the final confluence of the 'heresies' of the spirit and those of desire, which had both come from the one East along either shore of the Civilising Sea, there was born the great western model of the language of passion-love." (5)

Rougement's views are not, however, universally agreed. In fact, the debate about the historical basis of courtly love continues to be conducted. Some later scholars prefer to dismiss its historical foundations out of hand and assert that texts relating to it were fantasy or fiction intended to underpin an ideology. But even if they represent nothing more substantial than an ideology that justified the moral standing of the aristocracy, their historical effects cannot be denied. The spiritual elevation of secular love incurred terrible reprisals from the Catholic Church. Love, an ideal in itself, rather than the means to the conception of children within the sanctity of Christian marriage, played a major role in the Albigensian Crusade and the wholesale extermination of the Cathars. Even Rougement's own final verdict is that the extremes to which devout Cathars took the spiritualising of love was a force of division rather than unification. (6)

Some Later Responses to
the Divinizing of the Erotic

A wide range of different texts have placed romantic love in a dimension lying outside the commonplace experience of the senses, and at times perceived as specifically sacred.

Elements associated with the Cathar and troubadour fusion of the divine and the carnal in romantic love appear intermittently in many times and places. In the guise of brotherly love, the romantic ideal sometimes surfaces in radical and utopian politics and the literature of rebellion. (7) It has also been a subject for feminist enquiry. In *The Feminine and the Sacred*, a long exchange of letters between Catherine Clément and Julia Kristeva, Clément explicitly considers the sacred as *sexual*, "the sacred authorises the lapse, the disappearance of the Subject, the syncope, vertigo, the trance, ecstasy."(8) In spite of various other disagreements, these women share the opinion that the religious and the sacred are two entirely different entities. Clément comments that, "the function of the religious always comes back to the organization of worship... The sacred does exactly the opposite: it eclipses time and space. It *passes* in a boundlessness without rule or reservation, which is the trait of the divine... The sacred is an immediate access to the divine." Furthermore, the sacred is naturally subversive and "can serve a good revolt." (9) Its inclinations also are distinctly feminine: "society governs by the pure masculine principle, whereas the sacred resists by the pure feminine principle," and, "Women's predisposition to the sacred better accomodates itself to naked rebellion." (10) Both Clément and Kristeva hold the political view that, wherever the sacred is severed from private or personal experience and converted into a public institution, totalitarianism and fundamentalism will result. Though it will not take place in the present context, this thought merits detailed discussion.

Luce Irigaray makes no apologies when she rejects the constraints of the masculinist order one might expect a philosopher and psychotherapist to observe. She reunites the physical and spiritual possibilities of love with disconcerting directness and refuses to allow the body to be diminished in value because of its long association with the feminine. After early struggles (11), Irigaray's abandonment of orthodoxy grows more confident. She discards all pretence of remaining moderate as she describes "a woman's voyage as she goes in search of her identity in love," and writes of a "love between the sexes .. which is both empirical and transcendental." (12) Jettisoning reserve and other academic baggage, she allows herself to voice open emotion as she pursues her elusive objective. In a fusion of the ethics and aesthetics of a sublime love with rapture of the senses, she echoes devotion to the lingam, symbol of a divine sexual union that is entirely foreign to western thought. Irigaray laments the "dissociation of body and soul, of sexuality and spirituality .. and of their distribution between the two sexes in the sexual act." The increasing rarity of romantic or uncontaminated erotic passion in popular contemporary conceptions of love in the West means that, "these realities remain separate even opposed to one another .. Their wedding is always being put off .. devalued ." (13) In sexual union, the man "renders her (the woman) profane through his transcendence and relation to the divine." Irigaray firmly rejects the constellation of the spiritual-intellectual masculine and the material-emotional feminine, remarking that its inevitable outcome is "Sensual pleasure .. which does not know the other." (14)

Most feminists recognise the need for an improved analysis of feminine sexuality, but it is not commonly mentioned that discussions of sexuality which do not include an associated possibility of love have already succumbed to an androcratic definition. Belief in the exclusive and objective verifiability of scientific method forces discussions of love and the erotic to exclude whatever cannot be precisely quantified. Freud took a classic masculinist and dogmatically rationalistic stance when he pinned his ideas about human love to a demonstrably male sexual drive. Lacan refers bluntly to the efforts made in the Freud-Charcot era "to reduce the mystical to questions of fucking." (15) In a culture of science, irrational feelings and behaviours (most crucially all those 'feminine' problems of hysteria) must be persuaded to submit to reason. The ambition of psychoanalysis was to transform all these irrational and neurotic disturbances into commomplace and orderly discontent.

Freud did not share Stendhal's accomodating attitude towards sexual passion and was made deeply uneasy by women's apparently untroubled relations with this unregulable force. (16) But the androcentric value of objectivity is not necessarily central to scientific enquiry; science can also prosper in a gynocentric climate of empathy. A feminist and specialist in mathematical biophysics is of the opinion that, "We need to pay particularly close attention to the science produced by those who have seen their relation to their material in erotic rather than adversarial terms." She praises the work of a geneticist for " the intimacy she experiences with the objects she studies .. a wellspring of her powers as a scientist." (17)

Very few scientists have explicitly located the source of creativity in love. Rather surprisingly, it is a Jesuit palaeontologist who speaks out for love as "the one natural medium in which the rising course of evolution can proceed". He goes further: "Love cannot and must not dispense with matter", he tells us. "It is a fundamental law of creative union that the fusion of spiritual apexes presupposes a coincidence of their bases." His reading of the evolution of mental process stresses that love between the sexes is sacred and knowledge of the other sex is indispensible to the evolution of consciousness. This quietly reinstates essential features of the Church of Love and supports exactly the same principles that the Catholic church once laboured so brutally to eradicate. His texts are thickly populated with Platonic thought, his *Feminine Ideal* taps into ancient roots and undeniable residues of courtly love. He writes, "The more I become Feminine, the more immaterial and celestial will my countenance be." (18)

Courtly Love, Infidelity and Feminism

Though the psychoanalyst, Jacques Lacan, is almost as prone to abstractions as the Jesuit, his view of love is emphatically less ethereal and a great deal more ruthless. He supports the idea that extreme phallic dominance makes a fantasy out of woman. "Lacan argues that the sexual relation hangs on a fantasy of oneness, which the woman has come classically to support. He traces that fantasy through a sustained critique of courtly, religious and ethical discourse." (19) It follows naturally that Lacan should see "courtly love as the elevation of the woman into the place where her inaccessibility stands in for male lack," (i.e. lack of an assertive penis), and that for "the man, whose lady was entirely, in the most servile sense of the term, his female subject, courtly love is the only way of coming off elegantly from the absence of sexual relation." (20)

It is particularly intriguing to observe Lacan's very untypical introduction of a "female subject" here. He also refers to the man in this romantic situation as "servile". The man who for some reason cannot dominate a woman in a sexual sense loses his mastery over her altogether. Lacan is here celebrating himself as a male chauvinist of a fully deliberate order so it is no surprise that he regards courtly love as a "fraud" and sees it as a means of covering up the absence of sexual relations with the pretence that an "obstacle" has been deliberately inserted. This is a sign of "supreme decadence" and of "such depths of political degeneracy, it must have become noticeable that on the side of the woman, there was something which really would no longer do." He adds that courtly love is "an enigma" and "was assigned to its original futility by .. scientific discourse, that is, something owing nothing to suppositions of the ancient soul." (21)

Lacan insists that, irrespective of the necessary existence of two sexes, it is the "phallic term" or *male* organ that "is the mark of sexual identity". He regards the jouissance (the word is an amalgam of 'to play' and 'to enjoy') of a woman as differently constituted from that of a man. Where a man is chiefly concerned with achieving orgasm, a woman's jouissance leaves behind a jumble of questions and residues. And unfulfilled desires. Lacan maintains that, for a man, "his *jouissance* suffices which is precisely why he understands nothing." (22) Irigaray abruptly pulls Lacan's ruminations on jouissance into shape with the laconic remark that woman "always wants *more, encore*, we are told by certain psychoanalysts (Jacques Lacan in particular) who equate this *more* with pathology." (23)

But what is this *more*? When courtly love made efforts to establish an alternative to the loveless marriages of feudal society (24), a priest-ridden patriarchy rushed to excise it. This is the same repression of desire that conditions Lacan's *Name of the Father* and that governs in the name of the Lacanian *Law of the Father*. Both wish to erase independent feminine sexuality and ensure that culture remains centred exclusively round phallic symbolism. Irigaray pinpoints exactly what the Freudian scenario demands of women: "that woman has to put her love for her mother and for herself aside in order to begin to love a man. She has to stop loving herself in order to love a man who, for his part, would be able, and indeed expected, to continue to love himself." (25) Her analysis suggests that the essence of this *more* is the excluded love of the woman who is both another and herself.

Opposition to the ideal of marriage and to sexual fidelity is complex, whether ancient or modern. As a deliberate strategy, "Infidelity then is a feminist practice of undermining the Name-of-the-Father .. Infidelity is *not* outside the system of marriage, the symbolic, patriarchy, but hollows it out, ruins it, from within." This is, of course, referring to infidelity on the part of the woman. The statement is prefaced with the comment that, "Any suspicion of the mother's infidelity betrays the Name-of-the-Father as the arbitrary imposition it is." (26)

Every so often, some pearl of feminist observation reveals its debt to the extreme irritant of Lacanian opinion.

Three Fictional Portrayals of Romantic Love

Fiction, genre fiction in particular, does not need strategies of this kind. It is free to erase the rules when and where it pleases. Science fiction, fantasy, horror and the gothic, as well as surrealism and magic realism need no gesture of apology before they brush aside the sober 'realities' of the master narrative and embrace the irrational or purely imaginary. With widely varying degrees of allegiance to realism, Tanith Lee's *Madame Two Swords,* (27), Sándor Márai's *Embers* (28), and David Lindsay's fantasy classic, *The Haunted Woman*

(29), all have common elements. Lindsay and Lee both construct narratives that operate on two planes simultaneously, one set within the bounds of normal experience, the other stepping beyond ordinary reality into a physically altered, supernormal dimension. Each of these narratives makes use of residual traces from a past that is historically distant, both use other-worldly elements to fuse sexual passion with love that possesses a transcendental aspect. *Embers* remains attached to linearity and normal reality and is narrated in a retrospective conversation.

The protagonist in Lee's novella is simultaneously a young girl and a long dead, adult man: at the same time, she is herself and a reincarnated version of a political writer and activist, Lucien de Ceppays, who was guillotined during a time that suggests the French Revolution. (30) The main narrative takes place well over a century after his death. The young girl is not aware of her double identity as she buries her mother and is confronted by the brutal realities of penury in a big city. Her one personal treasure is a faded booklet of de Ceppays's political writings which includes a small watercolour portrait of the author. Unaccountably rescued from the streets, she is taken into the household of a strange old woman, Camélie de Ceppays. She begins to remember her former identity when a mirror reflects Lucien's image in place of her own. She slowly ceases to be that "nervous innocent feminine person I had been for twenty-two years". Camélie has been kept alive for an impossible number of years by her fierce desire to be reunited with her beloved, Lucien; the intensity that has accumulated during the long wait is condensed into a single night, as the protagonist holds the dying woman in her arms. After Camélie dies, the girl takes courage from her knowledge of her former self. She finds a job in a laundry and becomes a fearless and eloquent advocate for the rights of oppressed women workers.

Lee's alignment of emotions and persons here is complex and full of unexpected insights. The girl describes her original childish feelings at the sight of Lucien's portrait on a market stall: "..poised on the threshold of readiness, of *need*, longing, or some form of blind desire (and I do not necessarily mean sexual desire) must occur. It is the only way to find beauty or adventure, and they are the universal dreams of mankind, beauty and adventure, and love." The ambiguity of a desire that is sexual and yet something other also, the merging of two identities in one person, the fusion of two consciousnesses, embody all the *sacred* elements of romantic love and of the feminine that Clément and Irigaray defend. This desire sets up a circular flow of energies, and, with inner and outer united, the girl becomes both actor and spectator. Active, passive, subject, object, all of them fuse; she is no longer locked in solitude. Her single experience of intense oneness with Lucien and of the love that exists between Lucien and Camélie, restore to her both the lost mother and her desire for the excluded feminine. This double helix of male and female identities and of numinous and sexual energies is drawn with the detailed precision of an anatomical study. "..love binds. Yes, he had been hers... That part of him retained in me was bound to her yet... But also mine. Lucien was mine. He would be mine for ever."

David Lindsay does not imagine a permanent transformation or a love that stretches over to change the course of an entire life. The other dimension he introduces is located in an ancient long-vanished part of an old house. Sometimes stairs to this former part of the building materialise, although it is only people of "passion" who have access to it. The central character, Isbel, engaged to a worthy young man, is incurably restless, and when she meets with an older man in a metaspace that is contained in the house, she falls passionately in love. Once they are back in a normal continuum, however, neither is able to remember the meeting. The lack of continuity with daily life leaves only fragments of the experience of boundless emotion. Yet Isbel believes that women are "the sex which worships the heart and believes it higher than the highest morality." She holds that "no woman can feel really safe until she has experienced this feeling." She slowly begins to understand what has happened to her and in the conflict between her love for the older man and fidelity to her fiancé, she breaks off her engagement. The older man suddenly dies of a heart attack, possibly signifying that he has, either heroically or fatally, damaged or sacrificed himself by failing, in the words of Lacan, to "reduce the mystical to questions of fucking." Sadder and wiser, Isbel prepares to be reconciled with her fiancé and to retreat into the security of a passionless marriage. She has tasted the forbidden fruit but, reduced by her amnesia, she lacks the resolution through which it might have permanently transformed/ informed her. Though she seems to have gained more than the Lacanian man, who "understands nothing" as a result of his sexual pleasure, romantic and 'real' are unable to reach a consummation or outcome in this novel.

In *Embers*, the torment of infidelity – the infidelity of a wife and the infidelity of a friend – is the central issue. Two old men, inseparable friends during a boyhood spent in a military academy, meet after an estrangement which, by the calculations of the General, has lasted "forty-one years and forty-three days". The General has lived on into a solitary old age only for the sake of a reunion with Konrad, friend of his youth and seducer of his wife. The two men spend an entire night in conversation. Like his father before him, the General has remained faithful to military honour and its core of loyalty to comrades. Konrad is "a different kind of man", a musician, a failed soldier, a man with a strong feminine streak. From childhood, Konrad's love of music and of beauty has outweighed his commitment to masculine concepts of probity: ".. melodies did not speak to the rational side of his mind... Music dissolved the world around him ... and at such moments Konrad ceased to be a soldier." The two men have lived by different codes, but both of their lives and that of the woman they loved have been destroyed by Konrad's infidelity.

The General is obsessed with learning the meaning of these long past events, desperate to understand Konrad's experience of them. The night's conversation leads to one final question:"Do you also believe that what gives our lives their meaning is the passion that suddenly invades us heart, soul and body, and burns in us forever, no matter what else happens in our lives? And that if we have experienced this much we haven't lived in vain?" "Why do you ask me?" Konrad replies quietly, "when you know the answer is yes." However, it is the General, not his friend, who sums it up: "... we know that all our offended, cowardly, haughty masculine intelligence has won us nothing at all..."

In each of these narratives, the protagonist is changed – each with a varying degree of conscious-ness – by entering a space that is mysteriously unlike the 'normal' realities they know. Access is always difficult . This 'other' space links the mundane continuum with another stratum of existence where, whether temporarily or permanently, interior and exterior are unified. As Lee's fragile young woman is united with a long buried, interior self, she grows strong. The haunted woman of Lindsay's novel is able to feel "safe" or even, as a reader might guess, whole. Maráis's aged general is released from his endless, stoical wait when, through his friend's less dedicatedly masculine perspective, he understands the meaning of his own past and is able to piece together the fragments of his life.

Irigaray tells us with inimitable simplicity how love which permits a meeting "between the inside and the outside, the outside and the inside, and of their distribution between the two sexes in the sexual act" is what also permits the discovery of "identity in love". (31) But of exactly what sort of identity are we speaking? Certainly, none of the three novels just discussed is limited to the phallic sexual identity prescribed by Lacan. Isbel is haunted by an intense desire for romantic love, but is not prepared to sacrifice her more worldly needs to it. She chooses to put aside her transcendental experiences. In discovering the full scope of his own personal identity, including its feminine aspects, the General is able to accept the lawless morality of love. Even so, the real game has been played out between the two men, the real infidelity has been Konrad's. It is only in the Lee novella that, in spite of the many obstacles of appearance, gender, age and time and through all the dense obscurities of difference, male and female are able to recognise and unite with each other without losing anything of themselves, and the young girl is able to discover her "identity in love".

In these narratives, a male who is imprisoned in a fixed identity finds his self-understanding moving spontaneously towards death as the solution to the loss of self that romantic love can engender. The female does not generally exist as an isolated unit. An individual woman is able to extend what she is in herself through relationships with other individuals and systems. Lee's novella portrays a female consciousness that is able to inhabit more than one identity, able to think and feel from more than one position, able to merge itself with another. It examines the way in which the experience of merging awakens an androgynous self, who, thereafter, finds she has capabilities she would previously have considered unattainably masculine. The portrayal foregrounds both the multiplicity and the care for the other that various feminist writers have regarded as essential to serious understanding of the feminine.

However, all three accounts of love suggest that to know the Other it is necessary to make use of measurements and judgements that insist on another dimension and transcend the belief that the mundane is all that there is. Something else – "something *more*, encore" – is needed, something that does not depend on exactly balanced reasons or binary forms of logic, something that will not accept that such a thing as 'feminine' desire only exists inside the realm of fantasy. *Rosy Apple, Lemon Tart.*

Footnotes

1) Stendhal, *Love*. Paul Elek, London 1959.

2) Denis de Rougement, *Passion and Society*, chs. 6-10. & p.74. Faber & Faber, London, 1962.

3) The code of courtly love is outlined in the *Treatise on Love and the Remedies of Love*, dictated by the Countess Marie de Champagne, the daughter of Eleanor of Acquitaine, to her unenthusiastic chaplain. The work states what a refined woman requires of a chevalier. C.S. Lewis describes this text at some length in his *Allegory of Love*, and quotes from it, "It is agreed among all men that there is no good thing in the world, and no courtesy, which is not derived from love.." Stendhal also transcribed the principal doctrines of the Code of Love.

4) The existence of this link continues to be disputed: it seems that both religious conservatives and atheist intellectuals feel obliged to oppose the close approximation of sacred and profane love.

5) op cit, p.107. De Rougemont describes Tantric thought and practice in Catharism and troubadours and refers to Mircea Eliade's *Techniques of Yoga*. The eastern sources are Zoroastrian and Sufi.

6) The extreme form of Catharism brought "the divinizing Eros ... everlastingly in anxious conflict with the fleshly creature and this creature's enslaving instincts." ibid, p.276. For a full discussion of the many different interpretations of courtly love, see Toril Moi, Chapter 9, *What Is A Woman* ? OUP 1999.

7) Elements of transgression are perceived as being common to both *romantic* and *revolutionary* eras and a connection has frequently been

239

made between them.

8) Catherine Clément and Julia Kristeva, *The Feminine and the Sacred*. pps 30 & 29

9) ibid p.176

10) ibid pps 53 & 54

11) Irigaray's stance so challenged (Lacanian) notions of academic authority and decorum that she herself became a kind of latter-day heretic. She "was dismissed from the newly re-organised department of psychoanalysis at the University of Paris VIII (Vincennes) on publication of her book, *Speculum de l'autre femme* (1974)." See See *Feminine Sexuality: Jacques Lacan and the Ecole Freudienne*. pps.53-4. Ed. Juliet Mitchell and Jacqueline Rose, Macmillan Press Ltd, London, 1982. Rose and Mitchell also describe Lacan as the instigator of the term Name-of-the-Father, and of this Father as author of the Law. As "a challenge to authority yet at the same time authoritarian and patriarchal.. Lacan was trapped in the circles of this paradox." They discuss the "problem of mastery and paternity which has cut across the institutional history of his work."

12) Luce Irigaray. *Elemental Passions*. pps 4-7. The Athlone Press. London. 1992. (Editions de Minuit. Paris. 1982.)

13) Luce Irigaray. *An Ethics of Sexual Difference*.p.15 The Athlone Press. 1993. (Les Editions de Minuit, Paris. 1984.)

14) ibid. p.206.

15) *Feminine Sexuality: Jacques Lacan and the Ecole Freudienne*. ed.

Juliet Mitchell and Jacqueline Rose, p.147. Macmillan Press Ltd, London, 1982.

16) In *The Freud/ Jung Letters* (Hogarth Press & Routledge Kegan Paul. 1974) Jung, always preoccupied with mythology, religion, archetypes of the collective unconscious and the occult, writes to Freud that he will be attending a lecture with colleagues, among whom "the feminine element" will have "conspicuous representatives from Zurich." Freud glumly replies that in his faction the "only lady doctor is participating like a true masochist in the Adler revolt and is unlikely to be present." The Freud/ Jung correspondence seems to hint that their final split was caused by the larger significance which Jung, to Freud's great distaste, gives to the *Mother* as much weight as he gives to the *Father* .

17) Evelyn Fox Keller, *Reflections on Gender and Science*, (pps 126 & 164). Yale University, 1985.

18) Teilhard de Chardin, as quoted by Henri de Lubac, S.J. in *The Eternal Feminine, A Study on the Poem by Teilhard de Chardi*n. pps 91, 12, 100. Collins. London. 1971. Lubac also quotes Nicholas Berdayev, who speaks of, "the transfiguration of human sexual relations, of the enlightening of the feminine element, of the turning of generative energy into creative energy.. This means finding the mystical meaning of love." (p. 213, footnote 31.)

19) Mitchell and Rose. op cit, p.137 & p.156.

20) ibid p.48

21) ibid p.156-7

22) ibid p.53

23) Luce Irigaray. *An Ethics of Sexual Difference* p.64.

24) On this subject, de Rougement, p.114, quotes Rene Nelli, who maintains that many troubadours either were Cathars or adhered to the same principles: "castle ladies .. exacted from them [troubadours] less the illusion of a sincere love than a *spiritual antipode* to marriage, a state into which they had been forced."

25) Irigaray. *An Ethics of Sexual Difference*. Pps.65-66.

26) Jane Gallop. *Feminism and Psychoanalysis, The Daughter's Seduction*. p.48. The Macmillan Press. London. 1982.

27) Tanith Lee. *Madame Two Swords*. Donald M. Grant. West Kingston, RI. 1988. (I am particularly pleased to include this work which space restrictions forced me to omit in my earlier book on Lee.)

28) Sándor Márai. *Embers*. (1942) Penguin Books. 2003.

29) David Lindsay. *The Haunted Woman*. (1922) Revised 1964. Victor Gollancz Ltd. London.

30) Camille Desmoulins, the protagonist of Lee's historical novel, *The Gods Are Thirsty*, approximates to de Ceppays. Lee's extraordinary short story, *After the Guillotine*, also features a post-mortem, disembodied Demoulins.

31) Irigaray. An *Ethics* of Sexual Difference. p.206.

13

Silence, Language, and the Female Voice.

Silence, Actual and Potential.
Over the course of history, women have only too often been urged to hold their tongues – the speech of females brought disorder and ill-luck. Often, women have not been permitted to speak in public, doubly so in places of worship, government and learning. Those who spoke out anyway were branded as strident, garrulous, gossips, scolds, nags, termagants, viragos, fishwives. The message has varied very little: women talk too much, and what they say is certain to be false, foolish, extravagant, ignorant, or plain malicious. Feminists have generally viewed the silencing of women as one further instance of their abuse by the dominant male. A few, however, have focused instead on less widely considered potentialities of silence to offer insights into the struggle for women's self-realisation.

The proposition that language is governed by patriarchal concepts and that this can make it difficult for women to present their own ideas is broadly accepted. But there is no consensus over how, given this situation, women could communicate without some degree of self-distortion. One view is that, since language, though patriarchal, is still our central or only intelligible means of communication, we should concentrate on using it as neutrally as possible. Those at the opposite extreme maintain that language needs to be adapted and expanded until it can enable women to think and express the 'feminine'. And then there is silence. Silence can be a wordless form of expression. It can become expressive in itself: "..the 'not-said' of a text might be thought of as an 'unspoken sub-text', that, by its very silence, interrogates and undermines what is represented by the 'official discourse'. [It is] concerned with identifying the 'gaps' in a given text and speculating on what they reveal." (1) Another observation is unequivocally confident: "I suggest that silence can be understood as an avenue to power. The simple equation of voice with authority, and silence with victimization needs to be reexamined .. The meaning of silence – being unwilling or unable to speak – can be seen as complex and multi-dimensional." (2)

Meanings bred out of silence are by definition formed separately from the surrounding discourse. However, they may also cause disturbances in the discourse that initially excluded them. The meanings located in silence are a little ghostly, without fixed shapes or limits, but they are still able to create an invisible excitation. Sometimes this has been perceived as suffering – perhaps sometimes it is. Xaviere Gautier endorses the idea of the silent victim when she asks how women can "*make audible* that which agitates within us, suffers silently in the *holes of discourse* ... blank pages, gaps, borders, spaces and silence." These attempts to communicate become "compromised, rationalised, masculinised .. If the reader feels a bit disoriented in this new space which is obscure and silent, it proves, perhaps, that it is women's space." (3) For some readers, Gautier's emotive style may not seem to help her cause, but even so her silent space represents an area that stands free of what already exists in language and at least indicates something beyond a blank refusal to collaborate with what has already been spoken.

Though it may lack the exactitude of speech, silence has its own expressive and unexpectedy parallel functions. Speech tends to be seen as essential to the construction and maintenance of group identity, but the Quaker meeting is a good example of a silence that is just as central to group cohesion. Silence can mark a sense of mutual contentment or be a formal mark of respect or common feeling – such silences emerge out of understanding, not repression. Silence may follow a release of energy and self-imposed silence can be used to create new energies, but meaning that is silenced or prevented from taking form may behave differently. Repressed material tends to erupt in involuntary bursts such as giggling and what escapes from the 'holes in discourse' may not conform with social expectations or integrate readily with established concepts. New meanings may take strange or grotesque shapes, but once a new meaning has been recognised, it cannot be casually brushed away.

Drawing on fictional portraits of three women, all silenced by different circumstances, this chapter will try to tease out a few strands of the surprisingly communicative complexities of silence. In their common fascination with meanings found in silence, these narratives describe the results of either the abandonment of speech, the loss of speech, or the repression of speech. Each author reflects on ways in which compensatory forms of communication may come welling up in the place of speech and how imposed silences can create conditions out of which alternative forms of expression emerge spontaneously. The results may not always resemble speech as it is normally understood, but anything that conveys a human response to reality is performing a function that belongs to human language. The three texts under discussion are all written by women who set out to examine silence as a matrix in which nameless but urgent meaning is waiting to make its way into the world outside themselves.

The lapse into a non-verbal state in Sylvia Townsend Warner's story, *The Mother Tongue*, (4) is a result of unfortunate circumstance rather than malice or deliberate repression. Unlucky isolation from her ethnic group and a lack of everyday, spoken communication gradually reduce a young, already traumatised refugee to absolute silence. Eventually the accumulated tension of her silence produces a more intense expression of her experiences than speech could ever have done. Dacia Maraini's novel, *The Silent Duchess*, (5) explores the life and development of a deaf-mute woman (also traumatised), who acquires odd, compensatory talents and engages in a long, silent struggle towards a freedom from conformity almost unknown among aristocratic, eighteenth-century Sicilians. Suzette Haden Elgin's trilogy inhabits a dystopic future, in which a patriarchal community prohibits women from voicing opinions. Over many decades, the women secretly create a private language to express their thoughts and, as new ways of thinking become embedded in their language, the balance of power very gradually begins to shift. (6)

The discussion that follows does not engage with debates over whether it is possible to 'represent' woman in language made to express masculinist values. Nor does it deliberate on whether woman is "the ruin of representation" (7) as one succinct feminist phrase has put it. The focus here will be close, resting on some unusual perceptions of positive if sometimes painful uses of silence.

Language and the Voice

Sylvia Townsend Warner's story follows the progress of, Magda, a young, not very promising refugee who speaks only a few words of English. When she is found a placement as a servant on a farm, her initial efforts to talk are hesitant, and she soon lapses into the silent performance of her duties. "Clean floors, washing on the line, food for hens and food for pigs, these were the things required of her, not conversation." The author situates her commentary on language inside a plausible, commonplace setting. It is the plain, unvarnished character of language and its

function in ordinary social contexts that interest her. "..
language is a thing which can only be possessed by
those who possess it in common. Language is a dozen
voices clinging to the rope of a litany. Language is a
hundred voices clattering against each other in the
market place. Language is the lamentation of
thousands crying out in terror and anguish. Language
is the uproar of millions, a rustle of questions
sprouting thick as corn..." Language, then, is the
vehicle of shared discourse, the thread that holds
people together.

An unconversational present and a past too painful
to describe exclude the girl from social interaction.
She comes closest to expressing her past history when
one night she wakes up screaming. Her summation of
her distress is expressed so simply it becomes ambiguous: "All gone," she says. "Magda discarded her
English... She retreated into her native language as an
animal goes back into the wood." Soon, speaking
neither English nor Polish, she has "entered a limbo of
almost no language at all". But even this is not the
final destination of her retreat, for, ".. behind the wood
lies the forest, dusky, pathless, and unsignalised.
Behind not speaking lies the unspoken."

It is this unspoken on which the author wishes to
fix our attention as she brings us to the threshold of a
silence that goes far beyond simple non-participation
in speech. When a farm labourer dies in an agricultural
accident, the farmer's wife takes Magda along with the
family to attend the funeral. The ceremony proceeds in
the normal way until the moment the coffin is lowered
into the grave. Suddenly, then, "Magda heard her own

voice .. something had broken and she had found her speech .. she threw herself down and began to lament .. she sobbed and wailed and dug her nails into the ground, grovelling face-downward and filling her lamenting mouth with the taste of earth." Making a precise distinction between language and voice, the author tells us that "her outcry was of no language." The rest of the congregation understand "the vast tract of human misery from which she came, and the innumerable dead she bewailed, lying on the brink of a stranger's grave." When she has finished, "no one could think of a word to say." She stares "round on them as if interrogating their silence", seems relieved that no one speaks and then gets to her feet, "all the while gazing down into the grave as though she were intently listening for a reply."

Magda's lament is addressed to the dead, to a place beyond speech. The fullness of her feelings goes beyond what could be put into speech but still she conveys the anguish of her "innumerable dead" and her past to the mourners of her present. With the palliative functions of everyday speech torn away, her silence exposes a wordless void, a subterranean reality that she cannot speak.

The Compensations of Silence

Dacia Maraini is a novelist, critic and playwright, who has been active for many years in Italy's feminist movement. (8) The story told in *The Silent Duchess* is based on the life of one of her ancestors. In her memoir, *Bagheria*, (9) Maraini speaks of a visit to the eighteenth-century family villa in Sicily, built by the

Duchess Marianna, the deaf-mute wife of Duke Pietro Ucria. She describes a portrait of Marianna, who "holds a sheet of paper in her hand, for writing was the only way she could express herself: she was called 'the dumb one'." (10)

The Silent Duchess "is not a radical feminist novel denouncing men but a complex attempt to forge a feminine identity within a social and cultural system which would suppress it, to express female desire in a society which would deny it."(11) It demonstrates how, even in the most unpromising and unlikely circumstances, silence can become a source of personal growth and freedom. The third person narrative is largely observed from the viewpoint of Marianna. At the age of five she is savagely raped by the uncle who will later become her husband. After the trauma she is afflicted with lifelong mutism and deafness. Her memory of the event is repressed and her father lies about the origin of her condition and his condoning of it. Her exclusion from spoken language becomes a continuing denunciation of the patriarchal aristocrat's licence to abuse his womenfolk and servants without penalty. When Marianna's father marries her off at thirteen to her ageing rapist uncle, he tells her that no-one else would have a wife with such severe disabilities and, ominously, comments that this repulsive old uncle has always had a special fondness for her. (Here, Maraini drily informs the reader that this uncle had also had a special fondness for a goat when he was a boy).

Dim memories of having once heard voices are overridden as she tries "to convince herself that she had only dreamed up those distant voices, unable to admit that her sweet gentle father, who loved her so much, could lie to her." (12) Belatedly but never quite perfectly, Marianna recalls being raped as a child by "uncle-husband". She comes across random clues in her father's posthumous papers, Duke Pietro's savage sexuality, and in their son's face as, "She recognises in it the sudden secret lust for rape." (13) Later, in the course of a feverish illness, ".. for the first time in her life she comprehends with a diamond clarity that it was him, her father, who was the one responsible for her disablement .. who cut her tongue .. who filled her ears with molten lead so that she can hear no sound and circles perpetually in the kingdoms of silence and fear." (14) Such moments of recognition can be found in the lives of many women when they abruptly realise that they have been deceived and betrayed by patriarchal agencies that have taken advantage of them rather than afforded protection.

Marianna never ceases to resist. She cares for her children, loves her youngest son, but refuses to be consumed by maternal duties. When she constructs the villa in Bagheria, she disengages herself from social obligations, abandons the habits of the Sicilian aristocracy and achieves her desire for seclusion, independence and learning. Modestly, hesitantly, barely aware of what she is doing, she converts her disability into advantage and uses her isolation to understand and realise herself. Maraini's ideal of feminist independence seems to entail some cultivation of solitude or loneliness. The duke leaves his wife to her reading and writing. ".. he dare not oppose it .. he knows that for Marianna reading is a necessity... He himself avoids books." Like other aristocrats of his time, he experiences no need for thought. For Duke Pietro, "reality consists of a set of immutable and eternal rules" (15) but independent thought forms the core of Marianna's rebellion. At first she regards thinking as "something daring that tempts her as an exercise she can secretly indulge in", but soon a philosophical question adds itself: can she "retain something of her own that does not originate in other minds, other constellations of thought, other interests?" Aside from its general applications, the question stresses the damage done to women's self-esteem by language that does not include their particular reality. Yet, in spite of self-doubt, Marianna continues to query the god-given certainties of a Sicilian aristocracy that blindly denies the possibility of what she recognises she is. She pursues her own thoughts even if they do stem from "the opaque brain of a dumb woman". (16)

Marianna's difficulty in distinguishing her own thoughts from those that come from books prefigures her telepathic experiences. When she asks an older brother, now an abbot, if she was ever able to speak, he recalls "all the whisperings in the family, the closing up of terrified lips" and the sight of "Marianna with her legs all bloodstained being dragged away," but Carlo tells her nothing. It is "a family secret... an affair between men", and when Marianna leaves weeping, he wonders if perhaps "she had heard his thoughts... if behind that deafness there might not be some more subtle hearing, a diabolical ear capable of unveiling the secrets of the mind". (17) The silence so often imposed on women is here being linked with a corresponding ability to listen. Maraini both represents listening as an integral part of the process of communication and, at the same stroke, exposes the depth of Carlo's misogyny and the priestly prejudice which causes him to attribute his sister's gift to a "diabolical ear" – a mere woman could hardly have got this preternatural talent from any other agency.

Marianna has, in fact, begun to overhear the thoughts of others as clearly as if they had been spoken. "Lately she has taken to dropping inside people, attracted by a lively fluttering of their thoughts.." Sometimes she experiences a difficulty to which women from many times and places commonly refer: "she becomes lost in them, swallowed up, without knowing how to extricate herself." (18) In narrating the life of a deaf and dumb woman, it is natural for monologue to replace dialogue. Often Marianna's extra-sensory perceptions produce a stream-of-consciousness account. Maraini's account redefines listening, showing that, without silence, listening does not exist, and that, without listening, understanding is stunted. Her telepathic gift has both comical and painful aspects: she overhears her daughter mentally calculating how much she will inherit on her mother's death, while the thoughts of her servant "almost attack her". She comes close to despair when a "silent voice refuses to stop" or "words take on a musty smell"(19) but, as time passes, she learns to take control. When she hands the parish priest a note reading, 'Curb your thoughts', he becomes "fortunately... impenetrable". (20)

This portrait of the duchess never ignores her sufferings or the slow pace of her persevering progress. It also captures the modesty of her self-appraisals. Though deaf mutism permits her to make unfiltered observations of the people around her, the silence she inhabits is always ambivalent. Her disability "has given her more insight into herself and others", yet she feels "she has not known how to elevate this talent into an art form". (21) Maraini writes, "Silence took possession of her like some illness, or perhaps like a vocation." Marianna is "so eager to be daring and so resigned to playing safe." (22)

As she grows older, her daring grows with her. She takes a lover of the servant class and discovers her sexual desire, but she declines to marry a judge who is captivated by her intelligence, erudition and perhaps most of all by her ability to listen. After making an extended journey through Italy accompanied only by a maid, eventually she finds herself alone, still full of questions, still searching for answers and uncertain whether to return home or if her apparently aimless travels may be "a premonition of her end". (23)

Maraini reportedly commented on how frequently the maxim, 'Io sono mio' – 'I am my own person' – appeared amongst the graffiti on the walls of the casa della donna in Rome. (24) Her duchess exemplifies a person who, despite the odds against it and irrespective of the era, found the strength to shake off the fetters of a patriarchal society and its female stereotypes and to become her own person.

Words First Spoken in Secret

As a linguist, Suzette Haden Elgin wrestles with the question of how and why new meaning finds a place in language and, as a feminist, she rewrites linguistic terminology to fit her purposes. In *Native Tongue*, the term 'encoding' is central. She explains that in its standard application, encoding means assigning a name to a recognised "chunk of reality". However, she adapts this meaning for the book's central characters, the women of the linguist clans, who are inventing new words to install in a language they are secretly creating. "When we women say "Encoding," with a capital "E" we .. mean the making of a name for a chunk of the world that so far as we know has never been chosen for naming before .. a chunk that has been around a long time but has never impressed anyone as sufficiently important to *deserve* its own name. .. They are therefore very precious." (25)

Elgin suggests that, despite its recondite character, this activity could take root if exactly the right circumstances were to precipitate it. The linguists are hated both for their wealth and their apparently unique ability to translate the languages of alien species wanting to trade with Earth. Driven to live in segregated communities, they are only tolerated as a commercial necessity. The women of the "Lines" are sent out to work because they can bring in as much money as the menfolk. In the outside world, they are despised as "lingoe bitches" and doubly damned because no decent woman would work for a living. Inside the linguist communities, the men exercise rigorous control and value their women only insofar as they can earn money and bear children. These conditions, along with the addition of exceptional, hothoused, linguistic skills, correspond to the requirements specified by Elgin as appropriate for the creation of an invented language such as Láadan.

Prolonged disputes on the language question have produced different opinions among different groups of feminists. Some "want women – who have been segregated into a special 'women's language' – to accede to the use of 'neutral language'." Others "see 'neutral language' as itself an area of oppression, the alienation of difference in the order of the same of the phallus".(26) Apart from being a virtual impossibility, a truly neutral language that lacked all difference would be inert and have no potential for change or fresh meaning. (Or for the unsettling of masculine prototypes.)

Elgin's Láadan is anything but neutral: it is not only made to express unrecognised feminine needs and desires but to give form to undiscovered concepts. In her detailed account of the theory of its construction and its long-term effects, Elgin takes a clear position over the implications of gender differences in language, and in inventive references to linguistic theory, she substantiates the possibility of finding languag e expressive of new and unknown meanings. Using her own variant of Goedel's theorem, she makes the point that if new and previously non-existent concepts enter a language, then the position from which reality is viewed, and therefore also the reality itself, will be forced to give way to a new reality.

REFORMULATION ONE.

Goedel's Theorem: For any language, there are perceptions which it cannot express because they would result in its indirect self-destruction.

REFORMULATION ONE-PRIME

Goedel's Theorem: For any culture, there are languages it cannot use because they would result in its indirect self-destruction." (27)

In the sequel, *The Judas Rose*, Elgin moves her narrative forward to a time when the secret dispersal of Láadan amongst female populations outside the linguist communities has begun. As the narrative follows the covert spread of Láadan across the world, digressions on linguistics become more frequent and more ironic. The collision between extreme misogynist prejudice and a female consciousness of self that is no longer handicapped by the limitations of masculinist understanding becomes openly comical. A male academic gives a paper that refers to a hypothesis, "known quaintly as the 'linguistic relativity hypothesis'," in which Sapir and Whorf once suggested that "language controls perception". This hypothesis, he tells his audience, "lies buried beside the Flat Earth Hypothesis, and the dear ladies have been restored to their proper place in the world, allowing us all to both work and rest in peace." (28)

Both novels feature damaged children , unable to speak because they have been traumatised by experimental exposure to "non-humanoid" aliens with brain patterns that are incompatible with their own. The linguists explain that, "these children have their heads full of nonverbal experiences and perceptions for which no language offers a surface shape .. experiences for which no lexicalizations – no words, .. no signs, no body-parl units – exist." (29) The analogy with some feminist analyses is very clear: if there are no signs or words to equate with thoughts or experiences that are specifically feminine, then silence is the only alternative.

As *Native Tongue* draws to a close, Nazareth Chornyak, a central contributor in the long labour of creating Láadan sums up: "there was only one reason for the Encoding Project, really .. The hypothesis was that if we put the project into effect it would change reality." A friend objects, "How can you plan for a new reality when you don't have the remotest idea what it would be like?" Nazareth agrees, "We have pseudo-sciences, in which we extrapolate for a reality that would be nothing more than a minor variation on the one we have .. but the science of actual reality change has not yet been even proposed.." Here she comes to a halt, unable to bring herself to say that she has been acting on faith – "that dreadful word, with its centuries of contamination hiding the light of it." (30)

Elgin represents the creation of Laadan as a vast and dauntingly difficult feat. Producing the merest rudiments of this new language is the work of well over a century. And consequent changes will take much longer. The women are adept at finding small ways to spread it among themselves, but men, both outside and inside the linguist communities, take far longer to respond. The time scale is made apparent in the aged Nazareth's diaries: "I was so very slow to grow up .. to discover that almost everything that made

up the reality in which we lived was simply lies ..
Every lie was intertwined with every other lie; every
lie was wound into a dense fabric that seemed
impenetrable .. I was ill-prepared to set my mind to
plans that must be based upon thousands and
thousands of years. Nothing about me was large
enough to stretch itself to such a scale." (31)

Each of these texts gives its alternative and
positive value to silence, each perceives it as a
medium able to elicit new forms of communication.
Magda's lament, Marianna's silent listening, the
Encodings of the women linguists all carry similar
messages: thoughts that have either been beyond the
reach of words or that are held to be too full of
destructive potential to be allowed a voice can
sometimes find their way into language. It does not
matter whether this is done through a primal lament, or
a life spent in study and acquiring self-knowledge, or
through the barely imaginable collective labour of
inventing a new language. Each one shows how
silence may contain the germ of growth.

Footnotes

1) Sara Mills, Lynne Pearce, Sue Spaull, Elaine Millard, *Feminist Readings/ Feminists Reading* (p.192.) Harvester Wheatsheaf, 1989. Pearce and Mills.

2) *The Problem of Silence in Feminist Psychology*. Maureen A. Mahoney. Feminist Studies, Fall 1996. (Mahoney is citing Carol Gilligan's equation of voice with authority and silence with victim in *In A Different Voice*, Harvard Univ Press, 1982)

3) Xaviere Gautier, *Is there Such a Thing as Women's Writing? New French Feminisms, ed.* Elaine Marks & Isabelle de Courtivron, p.63-4. Harvester Press ltd 1981.

4) Sylvia Townsend Warner, *The Mother Tongue, One Thing Leading to Another* (p.135) Virago Press, 1990.

5) Dacia Maraini, *The Silent Duchess* (translated Dick Kitto and Elspeth Spottiswood) Peter Owen, London, 1992.

6) Suzette Haden Elgin, *Native Tongue, The Women's Press, 1985. See also The Judas Rose*, The Women's Press, 1988, and (not discussed here) the final volume, *Earth Song*, Feminist Press, City University of N.Y. 2002.

7) Michele Montrelay, *Inquiry into Femininity.* m.f. 1978.

8) Maraini's work has focused on the lives and circumstances of women as different as a murdered prostitute (Isolina) and a nun intellectually persecuted by the Catholic Church (Suor Juana). She has also engaged in initiatives ranging from actions supporting abortion rights to founding a

cultural centre for women and an all-female theatre in a poor neighbourhood in Rome. For a brief account of Maraini's activities, see *Liberazione della donna, feminism in Italy*. Lucia Chiavola Birnbaum. Wesleyan University Press. USA. 1986.

9) Dacia Maraini, *Bagheria*, Peter Owen, London, 1994.

10) Although largely self-educated, Marianna was able to read and write; this seems to establish that at one time she had also been able to hear and speak.

11) Sharon Wood. p.228. Journal of Gender Studies, Nov 1993.

12) Maraini, *The Silent Duchess*, p.17.

13) ibid p.179,

14) ibid p.172,

15) ibid p.48.

16) ibid p.99.

17) ibid p.187.

18) ibid p.60.

19) ibid p.120.

20) ibid p.146.

21) ibid p.180,

22) ibid p.99.

23) ibid p.233ⁱ.

24) Birnbaum. op cit. p.147.

25) Elgin, *Native Tongue* p.22. Láadan is not unprecedented in the real world. The ancient Chinese language of Nushu was created by women for private use among themselves. Reported extinct in 2004, Nushu has lived on and become a cultural attraction in its native region. Nushu may not have innovated unknown concepts but it expressed forbidden feelings of rebellion and grief, and demonstrates the intensity with which women living under oppressive conditions desire to communicate among themselves thoughts and sentiments that are unacceptable to a male-dominated society. For an account of of Nushu see The Forbidden Tongue, Jon Watts. Guardian 23 09 05. Because of its widespread use by Elgin enthusiasts, Láadan has been officially recognised as a spoken language.

26) Jane Gallop, *Feminism and Psychoanalysis*, p.46. The Macmillan Press, London, 1982.

27) Elgin, *Native Tongue*, p.145.

28) Elgin, The Judas Rose, p. 160-1.

29) Elgin, *Native Tongue*, p.167.

30) Elgin, *Native Tongue* p.296.

31) Elgin, *The Judas Rose*, p.292.

14

Feminine Writing Comes
in Many Shapes and Sizes

Feminine and Feminist

This chapter hopes to show what a wide diversity of 'feminine writing' can coexist on both philosophical and popular levels. It will also touch on the distinction between 'feminine' and 'feminist' and the connections between both terms in general and in writing.

In a book written in conjunction with Catherine Clément, *The Newly Born Woman*, Hélène Cixous writes: "Everyone knows that a place exists which is not economically and politically indebted to all the vileness and compromise. That is not obliged to reproduce the system. That is writing. If there is a somewhere else that can escape the infernal repetition, it lies in that direction, where it writes itself, where it dreams, where it invents new worlds." (1) Her co-author, Clément, takes a less sweeping, less categorical position: of course what passes as objectivity is prejudiced, controlled by men and bent on excluding women, but she does not think it politic for feminists to renounce canonical thinking/ writing out of hand. However biased they may be, these structures of thought and language have emerged out of material human experience and to discard one is to risk losing the other. Even the histories that have been most distorted by masculinist seizures of power are able to provide some sort of control over ideology's worst excesses. Without history – and language is a fundamental part of history – ideology would be answerable to no one. Elsewhere, Clément points out that, to reach the material foundations of 'objective' reasoning, "One would have to cut through all the heavy layers of ideology that have borne down since the beginnings of the family and private property: that can be done only in the imagination. And that is precisely what feminist action is all about: to change the imaginary in order then to be able to act on the real, to change the very forms of language which by its structure and history has been subject to a law that is patrilinear, therefore masculine."(2)

Where Cixous is bent on inventing new worlds, Clément wants to re-invent the present one by replacing its imaginary basis. Both are grappling with a reality that does not yet exist but their conceptions of this nonexistence vary. Clément is struggling to construct a doorway leading out of the constricted space of patriarchal ideology, Cixous is prescribing the purgative which will cleanse the feminine of patriarchal pollution. And though each makes concessions to the other, whether they are always speaking of precisely the same subject remains debatable. In their closing dialogue, Clément seems to be stressing this possibility. She emphasises the importance of diversity, remarking, "there can be two women in the same space who are differently engaged, speaking of almost exactly the same things, investing in two or three different kinds of discourse ... There is no reason at all not to steal that discourse from men .. we are within the same cultural system. Granted it is a phallocentric cultural system, but trying to make another in advance is unfounded." (3) Cixous fixes on the historical multiplicity of the feminine and the need for universal inclusion: "There has always been a split between those who are in possession of knowledge and culture and who occupy a position of mastery and the others... I am not saying that knowledge is always associated with power, or that it must be; but that is its danger. And I am not saying that women are never on the side of knowledge-power. But in the majority of cases in their history, one finds them aligned with no-power or knowledge-without-power." (4)

However, neither Clément's diversity of methods nor Cixous's efforts to collectively embrace all women tell us precisely what constitutes the difference between feminine and feminist discourses. This question has been addressed more systematically elsewhere: a text is usually "recognised and incorporated as feminist" if it comprises "writing about the work of women only, writing only about the production of woman; addressing feminine writing to feminine readers/ putting feminist questions to masculine texts." This is not the same thing as feminine writing or writing "as a woman." (5) Though specific requirements are proposed, even this detailed definition uses the word feminine ambiguously and we cannot predict whether the reader will construe it according to the usual stereotypes or within the boundaries of a newly defined identity. However, a third position also exists. Luce Irigaray resists "definition as feminine" – her "feminine is conditional or future tense, an interrogative mood." And, "Irigaray remains the recalcitrant outsider at the festival of feminine specificity – she lounges ironically at the door. For what goes on inside, celebrated in the joyful present tenses of Hélène Cixous or Marguerite Duras, is nothing more powerful than literature." (6)

A desire for a specifically feminine language did not originate with modern feminism. In antiquity, a language which was conceptually different from language constructed by a male-dominated society was conceived. For intimacy and understanding, and for freedom from constraint, somewhere between 1600 and 1100 B.C., some Chinese women constructed a language for use solely amongst themselves. It was elaborate enough to have a script, syntax and grammar that differed considerably from other forms of Chinese and, astonishingly, it survived up to the present day in a small region of provincial China. Perhaps to an extent that is no longer fully imaginable, this archaic language perceived a common identity in what we now divide into feminine and feminist.

The Chinese language has been said to be predisposed towards "a pre-Oedipal phase – dependency on the maternal, socio-natural continuum, absence of clear-cut divisions between the order of things and the order of symbols." (7) This is to say that where western thought and language systematically polarise things and symbols, Chinese constructions fuse them and thus rescue material existence from the domination of theory. Western culture does not so easily perform the task of healing the split between a material reality defined as feminine and a consciousness defined as masculine.

So What Exactly Is 'Feminine' Writing?

"I think 'feminine literature' is an organic, translated writing .. translated from blackness, from darkness. Women have been in darkness for centuries. They don't know themselves. Or only poorly. And when women write they translate this darkness... Men .. begin from a theoretical platform that is already in place, already elaborated. The writing of women is .. like a new way of communicating rather than an already formed language... Behind them, there is darkness. Behind men, there is distortion of reality, there are lies." (8) Though this summation may be more descriptive than prescriptive – spoken more in harmony with the demands of art than in the didactic language of politics – it expresses the perceptions of many women.

In his later texts, Jacques Derrida speaks about writing and gender as if about a musical form. He comments on disparities between masculine and feminine voices, ".. it has always seemed to me that the voice itself had to be divided in order to say that which is given to thought or speech. No monological discourse – and by that I mean here mono-sexual discourse – can dominate with a single voice, a single tone ... I have felt the necessity for a chorus, a choreographic text with polysexual signatures." He then goes on to denounce "the apparently least suspect sexual neutrality of 'phallocentric' or 'gynocentric' mastery" in "what remains irreducibly disymmetrical." The ultimate goal is "the area of a relationship where the code of sexual marks would no longer be discriminating." (9) To Derrida, discourse means a developed enunciation of human understanding which can only reach its ideal state when the masculine and feminine voices have both been included, each one in its own right, neither seeking to oust the other. Lacan thinks otherwise and his very different stance amply fulfils our expectations. His position as it relates to women has been summarised very bluntly: ".. castration for Lacan is not only sexual; more important, it is also linguistic: we are inevitably bereft of any masterful understanding of language, and can only signify ourselves in a symbolic system that we do not command, that, rather, commands us." (10) In reality, all feminists face a paradox: if they address themselves solely to "translating darkness", they are renouncing all authority within the controlling discourse; if, on the other hand, they position themselves inside the boundaries of the controlling discourse they are giving up participation in a discourse that is dedicated to representing an uncontaminated feminine.

Clément sees this dilemma as more obdurate in theory than it is in practice. She calls for a less consistent, less fastidious, but still radical pragmatism.

She is prepared to use all available forms of reasoning, compulsively symmetrical or otherwise, so long as they advance feminism. She "defends the strategic value of using coherent public discourses, however tainted by masculine mastery; otherwise, she asks, what happens to the possibility of debate among women as well as between women and men?" (11) If women abandoned dialectics for the sake of feminist purity, women would not be able to "use thought to help free themselves," and "that would mean that language is always masculine." If women "renounce the exercise of thought, it then belongs to men." (12)

There are also, of course, questions regarding what is meant by a *form* or *style* that is specifically feminine. This is frequently seen as writing that drifts out beyond the limits of cause and effect that is lodged in the fixed structures of conventional narrative, and becomes fluidly accretive. The novels of Virginia Woolf have been taken as a prototype of this kind of writing, but it appears in a variety of different guises. Ursula Le Guin's *Always Coming Home*, in itself an excellent example of 'feminine writing', makes some interesting comparisons between narrative modes. She writes, "The principal mode of our thinking is binary: on/off, hard/ soft, true/ false etc. Our categories of narrative follow the pattern. Narrative is either factual (non-fiction) or nonfactual (fiction). The distinction is clear... In the [tribal location of the novel] the distinction is gradual and messy.... If fact and fiction are not clearly separated ... truth and falsehood, however are. A deliberate lie (slander, boast, tall tale) is identified as such and is not considered in the light of literature at all. In this case I find our categories perhaps less clear than theirs. The distinction is one of intent…" (13)

What constitutes feminine form will not be discussed further in this chapter as the arguments on which it depends are put forward in the epilogue. New aspects of the debate will undoubtedly continue to emerge far into the future.

Writing from a 'Feminine' Preserve

A small sampling of methods and perspectives in the fiction of four different feminist authors should, hopefully, add some solid substance to these rather theoretical questions. Esme Dodderidge and Pamela Zoline lay claim to feminine territory by taking up subject material that has largely evaded masculine interference. Catherine Clément breaks apart the myth of a major patriarchal icon, Sigmund Freud, by reassembling his life in accordance with the feminine influences surrounding him in daily life and subjecting him to a kind of feminist re-education. Clarice Lispector's protagonist who, in her own eyes and as she is revealed to the reader, starts out with only the barest rudiments of a conscious identity is also an embodiment of feminine endurance in the face of sexist oppression and contempt. (Isn't endurance the most common form of courage shown by women?)

Where male interest is at stake and 'feminine' spheres have been transferred from the governance of women, where manuals map out routes to male-defined sexual pleasures and women who do not enjoy them are pathologised as frigid, where pregnancy is medicalised and maternal responses to the child are swamped by legal and moral masculine authority, unadulterated feminine subject matter may seem hard to come by. But not everything has been entirely colonised. Humbler and often particularly exploited aspects of women's lives may be left untouched. Housework, for example, stirs very little masculine interest. Unless hired out, housework is unpaid and a widespread lack of male participation means that ".. the modern concept of work, as the expenditure of energy for financial gain, defines housework as the most inferior and marginal work of all." (14) Apart from the inevitable intrusions of product advertising, women have been left to perform domestic chores with comparatively little meddling from outside. Instruction is mainly of interest as a sales technique. Very little is said about the endless chaos that agitates at the heart of the micro-universe of home and family. Perpetually receding horizons prevent the the final completion of any domestic chore and the requirements of others infiltrate many sexual and maternal functions. These effects are seldom mentioned: the home is supposedly peaceful and orderly, kept that way by the efficient housewife. And yet, though housework is condemned to a limbo of dullness, in the writings of both Esmé Dodderidge and Pamela Zoline, it gains a sudden rush of imaginative and revolutionary potential.

In *The New Gulliver*, subtitled, *The Adventures of Lemuel Gulliver Jr in Capovolta*, Esmé Dodderidge reverses the usual roles and the distribution of power between men and women. (15) The question of household duties crops up almost at once and remains a continuing theme. Gulliver, who is living as the guest of a Capovoltan family, protests when the husband he had assumed must be the head of the family stays at home all day engaged in menial labour, then waits on his wife and daughter when they return from their office jobs. The wife counters with the reasoned explanation that, "It is perfectly clear from their physique that men were biologically designed for their function as labourers and performers of heavy work .. it seems to me very wrong that women, with their inferior physique, should be engaged in work which you look upon as too heavy for my husband here." She clinches her argument that it is only logical for domestic work and the rearing of children to devolve upon the Capovoltan male with the point that, "men cannot give birth .. truly they can never perform the most important function in society and so can never receive the highest monetary rewards." (16)

After his marriage to a Capovoltan woman and the subsequent birth of twins, the new Gulliver has to confront the drudgery and exhaustion that are the daily lot of a houseman. His wife rebukes him: "I come home to an untidy, ill-kept house, to the noise of crying children, which after a day at the office gets on my nerves unbearably, and to a husband who instead of appreciating his luck and being grateful is late with the meals and complains about being tired .. I expect some comfort from you who are at home all day with nothing else to do except look after two small children." (17) When his wife deserts him for another man, he undertakes to care for and support the children singlehandedly. Though wifely fidelity is clearly not a prevalent characteristic in Capovoltan women, he is undeterred by a strong possibility that the children may not be his own. Dodderidge emerges from her narrative with the moral that all labour is valuable and that, while either sex wields power over the other, society can never be a benevolent institution.

But housework does not begin and end with its practical execution. The fact that a 'housewife' enters into a quasi-marital union with housework might of itself seem like a sign of mental disorder that prepares us for probable psychological repercussions. However essential it may be in everyday life, Freud never cares to investigate the psychopathology of housework and the masculine back remains resolutely turned. Pamela Zoline's short story, *The Heat Death of the Universe* (18), is written in a tone that is at times ironic, at times poetic. In the details of a single day, Zoline captures the irreconcilable contradictions that are provoked by the stifling limitations of domesticity. Trapped in its narrow confines, a housewife descends into madness as she struggles to connect the enclosed, material limits of home and family with the vast, unfettered abstractions of a scientific universe. She is struggling to give meaning to work that is not recognised as having any meaning because it has been given no meaningful (masculine/ phallocentric) definition. "Sarah Boyle is a vivacious and intelligent young wife and mother," who, nevertheless, "writes notes to herself .. on every available surface in a desperate attempt to index, record, bluff, invoke, order and placate." (19) She wards off "ammoniac despair" with a lipsticked inscription on the nappy bin describing the nitrogen cycle She knows the number "of objects (819) in the living room" and, as "quantities of waves or particles of very strong sunlight speed in through the window, and everything incandesces", she realises "that the dust is indeed the most beautiful stuff in the room" and thinks how "Duchamp set with fixative some dust that fell on one of his sculptures, counting it as part of the work." (21)

Sarah's heroic efforts to achieve order against a tide of disruptive forces reach a peak at a child's birthday party. The children sit down to tea "exhausted and overexcited .. some are flushed and wet, others unnaturally pale." They resemble "a dinner party of debauched midgets." (20) Sarah sourly ruminates, "How fortunate for the species .. that children are as ingratiating as we know them. Otherwise they would soon be salted off for the leeches they are." (22) This is to be her day of reckoning: it will culminate in an explosion of weeping and vandalism. She smashes plates, jars of jam, the kitchen windows, and recalls that "the total ENTROPY of the Universe is increasing, corresponding to complete disorder of the particles in it", and that, "a time must finally come when the Universe 'unwinds' itself." Housework becomes a microcosmic reflection of the second law of thermodynamics as "The sand keeps falling, very quietly in the egg timer," while, "eggs arch slowly through the kitchen, like a baseball, hit high against the spring sky .. They go higher and higher in the stillness, hesitate at the zenith, then begin to fall away slowly, slowly, through the fine, clear air." (23)

At first, Zoline seems to be representing Sarah's madness as just one more outbreak of 'typically female' hysteria, but we soon recognise that she is itemising the exclusion of the feminine from public meaning. In the small compass of this story, as the protagonist bursts out of the straitjacket of domestic order, she acquires a kind of heroic stature. As the pretensions of science and aesthetics fail to save Sarah from her domestic insignificance, she allows herself to be swept away as if by involuntary forces.

Femininising the Patriarch

Catherine Clément's *Bildoungue Roman.* (24) interweaves the sphere of women – those of Freud's own household as well as those encountered in his professional life – with the more abstract and thus supposedly edifying theories of the Father of Psycholanalysis. Though her account is not unkind, her humour is irrepressible. She writes with a deflationary mixture of irony, comedy and sympathy for his self-imposed but seemingly inescapable predicament, so that her Freud is less lofty, less inflexible, finally less portentious than the Freud to whom we are accustomed. Unlike most of Freud's biographers or his own representations of himself, Clément portrays a Freud who is deeply dependent on others, especially his womenfolk.

"One knows almost all there is to know about his life," she tells us. "What he liked to eat, his phobias, pecularities, his smallest pleasures, his great desires." (25) Her intention is to trace the history "of a highly celebrated, notoriously phallocratic, somewhat perverse gentleman" (26) in "the kitchen version. There where the pastry for the tarts and the boiled chickens would count as much as the masses of theory, the hours of work and listening. There where a work built itself on Freud's feminine entourage, from his wife to his daughter." She is about to turn "the idol upside down in order to look at its underparts."(27)

Paradoxically, the closer Freud is approximated to the ordinary man – and at the same time to the reader also – the more complex and multi-layered he becomes. Clément is well aware that a person shaped by both male and female qualities is necessarily more elaborate than a monosexual, patriarchal icon. With a decidedly 'feminine' version of egalitarian ,which in a less incisively clear writer might be seen as typical of fuzzy feminine thinking, she draws no sharp lines between the sexes – she leaves that work to Freud. Nor does she recognise a firm distinction between events located on different planes, whether they happen to be physical or mental, external or interior, real or imaginary, past or present. The barefoot figure of the fictional Gravida (28) is waiting for Freud in the ruins of Pompei; fear of entombment conjures up the fantasy of a night locked into the Roman catacombs in the company of a wizened old woman; the figure of a sleepwalker imagined in his childhood years mingles later with a performance of hypnosis, and, later still, with on-screen images at an outdoor cinema in Rome.

Perhaps Clément's Freud has been less reconstructed than restored – restored to a more authentic self and a more chaotic condition where dreams, desires and sufferings cannot be subordinated to the psychoanalytic process. Hers is a Freud who is moved by the cross-currents and ambiguities of the novel, not one cut down to fit the preconceptions or timetables of the consulting room. In this feminine and feminising account of Freud, Clément remains comfortable with both masculine and feminine polarities. She takes the knowingly masculine step of including footnotes to annotate her sources but at the same time refuses to be categorised, saying of her account that, "Nothing is truly true in this fantasy: neither is anything truly false." (29)

Clément is also fully aware of the political aspects of housework. Her Martha Freud, and her Mme Victoire in her non-fictional text, *The Weary Sons of Freud*, are both conspicuously chained to domestic life. The cleaning woman who learns to be such a supremely expert listener would, in Clément's opinion, have made an ideal and uncoercive analyst, but, although Mme Victoire overcomes vast personal obstacles, she does not have the formal education that is essential for entry into a middle-class profession. And Martha Freud, forever the bourgeois hausfrau, is weighed down by the prejudices of her husband, her social group and her era, and seems to have more talent for childbearing than listening. But the two women, each in the manner of her own class, both roll up their sleeves and get on with the job, while Clément muses on their subversive potential.

The gleeful application of Freudian theory to reveal the "underparts" of Freud produces some surprising scenarios. Clément roots Freud's psycho-analytic technique in a childhood experience, when a

Catholic nursemaid takes Freud to a church. As she kneels in prayer, the three-year-old Freud, who is playing house in a confessional box, becomes an inadvertant confidant as a female penitent recites her secret sins. The novel draws on both plain and embellished versions of early experiences and uses them as sources of disturbance and of theory. Cross-referencing the theoretical and the fantastic, the personal and the professional, Clément inserts dream material into the visible fabric of Freud's everyday existence. She tampers with chronology and identity and sometimes puts him to work on the interpretation of his own early fantasies rather than those of his patients. Freud's childish experience of waking from his siesta at the noise of a horse-drawn cart in terror that the horse might bite him, reappears much later in his five-year-old patient, Little Hans. A childhood hallucination of a skeletal old man with a coffin under his arm later fuses with a demonstration of hypnotism Freud attended in Paris. Right though his years of celebrity in Vienna, the phantasm of this malign hypnotic subject continues to haunt Freud, lurking under the couch in his consulting room or behaving indecently with his patients.

Clément's Freud is a perpetually anxious figure, assailed by fantasies and appalled by realities, obliged to confront his own weaknesses and humiliations. He is repeatedly seen in flight, both from external threats, such as the jeering of prostitutes when he becomes lost among Roman streets, or from his own phantasms, as he runs from Michelangelo's statue of Moses, pursued only by the echo of his own footsteps. In almost every chapter he is caught in the act of fleeing horrors, even on one occasion from the obscene sight of his wife laundering her sanitary napkins. His cocaine habit is another recurring theme. He rashly recommends the drug to patients and friends until an overly large dose kills his friend, 'Wilhelm'. He "knew "that the death of Wilhelm would never go away" (29) and imagines an old man found dead in a beach chair is Wilhelm. Everything overlaps. Freud's children initiate fantasies that later appear in the case histories of patients. A dream which Freud analyses in The Interpretation of Dreams, where he administers an injection to a female patient, is fused with a touch of humour with his sexual relations with Martha and his resentment at her many pregnancies.

Finally, Clément provides two versions of Freud's death. In one an attending doctor ends his sufferings with a lethal injection, while Freud imagines the girl he loved when he was sixteen is smiling at him; in the other he dies "surrounded by his women, in the style of Greuze. They would all hold their hands to their mouths with appalled expressions but no one would be able to make a sound." (31) This image is more expressive of hysteria than sorrow.

In her more conventionally articulated critique of psychoanalysis, The Weary Sons of Freud, Clément comments that, "analysis is not meant to cure .. it is a cultural intervention .. a mode of thought, a life-style. It's a quest. It's a way of life." (32) Another feminist makes a more extreme comment: "We can ask whether psychoanalysis was not articulated precisely in order to repress femininity."(33) but Clément only finds it regrettable that Freud is not ".. a man overflowing with love"(34), like his friend and colleague, Groddeck. She addresses Groddeck: "you wanted to make him laugh .. And that stiff, confined old Freud never liked you .. He never did anything but forget how to laugh ... (no more looks, no more gestures, nothing but speech, watch out, eyes, danger; keep out love, transference, threat), Freud turned [psychoanalysis] into a harsh system", while Groddeck "didn't trust science when it was taken so seriously; you thought that Freud was inhibited by the need for a nomenclature .. you took the opposite view; to you thinking meant allowing ideas to form and grow; everything that's on the mother's side." (35)

Clément's criticisms of the pontificating Freud are written in the language of the status quo, but their form is balanced by her teasing exposure of the man. She forgives him his egotistical fragility, but, while she considers him from a feminine perspective, she is simultaneously undermining his interpretations of female psychopathology and disclosing the desperately vulnerable underparts of this unrelentiing patriarch.

Writing, Nothingness and Feminine Identity

Clarice Lispector is an elusive writer. Through fleeting thoughts and images and moments of quietly stated tragedy or wry humour, she enters the unadorned situation of a very ordinary woman. Lispector's final novel, *The Hour of the Star*, (36) portrays a woman who at first seems utterly empty. She only begins to recognise the misery of her own existence when she consults a medium who remarks on it. Up till then, "Maca even thought of herself as being happy. She was no idiot yet she possessed the pure happiness of idiots. She did not think about herself: she lacked self awareness." (37) Even so, glints of humour light up the surface of this abyss of lack: "It goes without saying that she was neurotic. Neurosis sustained her. Dear God, neurosis counted for something; almost as good as crutches." (38) Her tragicomic idiocy can also be a saving wisdom: "She did not covet Mme Carlota's chocolates for Macabéa had discovered that things belonged to others."(39)

The Hour of the Star pays conscious homage to tenets of both literary and feminist theory. Lispector tells us a great deal about the activity of writing and still more about the activity of writing as a woman. "When I write," she muses, "I am surprised to find I have an identity." (40) Published posthumously, this mutedly elegaic novel has fewer regrets about death than for her imminent parting with the writing that has sustained her existence. "I write because I have nothing better to do in this world: I am superfluous and last in this world of men .. were it not for the constant novelty of writing, I should die symbolically each day."

She adds, poignantly, "Now I only wish to possess what might have been but never was." (41) The sentence hints at a wistful hope that, even in a world in which the feminine has been ground into cultural non-existence, even where it is unable to recognise itself as anything, it will in the end acquire a conscious identity.

Macabéa represents the feminine sense of nothingness as an existentialist condition. To be nothing is also to salvage feminine identity from the phallogocratic constructions of language. Macabéa instinctively chooses to be nothing rather than to mask her lack by living as someone other than herself. Lispector tells us that, even in her nothingness, "The girl possessed what is known as an inner life Most of the time she possessed, without knowing it, the emptiness that replenishes the souls of saints."(42)

Lispector takes the curious step of initially introducing herself as a male narrator. He watches as Macabéa looks in a mirror which is reflecting his own unshaven face. On one level, this describes the male use of woman as his mirror but beneath that it is commenting on the longstanding appropriation of the written word by the dominant masculine and on the deprivation of the poor, especially the women among them, in a literate world. The device also seems to reflect on Lispector's own identity as a writer and on the status she must relinquish if she is to enter into the simplicity of her character. Lispector as male narrator only supplies a frame, while the steady leakage of feminine uncertainty exposes her ruse for what it is. "I am scared of starting. I do not even know the girl's name.... I must render clear something that is almost obliterated and can scarcely be deciphered." (43) At this point the male narrator fades away altogether.

The poorly educated protagonist, is a country girl from the impoverished north-east of Brazil and is swallowed up in the urban anonymity of Rio de Janeiro. As the fragments of her humble existence are assembled we are warned to expect no sophistication, that this is to be a "stark" narrative, that puts aside all "refinments" that might in any way distract from the reality of this simple and almost "obliterated" girl. ...The narrative soon produces a prototypically macho young man. Olympico's unfounded claims to power and knowledge would be quite laughable to anyone less naive than Macabéa, but, to Macabéa, everyone's sum of knowledge exceeds her own. In her efforts to learn, she turns to the radio and informs herself with a collection of curious facts: the local names given to the emperor Charlemange, or that the sexual disposition of horses is uniquely non-incestuous. Olympico, however, takes no interest in anything that does not directly enhance his ego and knows a good deal less than she does. But his preposterous claims to superior knowledge are consolidated by a patriarchal authority that Macabéa accepts unquestioningly as final and inescapable. "She thought and thought and thought. She decided that no one had ever really oppressed her and that everything that happened to her was inevitable.." (44) "The girl never complained about anything. She accepted things as they are – after all, who was responsible for organizing the land inhabited by men?" (45)

Nevertheless, as Lispector comments in an aside, "I know about certain things simply by living. Anyone who lives knows, even without knowing that he or she knows. So, dear readers, you know more than you imagine, however much you may deny it." (46) "Dear readers" attaches firmly to a female audience. In any case, who else would want to read a story about a girl without charm, beauty, passion or worldly allure of any kind? Who, in fact, other than a woman would so readily concede that she might lack knowledge? Above all, who but a woman would conceive a desire to create such a character?

Lispector balances the knowledge that inheres in culture with knowledge of an experiential kind in a single, gracefully poised comment: "Facts are words expressed through the world." (47). In creating a character she repeatedly refers to as difficult or even frightening from the authorial point of view, she is taking on the feminine 'nothing' and, without losing sight of its limitations or restrictions, is writing it into existence. Macabéa never relinquishes any part of her sense of nothingness and yet becomes a reality. Lispector explains, "She had transformed herself into organic simplicity. She had contrived a way of finding grace in simple, authentic things... Sometimes grace descended on her as she sat at her desk at the office." (48) Writing is the reality towards which Lispector remains unswervingly faithful. Confronted by death, her own as well as Macabéa's, she composes an epitaph for women everywhere: "To die is not enough. It fails to achieve my greatest need: self-fulfillment." (49)

To be a feminist is to engage, whether by hand or by brain, in securing a measurable and probably painfully slow, progression of improvement in the lives of women. To shape a feminine identity for oneself is the creative work of a lifetime. There will be many points of meeting and convergence. Feminism needs to be nourished in the rich medium of a specifically feminine identity so that it can provide shapes and channels through which the feminine can slowly infiltrate and rectify the balance and composition of society.

Footnotes

1) Hélene Cixous and Catherine Clément, *The Newly-Born Woman.* p.ix. Manchester University Press. 1986. (French edition 1975)

2) Catherine Clément *Enclave Esclave.* New French Feminisms, ed. Elaine Marks & Isabelle de Courtivron. p131. Harvester Press, U.K. 1981.

3) Hélene Cixous and Catherine Clément, *The Newly-Born Woman* pps. 136-7

4) Hélène Cixous and Catherine Clément, *The Newly-Born Woman* p. 141.

5) Meaghan Morris. *The Pirate's Fiancée* p. 75. Verso, London & N.Y. 1988

6) ibid, p. 64.

7) Julia Kristeva, *About Chinese Women,* p.56. Marion Boyars, London, 1977 (France 1974). (For feminist reasons, Clément and Lispector both blur the distinction between thing and symbol.)

8) Marguerite Duras. New French Feminisms p174. Signs. Winter 1975.

9) Jacques Derrida. Choreographies. Diacritics, p.75. Summer 1982.

10) Jane Gallop, *Reading Lacan*, p20. Cornell University Press, 1985.

11) Ann Rosalind Jones. Editor's Introduction to Catherine Clemént's *The Weary Sons of Freud.* p.4. Verso 1987

12) Catherine Clément. Enclave Esclave. New French Feminisms p. 132. (L'arc no 61, 1975)

13) Ursula Le Guin. *Always Coming Home*. p. 536. Bantam.1985,.

14) "Menial" comes from a French word meaning household, and "should properly be used to describe only housework." Ann Oakley. What is a Housewife? British Feminist Thought, ed Terry Lovell. Basil Blackwell, 1990.

15) Esme Dodderidge. *The New Gulliver*, pps.11-16. The Women's Press. 1988.

16) ibd. p.18.

17) ibid. p.173,

18) Pamela Zoline. The Heat Death of the Universe. *Busy About the Tree of Life*. The Women's Press. London. 1988.

19) ibid p.52-3

20) ibid p. 56

21) ibid p. 62

22) ibid p.58

23) ibid p.65.

24) Catherine Clément. *Bildoungue Roman. Une Vie de Freud?* Christian Bourgois Editeur, Paris, 1978.

25) ibid p. 9.

26) ibid p. 10

27) ibid pps. 12-13.

28) The protagonist in Jensen's novel, *Gravida*.

29) ibid p.145

30) ibid p.99.

31) ibid p. 144.

32) Catherine Clément, The Weary Sons of Freud, p.16. Verso, London, 1987. (French ed. 1978)

33) Michéle Montrelay, Inquiry into Femininity, The Woman in Question, ed Adams & Cowie, p.267. Verso, London, 1990.

34) Clement. The Weary Sons of Freud, p.107.

35) ibid. 108-110

36) Clarice Lispector, The Hour of the Star. (Brazilian ed. 1977) Carcenet Press. Manchester. 1992. The present account is restricted to particular aspects of this one work and does not refer to other writings or broader critical readings of Lispector.

37) ibid p.68

38) ibid p.34

39) ibid p.73

40) ibid p 15

41) ibid p. 21

42) ibid p.37

43) ibid p.19. This theme has already been discussed in reference to correspondence between Alice Sheldon, Joanna Russ and Ursula le Guin in chapter 7.

44) ibid p. 40

45) ibid p.34

46) ibid p.13

47) ibid p.70

48) ibid pps.62-3

49) ibid p.63.

15

Darkness Is More
Than an Absence of Light

Darkness Has Its Own Agendas.
Incarnations of darkness have been too numerous to count. Darkness represents ignorance, the unconscious, the unknown. It hides secrets, sins and evil deeds, it colours unsanctioned sexual liasons and, in some ways, all sexual acts. Dark thoughts and dark deeds must not be permitted to contaminate our rational social order. In fact, the continuance of civilized existence depends on our unwavering efforts to keep darkness at bay. Madness darkens the mind and, along with criminals, lunatics and deviants, foreign places and people are murky and menacing. And if these perhaps seem like a hapless, ramshackle lot, let us not be deceived into relaxing our guard. Or so the story goes. And it goes without saying that women are specially and inextricably linked with darkness. The feminine, Yin, is dark, Yang, the masculine, is light. Day and the sun are masculine,

moon and night feminine in the majority of gendered languages. In both reality and myth, the relationship between women and the dark has produced complicated prescripts and mysterious messages, most of them sinister. There is also the desire to keep women in the dark, which stretches back into the unalleviated blackness of the far past.

Fiction teems with narratives where darkness is a central motif. In the tale that is told to the stolen bride in *The Golden Ass* (1), Amor cautions Psyche that, unless she ensures that the darkness alwaysremains absolute during his visits to her, the consequences will be disastrous. Inevitably, Psyche lights her lamp, and, as Love lies sleeping, a drop of burning oil falls on his shoulder. Amor flies off and the promised misfortunes follow. In fact, Psyche even manages to err twice over: her divine lover has clearly warned her that she must never disclose his identity to anyone. But, though she herself has failed to identify him – she is still in the dark – somehow she has allowed her less naive sisters to guess he is a god. Yet it is her error that takes her on a journey which ends in immortality. Depictions of the god of love frequently portray him as wantonly cruel, a tormentor of souls and butterflies, but in this story it is Psyche who wounds Amor and forces a painful and initially unwelcome consciousness of himself upon him. Before she sheds light on him, Amor has existed in a darkness where god and monster are inseparable and indistinguishable. But Amor is love, and to become aware of himself is to become aware of love. However, though Psyche may have started out in the dark, this does not mean that the legend is a simple story of dispersing primitive darkness to make way for light. The division into polar opposites such as good-bad or light-dark does not get to the roots of a story so rich with the interplay of meanings that the most cunning strategies of the divine Aphrodite can be defeated by an apparently powerless girl, and in which the god of love finds both love and himself in the simple heart of a human. In this tale, darkness is the precise element which engenders the desire for self-discovery. Finally, Psyche's transgressions are closely matched by those of the narrator, Lucius. Like Psyche, this central protagonist of the book is provoked into the search for consciousness by a curiosity born in darkness. His indiscretions leave him trapped in the body of an ass, but, unaware that he is all the time under the direction of the goddess Isis, he too is acquiring painful wisdom as he travels along the winding and often comic byways of worldly folly.

Biblical reactions to self-determined women are not so indulgent. When the Foolish Virgin lights up her lamp she is met with unmitigated disapproval. To the sound of platitudes about good housewifely management and self-restraint, we are exhorted to fix our eyes admiringly on the conduct of the Wise Virgins and to deplore the behaviour of the Foolish Virgin who, instead of reserving the oil in her lamp for the illumination of the illustrious bridegroom, burns it on her own behalf . The bridegroom's retaliation is absurdly predictable: when the Foolish Virgin fails to light up his arrival, he refuses her entry to the wedding feast. But darkness has its own agendas and it is precisely the withdrawal of his patronage and protection that will lead her to take responsibility for herself. This is more than her eagerly cooperative companions seem destined to accomplish. Whether or not she knows in advance what the effect of her action is liable to be, by declining to sit about submissively waiting in the dark, the Foolish Virgin becomes her own person. She may not inhabit Psyche's poetic world, and, like the bridegroom, the bible may treat her dismissively, but none of these differences diminish the significance of the un-narrated journey that lies ahead of her.

Back in mundane reality, women have typically been associated with interiors and dimly lit spaces. They have been installed behind bedroom curtains, or down in kitchens at the backs or basements of houses, or, in certain cultural contexts, secluded in enclosed and often shuttered quarters (nunneries, harems, purdah) that were, or still are, specifically dedicated to women. Where churches or other public places did not automatically exclude women, it was quite common to keep them veiled or out of sight entirely. Conventions regarding lighting and visibility have all had their effects on the characterisation of woman. (2)

Even in the most everyday conditions, darkness comes with an undertow of uncertainty, suggesting hostile or possibly supernatural presences. It provides a natural haven for secrets. But secrets inhabit a web of complex motives and those who habitually struggle to keep others in the dark will almost certainly be doing so in order to keep secrets of their own. Issues beyond a simple desire for power seem to lie at the roots of resistance to the emancipation of women.

Does the desire to keep women in the dark, whether as unseen, unheard, uneducated, unenlightened, unpoliticised, unprofessional or merely unpaid for their 'women's work', stem from a desire to keep the falsehood of male supremacy under cover? Concealment on such a scale and in such elaborate forms is bound to have psychological repercussions: inevitably those who go to such zealous extremes to keep women in the dark will become convinced that those they are oppressing must be hiding guilty secrets. And so, characterisations of women become further embellished with dark and sinister attributes.

Women of Darkness in the Male Imagination

Woman is commonly said to be 'a mystery'. Like everyone else, women will have things to conceal, but the woman of mystery is an especially exotic fabrication. Essentially she is the woman who has eluded male control. She is the woman with a 'past'. She is at her most dangerous in the form of the alluring 'femme fatale'. This figure, classically fetched up from the male imagination, is indispensible in hardboiled crime fiction and 'film noir' along with the celebration of masculine violence and the struggle for power. If the femme fatale knows a little more than she ought to about the secrets of others and may not have their good at heart, the real fear which she inspires thrives on irrational and atavistic residues. She is really a throwback to more sorcerous forebears and endowed with powers of fatal attraction. There is no limit to what a woman with her resources might do to a man. Even the keystone of male authority, the lawman, is liable to be sucked irresistibly into her intractable darkness. Often it is some waywardly individualistic private eye who imagines he has found his equal and counterpart in her. Or perhaps – this temptress has been described as a man in drag – he is just enjoying an equal contest of male strength. But whatever the homosexual undertones of this genre, the best man is always destined to win, the femme fatale usually to die, and proper order to be once more restored. On rare ocasions the male protagonist also dies.

Franju's cult classic, *Eyes Without a Face*, reverses all the usual values, even though it retains the cinematic properties of film noir. In this film, patriarchal violence is overcome through the quiet endurance hidden in the darkness and silence that shroud an apparently defenceless young girl. All but annihilated by a dangerous and tyrannical father, she haunts dim interiors, lingers wraith-like behind drawn curtains in her bedroom, murmurs of her despair and desire to die, and once whispers the name of her beloved into the telephone. Apart from her sad eyes, a mask hides a face that we learn has been horribly disfigured in an accident and obscures all trace of a personal self. She seems ultimately submissive, cowed by the will of the mythically powerful father who has vowed to restore her face. We soon discover that his true obsession is not his daughter's restoration, but his own performance of a successful facial transplant. In a secret basement suite, he operates on young women, abducted on obscure back roads at night. One by one, they die beneath his knife, while the daughter spys on him wordlessly from behind her impassive mask. Shot in black and white, the film's shadowy interiors are relieved only by the brilliantly lit cruelties of the basement surgery. The daughter's vulnerability makes her transgression all the more potent when she releases her father's final victim and sets free the caged dogs he uses for vivisection and leaves them to tear him to pieces. In the final sequence, she is transformed. She steps outside into the light, a dog by her side and a flock of doves which she has also released circling overhead. As the film tapers off into glimmering woods, we see that from the beginning an irresistible urge for freedom has been masked beneath her silent exterior. No terror, no confinement or cruelty, not even her obliteration in faceless isolation, is enough to force this seemingly powerless feminine being into final compliance.

**Doorways into the Dark: Witches,
their Analogues, Mirrors, and Stories.**

In Lacan's psychological schema, when the Father breaks in and shatters the initial union with the Mother, the Symbolic (reason, language, consciousness) replaces the Imaginary (the irrational, fantasy, the unconscious). However, this Imaginary cannot evaporate into total nothingness. It/ she remains behind in atavistic shapes and figures which swarm in an unfathomable darkness. Lacan is by no means alone in this view of the Mother/ woman. (3) Anthropologists have noted recurring primitive superstitions about women as bringers of bad luck who may depotentiate and pollute the male merely by being in his vicinity. (4)

Women, with their lunar cycles, are unavoidably associated with darkness. The enchantress and the crone are both invested with unholy knowledge and occult powers, and male fantasy reads something especially sinister into woman's sexual allure: "The eternal taint wears beauty like a mask." (5) The dark lady of male fantasy appears in many forms, but, whether she is irresistibly tempting or hideously ugly, the threat of evil and corruption remains the same.

In the era of witchhunts, it was held better to burn witch-women rather than risk having them take control over men. While millions of women were condemned only a tiny number of males went to their deaths as witches. A nineteenth-century text, *La Sorciere*, opens with a quotation: "For one sorceror, ten thousand sorceresses." The author continues, "Nature made witches – it is a particular characteristic of Woman and her constitution. She is born a Fairy." He describes the witch with sympathy, ".. in the beginning woman was everything", but, "The first Christians would curse Nature herself." (6) Conversly, a handbook for witchfinders published in the fifteenth century provides meticulously cruel instructions for hunting out and disposing of witches. It concludes that, "it is better called the heresy of witches than of wizards, since the name is taken from the more powerful party." (7) In a later century, Freud would ponder over why "confessions extorted by torture have so much similarity to my patients' narratives during psychological treatment." (8)

A detailed history of the origins and practices of witches in Europe traces witches back to the cult of

Diana, the goddess of fertility who was worshipped during excursions made at night and by women. The book speaks of "innumerable testimonies to the gradual, centuries-long diabolization of a stratum of beliefs that has only reached us in a fragmentary manner, through texts produced by canonists, inquisitors and judges. The key fossil that makes it possible to identify this stratum is composed of allusions to mysterious female figures, venerated above all by the women." (9) Diana was worshipped as the great goddess in many ancient communities, then retitled the Queen of the Witches by a christian church seeking to diminish her influence A recital of names in *The Golden Ass* suggests the immensity of the goddess's identity. When Lucius prays to Isis to free him from his bewitched, animal shape, he addresses her by a long series of titles. She responds, "I am she that is the natural mother of all things .. chief of the powers divine .. manifested alone and under one form of all the gods and goddesses .. my name, my divinity is adored throughout all the world, in divers manners, in variable customs and by many names." Among the many names that Isis mentions are Ceres, Venus, Diana, Proserpine, Juno, Bellona, Hecate. (10) . "The patriarchy has taken the divine away from women. It has carried it off and made it an all men affair, and it often accuses the religious spirit of women of being the devil's work." (11)

The Witch As Protectress

Care was always taken to invite the witch's more presentable alter ego, the fairy godmother, to christenings. She had to be conciliated when children were invested with the Name of the Father and there might be dire consequences if she were forgotten. But apart from these ceremonial inclusions, the witch was generally left to her shadowy forest solitude and the silence of wild places, and largely put from mind until some abandoned or motherless girl came to seek her help. This scenario is steeped in nostalgia for the lost mother. Catherine Clément reminds us that in the theories of both witchfinders and psychoanalysis, the mother is the thief of the father's penis and that, "in this phantasmic mythology the sorceress and mother come together again – are one and the same .. The hysteric is indeed the witch's daughter." (12) Clément attentively compares the sorceress with the *hysteric:* "The sorceress .. incarnates the reinscription of the traces of paganism that triumphant Christianity repressed. The hysteric, whose body is transformed into a theatre for forgotten scenes, relives the past, bearing witness to a lost childhood that survives in suffering." (13) Irigaray comments that, "the mother-daughter relation must be the dark continent of the dark continent, the most obscure area of our social order." (14)

The witch as victim of patriarchal persecution occupies a special position for many women. Fictional representations treat her in diverse ways. Everyone knows of the witches and fairy godmothers of folk and fairytale, and modern versions of these seem to have had a particular appeal for women authors. The witches of modern fiction are diverse in spirit. Some come in forms as familiar as the aunt. The witch-aunt in Sylvia Townshend Warner's *Lolly Willowes* is an airy figure of female resistance; in James Morrow's *The Last Witchfinder,* the aunt is the pivot of an alarmingly witty moral and philosophical battle; in Leslie Wilson's *Malefice,* the witch is seen from a historical perspective that is distinctly feminine. (15)

Lolly Willowes is an insignificant maiden aunt. On reaching middle age, she moves to the country where she discovers freedom and independence and the delights of nocturnal dancing in a latter-day witches' coven. *Malefice* studies the gradual construction of a witch in a small village community in seventeenth-century England. Delight in darkness is a key element in both these books. The witch's estranged friend in *Malefice* recalls this in the youthful Alice: "And she said: 'Darkness.' Her voice was soft and deep and her eyes went to slits in her face. Something wriggled sweetly, deep in my belly .. And she said: 'Foxglove, velvet darkness. I want it." The night before she is hanged, the parson labours to extort a confession that will redeem her and his self esteem together, but she rebuffs his efforts: " 'Heaven? God's a man, what good can we expect of him.' " Facing death, she turns instead to early memories: "Mother, she thought, come back and hold me .. Mother, put your arms around me .. I never loved anyone but you, it was all a mistake. I only want you. Mother, kiss me to sleep in the warm. I don't know who I am." (16) The surrogate mother in *The Last Witchfinder* is a widowed and highly literate woman. She takes a strong and active interest in philosophy, experimental science and the education of her motherless niece. The girl is forced to stand by as her witchfinder father contrives the execution of his sister-in-law. But in the spirit of her aunt the child points out that, "the best counter to a malicious idea is a *bon mot*, not a bonfire." (17) The traditional gendering of the irrational is dextrously reversed as she pursues the path her aunt has opened and dispels ignorance, superstition and witch-hunting with logic, learning and language, and narrowly escapes burning by her quick-witted reasoning. These portrayals all configure the witch as a woman who defies the social order of the patriarchy by reconstructing herself according to her own designs and desires and refer to love of the mother or her substitute.

Mirrors Are Also Doorways into Other Worlds

The image of the wicked Queen-Stepmother-Witch interrogating her mirror in the story of Snow-White is deeply embedded in the imaginations of western children. In fact, the mirror has traditionally possessed magic properties and been an object of fascination believed able to capture the soul. The mirror shows us what is not otherwise visible to us and allows us to arrange what others are going to see in us. It is the classic emblem of a woman's desire for beauty and in it she studies herself as if she were another. It is also the basic tool in the impersonations of masquerade, making it possible for a woman to study a part that another has written for her. The mirror contains meanings and metaphors in more or less every culture, past and present. Saturated with dangerous powers of illusion, it is a natural vehicle for the occult. Simple reflective surfaces can induce trance and hypnosis. As a trap for the soul, a mirror had to be covered after a death. Myth, folklore and fairytale abound with mirrors, both magic and sinister. To see the Medusa's face brought death but she could be perceived safely in a mirror, whereas a vampire is recognised specifically by its failure to produce a reflection. The voodoo gods of Haiti live within a cosmic mirror and are invoked in mirror image. (18) Some of these supernatural meanings relate specifically to women. In India, the supreme goddess was known as the mirror of the abyss. These meanings all suggest that the mirror is a point of entry into other worlds – Alice discovered this one dull afternoon.

The study of psychology has also noted the role of the mirror or reflection in the psychic development of humans. Lacan inserts the mirror at the point of divide between the Mother and the Father, where it stands like a doorway between the Imaginary and Symbolic. Lacan's *mirror stage* marks the subordination of nature and woman. But the dark, subversive Imaginary is still the matrix out of which the Symbolic evolves and on which it depends and cannot be so easily discarded. And then, patriarchal culture continues to need a mirror that can show it as it wants to see itself – Virginia Woolf's reflections on woman as the mirror a man uses to fix himself in his world have been thoroughly integrated into feminist thought. But when Lacan places woman on the far side of the mirror it is clear that his aim is to keep her there. In permanance. It has been said that Lacan is a "ladies' man": he is keen to seduce women with a show of understanding, yet determined to relinquish nothing of his position.

His "coy flirtation" – a virtuoso rendition of the female predicament – freezes "into a rigid system centred upon the phallus as transcendental signifier." (19) The subjugation and exile of the Mother and the installation of the Father in her place results in ".. the assumption of the armour of an alienating identity, which will mark with its rigid structure the subject's entire mental development." (20) The armour, the alienating identity, the rigid structure, all these represent an obdurately masculine ethos in which "every instinctual thrust constitutes a danger, even though it should correspond to a natural maturation." (21)

The psychiatrist, D.W. Winnicott, portrays the mirror phase very differently. He describes how the infant's consciousness of itself is formed out of what is reflected back to it in its mother's face. The Imaginary and the Mother who represents this phase remain just as vital, just as substantial as the Symbolic. He remarks on "the delicacy of what is preverbal, unverbalized and unverbalizable except perhaps in poetry." (22) Rather than the inevitable brutality of installing a more socialised style of perception, he advocates the need for a great gentleness of touch in guiding a child through the painful loss of its early symbiotic union with its mother. A child has to be eased into its separate identity where its own needs as much as those of society must be met. The link with the "good enough" mother need not be lost forever and she who first held together the child's fragmentary perceptions of the world can continue to sustain the growing person. Winnicott also wisely said, "each was once dependent on woman, and somehow a hatred of this has to be transformed into a kind of gratitude if full maturity of the personality is to be reached." (23)

Finally, there is also the speculum or curved mirror which reflects what cannot otherwise be seen. Much used in gynaecology, the speculum is a central trope in what may be Luce Irigaray's best known book, *The Speculum of the Other* [Woman]. Irigaray uses this specially constructed mirror in a metaphor that reflects non-phallic consciousness. An ordinary mirror creates a "speculative mode, in which male reason claims to be able to know itself and its limits [but] leaves no space for self-determined representations of women, for women's self-reflections .. the speculum enables women to see themselves, to examine themselves, to see and understand their sexual specificity." (24)

Where the Imaginary Rules: Stories
The connection between the Imaginary and imagination is instantly visible. It marks the place where story enters the picture. As we all know, stories are under no obligation to adhere to the prescribed outlines of the world as we are collectively required to perceive it. However far-fetched, stories cannot be accused of lying. But neither can it be said that they are committed to telling the truth – or not, that is, the truth as it is laid down by the Father. In their fluidity, in the struggle to rewrite and recreate identity, in the demand for autonomy, a space of their own and freedom from canonical conventions and interventions, stories reveal some distinctly feminine inclinations. Story may thrive on fantasy, mimicry,

even excess, and, like hysteria, has an instinct for expressing things that have been repressed or that it is impossible to communicate by other means.

None of this is new. For the social reformer, Beatrice Webb, ".. writing labour history was writing the father's story, "stiff work", as she said, in contrast to the soft mother's work of fiction." (25) But that "soft mother's work of fiction" also serves serious purposes both in reality and fiction. Scherezade is the prime, fully explicit exemplar of just how indispensable the art of story-telling can be. In a cure as long and protracted as psycho-analysis, Scherezade heals her murderous and psychotic husband of his illness by regularly administered doses of story. This is the "talking cure" turned back-to-front. It is the patient who listens, and who, as he absorbs another's fantasies, eventually finds that his own imaginary horrors have been tamed and put to rest. An anthropologist speaks of the "healing power of symbols", (not to be confused with Lacan's Symbolic) and suggests that ritual healing is "a symbol of the matrilineal principle reaffirmed in its purity and solidarity – to the confusion of intrusive patrilineal segments and unbrotherly bretheren."(26) Thus story-telling becomes a form of spell-weaving as a "Zuni boy accused of sorcery cures his alleged victims by spinning fantastic tales." (27) This kind of behaviour does not of course fulfil the rational requirements of the civilised West and without doubt the 'savage' male has aspects that his modernised brother would prefer to remain undiscovered in himself. 'Primitive' practices such as *couvade* (male enactment of childbirth) and other initiation ceremonies for men often mimic female actions in stories where masks and masquerades that a modern man would find both humiliating and irrelevant can have curative properties.

Isabelle Allende's Eva Luna describes her mother's storytelling: "She placed at my feet the treasures of the Orient, the moon and beyond. She reduced me to the size of an ant so I could experience the universe from that smallness; she gave me wings to see it from the heavens; she gave me the tail of a fish so I would know the depths of the sea." (28) Endlessly regenerating and reconstellating itself, story revives distant pasts, distant prospects and distant thoughts. Almost everyone, man and woman, remembers being told stories, more especially at bedtime before the stories conveyed by dreams would come to claim us. Story can rescue us from the harsh concerns of the daytime world, it can melt away the icy grip of the Symbolic. Story allows us – sometimes only briefly but perhaps sometimes more lastingly – to escape the Law of the Father.

The notion of darkness is fraught with unstable and contradictory elements. These are often represented as characteristically female and stigmatised as irrational, certainly hysterical, possibly even psychotic. Darkness has been converted into a useful cultural scrapheap, an exclusion zone. In contrast to it, the steady appearance of unbroken reason and enlightenment can be sustained. Readings of history, works of fiction, interpretations of reality and the individual that undermine the dominant masculine consensus, all these can be dumped here. Nevertheless, meanings are prone to alter and things are inclined to sprout up unexpectedly in the dark. Without doubt, among the welter of cast-off signifiers, and somehow, by way of the perverse workings of entropy, (29) new varieties of a self-invented feminine will at this moment be germinating in the dark. Catherine Clément urges us to note that, "Somewhere every culture has an imaginary zone for what it excludes, and that is the zone we must try to remember." (30)

Footnotes

1) Lucius Apuleius. *The Golden Ass*. 2nd century.

2) Issues regarding the veiling of women in public places are conspicuously contentious. The root meaning of 'purdah' is 'veil'.

3) See Ch 2, p.27.

4) See, for example, Mary Douglas. *Purity and Danger*. Routledge & Kegan Paul. 1966.

5) Laura Riding. *The Mask*. Selected Poems.

6) Jules Michelet, *La Sorciere*, pps.31 & 45 Garnier Flammarion, Paris. This book, originally published in 1862, stirred up fears of censorship. The quote is from Louis XIII of France.

7) *Heinrich Kramer & James Sprenger, Malleus Maleficarum*, p123. Arrow Books, London, 1971

8) As quoted by Catherine Clément in *La Jeune Nee* p. 12.

9) Carlo Ginzburg, *Ecstasies, Deciphering the Witches' Sabbath*, pps 99-100. Hutchinson Radius, London. 1990.

10) *The Golden Ass*e. Lucius Apuleius, translated by William Adlington (1566) pps 263-4. Collier Books, N.Y. 1967.

11) *Luce Irigaray. Sexes & Genealogies*, p190. Columbia University Press. 1993.

12) Clément, Catherine in *La Jeune Nee* p. 52

13) Clément, Catherine in *La Jeune Nee* p.5.

14) *Meres et filles vue par Luce Irigary*. Libération. 1979.

15) Sylvia Townsend Warner, *Lolly Willowes*, The Women's Press, London 1978 (first ed1926 James Morrow, *The Last Witchfinder*, Weidenfeld & Nicholson, London, 2006. Leslie Wilson, *Malefice*, Picador, Pan Books, London. 1992

16) Leslie Wilson. op cit. pps 28, 96 & 57.

17) James Morrow, op cit. p.465.

18) See Maya Deren, *The Voodoo Gods*. Paladin, 1975, UK.

19) Gallop. op cit p.36.

20) Jacques Lacan, *Le Stade du Miroir (1949) Ecrits*, p.4. Tavistock Publications, London 1977. (Editions du Seuil 1966)

21) ibid p.5.

22) D.W. Winnicott, *Playing and Reality*, p 131. Penguin Books, UK 1974.

23) D.W. Winnicott, *Home Is Where We Start From*, p193. Penguin Books, London, 1986.

24) Grosz. op cit. p.xxii

25) Elaine Showalter, *Sexual Anarchy*, p 62. Penguin Books, UK, 1990.

26) Mary Douglas. *Implicit Meanings*. p.142. Routledge & Kegan Paul. London 1975.

27) Douglas. ibid, p 149.

28) Isabelle Allende. *Eva Luna*, pps 3&21. Penguin. 1989.

29) The literal meaning of entropy is transformation.

30) Clément, Catherine in *The Newly Born Woman* Hélene Cixous and Catherine Clément, , p.6. Manchester University Press. 1986. (*La Jeune Née*. 1975, Union Génerale d'Editions, Paris.)

16

When Not in the
Name of the Father: Traces

Maternal Uncles, and
Brothers and Sisters of One Womb

For as long as anyone can properly recall, the monolithic Father has cast his shadow unhindered across the world. Patriarchal societies have kept their persevering records of law and lineage and ownership and asserted that the male has been in command since the beginning of human history. Studies based on inference and more oblique sources such as myth, literature and archaeological remnants have tentatively proposed the existence of ancient matriarchies, but with nothing explicitly stated, no written records, their suggestions of primal societies organised on matriarchal principles have largely been dismissed as fantasies. Even so, tantalising indications remain.

A matriarchal society would have had exact identifying features. Matrilineal descent passes through the mother and certain positions that are defined by paternal relationships in male-dominated contexts would have attached instead to the mother's closest male blood-kin. This would be the mother's brother. A man would not acquire rights over a woman's children through the fact that he is their father. Until very recently, a father could not be certain of his paternity. Uncertainties attach to fathers also: a man might have fathered children with more than one woman and have divided loyalties. A father cannot necessarily be relied on to ensure the equal rights of all a woman's children, whereas children born of one woman and one womb may not share the same father, but they will all have been equally nourished by her blood and have the same claim upon her. In some ways a father remains a stranger and is therefore potentially dangerous. The maternal uncle is the mother's true blood relative – he shares the same mother's blood and originating womb with his blood sister, and in this way he is identically related to all of her children. The paramount importance of mother and child's security in a matriarchal society means that a blood brother is the only assured protector and guarantor of the equal rights and welfare of his sister's progeny. The sacred nature of blood ties is obvious when even loyalties sworn between two males have traditionally been sealed by joining their bloods together.

In his studies of the traces left by early societies, J.J. Bachofen, a nineteenth-century social philosopher and ancient historian, hoped "to discover, if possible, the universal law of history." (1) He is best known for theories which suggest that, at least in some instances, matriarchal societies preceded patriarchies. He explains his methodology: his evidence necessarily comes from literature, myth and the interpretation of artefacts rather than written history. Often using Mediterranean sources, he pieces together fragments of matriarchal social structures and observes the prominent role of maternal uncles. More conservative historians and scholars have dismissed the possibility of matriarchal societies in either ancient (Amazons, Lydia, Lycia, Sparta etc) or modern forms (tribes of Native Americans, Zuni, Sioux, etc).(2) And the debate goes on, predictably continuing to incline towards recorded evidence that seems to consolidate unbroken male dominance and to dimiss theories proposing that there are reasons for considering the possibility of prehistoric matriarchies. (3) Bachofen speaks mildly to his critics on the historical question: "The thirst for systematic knowlege has inspired many attempts to arrive at a picture of the origins by philosophical speculation, to fill in the great gaps in our historical records with the shadowy figures of abstract reasoning. A strange inconsistency: to reject myth as invention and to accept one's own utopias so confidently." (4)

This chapter will discuss theories relating to early matriarchies and certain classical Greek dramas in which the action hinges on customs and moral stances that distinctly suggest the existence of early matriarchies. Pressures to deny this possibility are strong. At times even Bachofen is prone to dismiss the implications of his own evidence, as when he proposes that relations between fathers and sons "require a far higher degree of moral development than mother love". Yet at the same time he extols the ethical character of mother-love as, "The relationship which stands at the origin of all culture," and, "the only light in the moral darkness" of a primitive period. (5)

As Freud would later do, Bachofen took a special interest in the story of Oedipus, although he drew very different conclusions from the story. Freud saw Oedipus, who unknowingly killed his father and married his mother, as a prototype for the desires and erotic entanglements of the (male) child, but Bachofen saw the narrative as a reflection of a pre-existent matriarchy. "Oedipus belongs to the race of the Spartoi .. [who] have no recognisable father but only a mother." (6) Then he discusses the matter of Jocasta's clasp, with which Oedipus blinds himself. The clasp apparently refers to the deities of an ancient matriarchy and Bachofen takes this to mean that Oedipus is "breaking the curse of Aphroditean hetaerism." (7) A feminist interpretation (myth is surely open to interpretation) might well prefer the explanation that Oedipus was seeking to propitiate the primal female powers, the Eumenides, the Fates and to observe his moral obligations to the Mother. His bond with these ancient female deities is further endorsed by the fact that Oedipus acquiesces to their demand that he should spend his last days in their sacred grove, where he will be buried in accordance with their wishes.

Yet even then the family tragedy does not come to an end. Creon is not only Jocasta's brother and the uncle of Oedipus, he is also the maternal uncle of the children his sister bore with Oedipus and is bound in equal duty to them. His position as ruler of Thebes is derived from his relationship to his sister's children. In Sophocles's later tragedy, the *Antigone*, Creon betrays these children born of the same blood and ignores his sacred duty in order to secure his own personal power and profit. "Creon, represented in the myth as a usurper, seeks to attain legitimacy through union with his sister Iocasta." (8) Worse is to follow. Though Creon buries his sister's elder son with honour, he forbids on pain of death the burial of her younger son, Polynices. As spirit could not go to rest in the underworld if its body lay unburied, his decree is not only installing the patriarchal institution of primogeniture, it is violating his religious duty to bury the dead in accordance with matriarchal practices and betraying his sacred obligation to his blood-kin.

A large part of Sophocles's drama centres round the burial of the dead. The dead are the representatives of the past. Creon is sinning against past loyalties and obligations: when Antigone disobeys him and buries Polynices by night, he does not spill her blood but instead condemns her to be entombed alive. His response suggests that the old matriarchal ethics which Antigone defiantly upholds have not been fully displaced and still pose a threat to his newly assumed power. The play revolves around the clash between the old female deities and the sacred needs which they upheld, and Creon's assertion of his power to oppose the ancient law. Antigone's 'bloodbond' with siblings born from the same womb commits her to burying her brother, whatever consequences may follow. Forced to choose between death and her bond with her brother according to the moral code of the matriarchy, she never falters. Creon's decree cannot "override the gods, the great unwritten, unshakeable traditions." (9) She cannot leave her "own mother's son to rot, an unburied corpse". But Creon is pitting himself against far more than a rebellious girl; he is seeking to topple a living culture, to push it over the brink into extinction. Antigone refuses to define her brother as an enemy, and makes a declaration of her moral identity: "I was born to join in love, not hate – that is my nature." Her poweful moral conviction contrasts sharply with Creon's self-seeking misogyny: ".. if love you must – love the dead! While I'm alive no woman is going to lord it over me."

The power of the Mother, though it is about to be superseded, still possesses an immense and fateful attraction. It is when Creon, duty-bound to ensure equality to siblings related through the motherline, refuses the same rights to each of Jocasta's children and yet occupies the throne in the name of his bloodbond with her that he becomes a usurper. He is determined to destroy every person who upholds the order from which he has snatched his power and status: "Sister's child or closer in blood than all my family .. she'll never escape .. the most barbaric death." He rejects his female kin so absolutely that, for one forgetful moment, he is on the brink of condemning Antigone's submissive sister, Ismene, to death also. Finally, in supporting the right to rule and to burial of Jocasta's elder son, yet refusing both to her younger son, Creon is asserting the patriarchal instution of primogeniture which privileges the firstborn son. He is committing a crime against the fundamental principle of absolute parity between siblings linked through their mother's blood.

A Short Digression
Regarding Some More Modern Uncles

To this day, the fact of having occupied the same maternal womb can continue to create intense loyalties. And some surprisingly joyous rituals. The anthropologist, Gregory Bateson, describes exhuberant performances among a tribe in New Guinea, where the maternal uncle acts as a symbolic mother or sexual partner in relation to his sister's children: "*Wau* (mother's brother) wears grotesque female attire; offers his buttocks to male *laua* (sister's child ..); in pantomime gives birth to female *laua* .. acts as female in grotesque copulation.." A description of the "grotesque copulation" provides details: "..the *wau* puts on a skirt and fixes an orange coloured fruit, *mbuandi*, in his anus and goes up the ladder of a house displaying this as he climbs. At the top of the ladder he goes through the actions of copulation with his wife, who is dressed and acts as the male .. The orange fruit represents an anal clitoris .. My informant told me that, after the *mbora* (the brother's wife), acting as male had copulated with the wau, the other women would all follow suit – and we may imagine a scene of considerable confusion round the unfortunate *wau*." (10)

This account is filled with ebullient good humour. The unregenerate innocence of the maternal uncle's performance reveals social relations of a kind long since forgotten in the more civilised world. But if one shifts these relationships closer to home, the present day picture often tends to grow darker. The uncle of the modern world has no preordained role or inbuilt obligations. *Avuncular* suggests familial kindness and support and, interestingly, the word derives from a Latin root meaning *an uncle to the children of a sister*. A contemporary uncle may have no avuncular qualities. In fact, he may not be an uncle at all. The custom of awarding the title of 'uncle' to a mother's extra-marital consort, to someone who has no legal status or genetic link with the family, seems to stem from a desire to embed a possibly dangerous stranger in a system of loyalties we can scarcely now remember. (11) Familial attachment cemented through bloodbond has a stability that is demonstrably absent from the more fragile bedbond on which the patriarchy bases its expectations of social cohesion. The worst abuses that belong to the patriarchal order are able to come into play when nothing beyond purely secular and rescindable man-made laws are left to guarantee the security of women and children.

Modern narratives abound with menacing and often sexually-charged real uncles. Hitchcock provides all the right blood ties for the wicked uncle in his film, *Shadow of a Doubt*. This maternal uncle's return to the family bosom and his doting female kin masks his flight from a police investigation of a chain of financially motivated wife-murders. When his initially adoring niece becomes suspicious, he attempts to kill her but in doing so causes his own accidental death.

The family has him buried with honour. Only his niece knows what he is. Angela Carter's a maternal uncle is more visibly sinister: "his presence, brooding and oppressive, filled the house... She could not link him in her mind with her mother, though the two of them had once shared a mother themselves. He seemed of a different texture and substance from her gentle and ineffectual mother; he was hewn or cut out of thunder itself. She sensed his irrational violence in the air about him." (12)

Brothers and Bloodkin

The story of Antigone has been reinterpreted by several subsequent playwrights, among them Berthold Brecht and Jean Anouilh. Antigone is pivotal to issues of moral definition and has also received considerable attention from philosophers. One feminist philosopher points out that in Sophoclean terms, she "brings divine law into the human community in opposition to the authority of the polis". Hegel, however, asserts that even if Antigone commits a crime against the law for ethical reasons she "must admit guilt" (13) Another feminist adds that Hegel accepts "the justification for Creon's desire to maintain the authority of the state, but at the same time, in spite of Hegel's reputation as a misogynist, he recognises the ethical superiority of Antigone and the way of life she upholds"; Hegel not only stresses the "ethical bonds of love" and "the 'feminine' quality of love," he concludes that, "in defying the patriarchal authority of the state, Antigone's actions are determined by an authentic relation of love."(14) The slight figure of Antigone brings love and its feminine ethic into collision with law and the masculine. The penalty is death.

Irigaray also discusses Hegel's interpretation of the ethical dilemma that *Antigone* represents. For her, the work of Sophocles "marks the historical bridge between matriarchy and patriarchy." The king "affirms his right as a father, as well as the complicity between family (patriarchal) power and that of the State." She adds, "the power of the father's name, had its right already been in force, should have prevented Oedipus from committing murder and incest." (15) Irigaray also points out that the children of Jocasta and Oedipus divide naturally into two groups. Etocles and Ismene ally themselves to Creon's new regime and the fatherright by which the city of Thebes will in future be controlled, while Polynices and Antigone adhere to the ancient laws of motherright. "Now, whereas Ismene is termed a sister because she shares *the same blood* as Antigone, and whereas Polynices is termed a brother because he is born of *the same mother*, Etocles is brother because he is the son of *the same father and the same mother*." (16) Etocles personifies the elder brother in his "relation to power, reason, property, the paternal successsion."(17) Polynices is described as weaker and younger, in fact, as less manly. To assert his right to share power with an elder brother is to flout the law of primogeniture. Irigaray points out that the patriarchal "rule of law" renders a brother or sister who is equal the "worst enemy" of the other. The hierarchical nature of the patriarchal order inevitably leads to competition and opposition and consciousness is irremediably divided by the rule of law and "must therefore make up its mind to act in accordance with that part of the ethical essence ... which would correspond to its natural allegiance to one sex." (18) Irigaray concludes that, in this scenario, male and female are remorselessly polarised. The female of the new patriarchal order, here represented by Ismene, can be shut up "in the palace, the house, with the other women, who are all thus deprived of their freedom" (19) and brought under the full control of men. ".. male and female will be split further and further apart," she tells us. "Blood is burned to cinders in the writing of the text of law whereby man produces (himself) .. in his son, and in his wife – and the colour of blood fades as more and more semblances are produced, more atoms of individual egos, all bloodless in different ways." (20)

In theory, in a society organised by essentially familial matriarchal principles, rather than by law and the state, there is nothing that actively ruptures the continuity between child and adult. As its mother's son or daughter, a child can attain adult form in an unbroken line without suffering an enforced renunciation of its original loyalties or identity, either through baptism, the shattering of the Oedipus complex or any other form of initiation into the patriarchal order. In those contemporary societies which are most acutely patriarchal, all male relatives are given a share in the control of female family members and their sexual conduct. A wife comes as a stranger into her husband's house, and all of those who have control over her are kin to her husband, not herself. Honour killings of daughters, wives and even mothers will usually be executed or commissioned by a father or a husband. Or an uncle. To those living in less extreme contexts, events like these appear mythologically savage – as if all the participants were acting under a spell in some sinister fairytale. Or in a classic Greek tragedy.

The *Orestia* of Aeschylus is particularly explicit in its discussion of the claims of 'bloodbond' – connection through the mother – over 'bedbond' – through which the husband and father asserts his claims. The tragedy begins when Agamemnon, "ravenous for war", sacrifices Iphigenia, his daughter by Clytemnestra, to the gods to obtain a wind that will carry his invading army to Troy. On his return, a vengeful Clytemnestra murders him and is then murdered by her own son, Orestes, who in patriarchal terms is under a moral obligation to avenge his father's death. The trilogy ends with a struggle between old and new gods, represented respectively by the Eumenides and Apollo, and takes the form of a divine trial. The outcome is decided by Athene who has the casting vote. This goddess was not born of a mother but out of the head of her father, Zeus, a birth that has been described as "a desperate theological expedient to rid an earth-born Kore of her matriarchal conditions." (21)

The Chorus in the *Eumenides* make the accusation that, "the new gods .. buried the older powers under the floors of their own shrines and ruled from new altars – altars drenched with blood." They claim that murder of a husband by a wife is not sacrilegious because "wife and husband share no lineal blood."

Apollo then accuses them of failing to recognise the "contract with the father" and Orestes pronounces Clytemnestra a double murderer, guilty of the deaths of both her husband and his father. Finally, Apollo gives a summation designed to leave no room for further discussion:

"The son is said to belong to his mother –
But she is not the real parent.
The mother is incidental.
...She may be entirely unnecessary."
The Chorus responds,
"The earth is overthrown.
Our laws are obsolete.
You younger gods
Violate creation!" (22)

Whatever the facts of prehistory may be, echoes of this lament for a lost world still linger on, still suffuse myths of an age of innocence and harmony with the intentions of nature.

Footnotes

1) J.J. Bachofen. *Myth, Religion and Mother Right (1861)* p.xi . Routledge & Kegan Paul. 1967.

2) ibid p.xxxiii

3) An uneasy 1957 introduction to a rather sprawling early twentieth-century text asserts that it is "spoiled" (sic) by a belief in "the former existence of a primitive matriarchy universally preceding the patriarchy." Robert Briffault. *The Mothers ,* (1927) pps 11 & 14. Allen & Unwin. 1959.

4) Bachofen, op cit p 76. It has been remarked that the history of women "still awaits reconstruction in its fullest particulars." This necessitates "exposing the ideological foundations of a hegemonic discourse that has dominated the discussion of ancient women and that continues to make its powerful influence felt .. at the present moment in history." Marilyn A. Katz. Ideology and 'the status of women' in ancient Greece, *Women in Antiquity* ed Richard Hawley & Barbara Levick, Routledge, 1995.

5) Bachofen, ibid. p. 79.

6) ibid. p. 180-181.

7) ibid. p 183;

8) ibid. p. 180-181.

9) Quotes from Sophocles *Antigone*, are all from the translation by Robert Fagles. Penguin Classics. U.K. 1984

10) Gregory Bateson. *Naven.* Cambridge Univ. Press. 1936.

11) To call a sexual partner an 'uncle' is more common in less affluent groups, who, with less property to transmit, have traditionally set less store by legal marriage. The dangers of such uncles is well known. "The murder of infants by stepfathers or mothers' boyfriends resembles the circumstances under which sexually selected infanticide evolved in other primates: males from outside the breeding system increase their own chances to breed by eliminating offspring sired by rivals... in North America when the father of offspring under two years of age no longer lives in the home and an unrelated man or stepfather lives there instead, this rare event [child homicide] is seventy times more likely to occur." Sarah Blaffer Hrdy, *Mother Nature*, p.236. Vintage. 2000.

12) Angela Carter. *The Magic Toyshop*. Heinemann. 1967.

13) Patricia Jagentowicz Mills, 'Hegel's Antigone', *Feminist Interpretations of G.W.F. Hegel*, p.69, ed Patricia Jagentowicz Mills. Penn State University, 1996.

14) Susan Easton 'Hegel and Feminism', *Radical Philosophy no 38*, pps. 3&4. Summer 1984, UK.

15) Luce Irigaray, *Speculum of the Other* Woman, p. 217 ff. (trans Gillian C. Gill) Cornell Univ. Press. USA 1985.

16) ibid p. 217

17) ibid p. 219

18) ibid p. 222

19) ibid p. 217-8

20) ibid p. 221 – 222

21) Jane Harrison, Prolegomena to the study of Greek Religion (1903), p.302-3. Meridian Books, USA, 1966.

22) Quotations from *The Orestia* come from a translation by Ted Hughes. Faber & Faber, London, 1999.

Epilogue

In Hindsight

This final chapter will highlight some perhaps less widely disseminated ideas produced by third-wave feminists and try to pinpoint their connections with second-wave feminist formulations – also, to a very limited extent, to note the newer surge that refers to itself as fourth-wave feminism. As this text was crystallising on the page, more recent theory was seeping in and bringing with it an increasing awareness of the many connections between past and present expressions of feminism. The second-wave feminist theory which is discussed in this book has tended to cluster around concepts of difference and self-definition. Similar central concerns also play an important role in certain strands of third-wave philosophical theory, but, this time, they install the metaphor of "becoming woman" as a basic precondition for liberation from a masculinist regime. And, this time it is crucial to their thinking that liberation through this "becoming woman" is extended to both sexes. Though second and third waves read woman's difference on significantly different levels of meaning and reality, each reading is appropriate to its time. The second wave was embattled by a still confident patriarchal tradition, and the third endured a "backlash" of derision and rejection on a popular level. During this difficult period, some feminist apologists took their stand in more philosphical and metaphorical arenas. Fourth-wave feminism is now enjoying a resurgence and has a broad and comparatively relaxed sense of its own freedom. But it is still early for useful predictions about what its eventual shape and influence will be.

Even as feminists of the sixties and seventies were doing their best to formulate 'reasonable' and acceptable demands regarding equality for women, it was becoming obvious that, if at all, these would be met only in part. Rights that would meet the particular needs of women, especially if they related to differences in women's reproductive situation, would not be included. But 'woman' as a free-standing element in the definition of 'human' threatened to shake the foundations of male primacy. Therefore the system rejected any demands that deviated from the 'norm' (in this case, male) and conceded only the *same* rights as men – which of course made it impossible to supply a solution that was appropriate to women. However, where half a century ago, these problems seemed insurmountable, we now take the benefits of women's hopes and labours for granted and often forget the vulnerable conditions from which they emerged. The obstacles seem only to have stimulated a determination to replace interminable haggling over minor inequalities with outright change.

Demonstrably, feminism has not come to a standstill or become a museum piece. In a steady historical progression, it has consistently addressed change and future prospects. Feminist thinking seems to turn naturally towards the future. Injecting new vitality and meaning into the understanding of our social and cultural behaviour – and of ourselves - it has altered many of the ways that people, including many outside the orbit of feminism, think and will come to think. Undeniably, feminism won the gender argument on moral grounds. However, this happened at the precise time when traditional moral values were in a state of visible collapse (thus raising the question of a possible connection (1)). Feminism responded to this new challenge by affirming the need for radical change and a social order that could generate fresh rather than recycled moral values. This meant taking a radical and forward-looking position that invalidated earlier representations of women, men and the social order, contested the worth of a society that was built on hierarchy and acquisition rather than inter-dependence and community, and seriously questioned the assumption that mankind is the most important form of life on earth. I unreservedly include myself among those women whose lives have been changed and continue to change under the influence of feminist thinking and interpretation.

This text has intermittently readdressed questions that are still being regularly aired and debated and has also introduced materials that have not been explicitly connected to feminism. It has not lingered on well-defined practical failures to deliver what was promised to women. More concerned with woman's consciousness and identity than with misogynist abuses, the central proposition has been the importance of woman's self-discovery and her openess to an evolving awareness that will no longer tolerate the fixed cultural identities that were imposed by male supremacies and have kept them in power ever since.

New Definitions

The emphasis on self-definition and the new surge of energetic theorising that typify third-wave feminism were apparently too subtle for a media that preferred the simplistic explanation that feminism was over with, and anyway too academic to have social or political relevance. This assessment conveniently overlooked its own political conservatism. But feminists persevered: ".a third wave concerns the effect of self-definition. In one sense this refers to the fragmentation of feminist theorising. While this fragmentation can be regarded as undermining the coherence of second wave feminism, there are also sound grounds (necessary for a plausible self-definition) for seeing it in a very positive light, as having led to a rich, dynamic and distinctive diversity within an on-going discourse."(2) Even if this comment may not fully recognise the number of feminists in the sixties and seventies who were heavily engaged from the start with questions about self-definition, and even if many strands of second-wave feminism were more flexible and amenable to loosely connected structures than the word "fragmentation" suggests, nevertheless, the assessment very nicely catches the close connection between these two waves of feminism as well as their joint concern with difference, diversity and the defining self.

Crass popular accounts once liked to portray feminists as 'bra burners'. Many representations of present day feminists insist on emphasising their explosive, self-assertive anger and incoherent rage and barely mention new or underlying ideas. Of course angry outbursts will inevitably erupt in the struggle to dislodge male domination, but attributions of undirected female fury make feminism into an empty term that could mean anything from a synonym for post-feminist to a description of women claiming to be feminists by right of "empowering" themselves through the exploitation of their own bodies. Interestingly, the image of a raging woman contains a strong element of masculinity. She exhibits an urgent desire for power and conquest, accompanied by overtones of an aggressive 'male' sexuality. Though this text never suggests that so-called 'active' or 'male' sexual desire is to be found only in males, it has several times pointed out that instead of acknowledging a sexual desire that is specifically 'feminine', masochism is installed as an inherent 'feminine' perversion. No thought is given to the possibility that masochism is a convenient comple-ment to thecharacteristic of supposedly 'masculine' sadism. Meanwhile, feminists are repre-sented as distinctly 'unfeminine', frigid, life-denying women, bent on wiping out 'normal' sexual pleasure and repressing a 'normal' female instinct to be whatever men desire.

Some of the connections between second and third-wave thought and theory seem absolutely natural. The icon of the self-inventing, infinitely various, female person, with her endlessly changing faces and moments of self-recognition, converts effortlessly into the "becoming-woman" (3) of later twentieth-century philosophy who is a focal point for much third-wave feminist theory. In their affirmation of an undefined, dissenting, enquiring, and perennially-to-be-explored feminine avatar, feminists and also a separate philosophical constituency are creating an iconic source of radical aspirations to change. Third-wave feminist theory expresses an unconcealed desire for freedom and the avoidance of immutable rules or an encapsulating containment. It rejects authority which is imposed by hierarchical ideas and structures. There is no way to foresee what will become of these aims over time or through the filters of the various cultures in which they may come to be lived, but it has been assumed that, since they shift the human position on such a neo-Galilean scale, they will require a 'transformation' of perception rather than endless minor tweakings and adjustments. Michèle le Doeuff's focus on the inescapable presence of the imaginary in reason already anticipates the realisation that mankind in fact exists only *inside* the universe. Man is not a privileged external observer and so must give way to the greater whole.

This epilogue does not set out to discuss third-wave feminism in detail. It hopes simply to remedy the most glaring gaps in the public perception of feminism during the decades following its heyday in the seventies and to trace relationships between some of the materials that have been discussed in this book and some expressions of third-wave thought. It hopes to show how naturally these two waves merge as they come together. (4)

Definition and Difference

Third-wave feminist theory is complex and requires a certain amount of unpacking. This book has repeatedly asserted that it is no longer *enough* to identify the women's movement through collections of aims that remain situated in a fundamentally unchanged society, regardless of how vital these aims may have been or continue to be. Chapter 1 opened with Colebrook's reading of Deleuze and Guttari's idea that " 'Woman' opens the human to new possibilities." To explain why this could not be man, she tells us,"it is woman who blocks or jams the conceptual machinery that grounds man." If man clings to his long history of appropriation and enshrines his right to indisputable primacy, if he elects himself as "the ground of all concepts and speech, how can he account for woman? This is why there can be no 'becoming man', for man or the human has always taken itself as the ground of becoming. Woman short-circuits the self-evident identity of man." (5)

Thus the active recognition of difference between the sexes becomes something more than a key component in the progress of the feminist undertaking: it not only has the goal of revolutionising woman's identity, but, ultimately, the meaning of *human* identity. And though Deleuze's "becoming woman" was never intended to be identical with feminism's 'woman', this does not invalidate her usefulness to feminist theory. Elizabeth Grosz comments bluntly that, "While Deleuze is no feminist, he may prove to be one of the few philosophers committed to thinking the new, of opening up thought and knowledge to the question of the future ..." (6) She also gives a very precise account of the problems attendant on a revolution that seeks out the absolutely new, and a future "which we can approach through anticipation, hope, or wish, [but] where we cannot and do not live." To focus on "the future, the actualisation of virtualities hitherto undeveloped" is to risk losing a grip on common realities. But to "remain locked within the frame [of everyday struggles] ... stuck in the immediacy of a present with no aspirations to .. something different, something better" is stultifying and drains away our energy for new undertakings. Grosz concludes that, for feminism, "transformation, the very logic of change, the capacity to initiate a pragmatics of change, is central to its formulation as a political and theoretical practice." (7) Happily feminism is not obliged to carry the dead weights of tradition, authority, or the Law of the Father, and its thinking is correspondingly light on its feet and generally able to keep a few steps beyond the grasp of the status quo.

The composition of this collage of a self-invented woman (perhaps for third-wave purposes she is better described as 'self-inventing') has been comparatively simple. Out of a theoretically infinite multitude, it has assembled sixteen almost random applications of feminism , all of which point in the direction of a less overbearing, less hubristic human identity. Deleuze's, "becoming woman" inhabits a place where humanity is perceived as a single evolving part of a vast and endlessly evolving whole. In this context, the human prototype takes a female form because woman has never claimed to be the representative of human identity or supremacy. Feminist thought is at a stage where many of its ideas and objectives have to become acts of the imagination *because* they need to get beyond refurbishing the same, established past and beyond ever more desperate shifts of the same kaliedoscope. Transformation means to become *different in kind*, to allow all-inclusive revolution and perhaps infinite flux to become the norm. This is a step into uncertainty. It opens up an intensely brave, (and, from the present standpoint, imaginary) new world.

There are many arguments that support utopian ideas and their "potential as a mode for envisioning social change that emphasises the transformative over the perfected vision." It recognises that "the perfected vision" quickly becomes a project with material applications that are soon fixed in processes that are neither utopian nor feminist. "What animates feminism *is* the productive potential of utopic vision even when some accounts of feminism disavow this connection; and the definition of utopia may be productively expanded and enriched through its association with feminism's multiple futures."(8) Atopic and utopic both lie outside the borders of what we are so interminably urged to believe is the total sum of what is possible. Both speak of things as yet unrealised, but, even if we

335

are not quite ready to confront such a sweeping possibility on a daily basis, then at least we can glimpse its potential. Feminism may never reach its utopian objective, but the journey towards it will surely change the rules.

More than thirty years ago, Michele Le Doeuff carefully remarked that, "a work is atopian if it finds no circle of witnesses or readers already able to receive it. This is to say, also, that it manifests its author's singularity." (8) *"Atopos",* so she tells us, "means that which has no place, but also that which is bizarre, extravagant, strange. An atopia is a text which cannot immediately be given one single correct meaning by its reader." (10) She is assuming that representations of women which did not damage their integrity could mainly be achieved only in an imaginary reality. Three decades later on, Genevieve Lloyd is able to say quite casually, "We feminist philosophers are not the bearers of clearly bordered identities occupying stable, newly won, speaking positions. .. We are shifting subjects, taking on multiple identities, multiple positions in relation to power." (11)

The roots of feminism go back into proto-feminisms that existed long centuries before any organised women's movements. In modern times, each new surge of feminism is charged with resolving difficulties that until then were still as tightly sealed as buds, yet each phase seems to contain an odd awareness of things to come. If Simone de Beauvoir is remembered best for her struggles to gain equality and her failure to establish the need to abolish the patriarchal context, at the same time she is also aware of its profoundlydestructive effect on men as well as women. "... he feels hostility for women because he is afraid of them, and he is afraid of them because he is afraid of the character with whom he is assimilated. ... He would be liberated with their liberation. But that is exactly what he fears." (12) And in a slightly later era, while Jacques Derrida sabotaged the rigid control of the patriarchy through his *deconstruction* and effectively democratised meaning and language, feminists were beginning to consider the need for women's difference to be established before anything further could be accomplished. Soon, fixed values, words and meanings had been thrown open to all comers and perceived to depend on the deploying consciousness.

We cannot leave the question of difference without returning to Luce Irigaray. Her work on difference is finely tuned and includes new subdivisions of meaning, such as her term 'sexuate difference', used to indicate differences between the sexes that are not fully determined by either biological or cultural factors. (13) A recent interview confirms that her position has never faltered. She has always insisted that difference between men and women is qualitative and must not be seen as a quantitive measure of how each performs in masculine terms. "Man and woman are irreducible, the one for the other ... because of a difference in being and existing, that is to say, a qualitative difference. Agreeing with this and putting it into practice constrain us to enter another logic." (14) She thinks, "it is better for a woman to cultivate her belonging through feminine values ... to enter a really different culture based on the relation between two subjects not subjected to one another." (15)

Directions, Connections, Dichotomies

Feminists after the seventies inherited a dilemma that the second wave had not been able to resolve: how can a person define, or even imagine, an uncontaminated female identity without resorting to the masculinist language and constructions on which communication is based? Claire Colebrook is very clear that a complex strategy is needed. This cannot be just "a simple intervention within an adequate field, but must also attempt to open other styles or modes of address, or a new field." For some time now, some feminists as well as others whose thinking shows a desire to change perception, have been making do with an intermediate solution that uses masculinist constructions "in the full knowledge that this complicity, with its corruption and contamination, is itself an action against a metaphysics that would present itself as pure, self-fathered and fully autonomous."(16) This text tends to take the position that women cannot altogether abandon male dominated language, but neither can they accept it without question. It is also possible to undermine the privileged situation of language by mixing in perceptions that reach beyond standard meanings and so confound them. Clément takes an interim position of this sort and her discussion of feminine writing with Cixous in chapter fourteen reveals the intensity of second-wave feminist efforts to resolve these language problems.

Third-wave, post-Deleuzian feminist theory also engages with the overall context. It has been noted that both Foucault and Deleuze regard "attachment to the .. negative passions of narcissism and paranoia" as integral to the status quo or "majority system."(17) Whereas the struggle to become the foremost species or race or gender is clearly delusional, tensions at once lessen if humans are seen as one among many interrelated species. The same holds true for feminist initiatives. Advances in philosophy, science and social and political structures need to coexist with a pragmatic search for material ways to create an unconditional and non-discriminatory equality that includes women, men and other life forms. Le Doeuff's analysis of logic, Irigaray's sexuate difference and the ethics that attach to it, and the innumerable questions relating to language, society, sexuality and tradition that preoccupy feminists may all move the grounds of feminist theory, but their links with practical action need to be kept intact, and pressure for equal pay, education and opportunity, the safety of women and children, the abolition of pornography, worldwide women's rights, and a host of other single issues has to continue.

Colebrook explains the need to perceive difference as something that is differently constituted rather than merely as the opposite of something else: "becoming must begin with his [man's] opposite 'woman'. But this becoming must then go beyond binary opposition and pass through to other becomings, so that man and woman can be seen as events within a field of singularities, events, atoms and particles." (18) To envisage humans "*within* a field" much broader than the human one it is necessary to move a great distance from the swaddled security of human apartheid. The huge imaginative leap into an exponentially enlarging and unstable totality inevitably imbues feminist ideologies with qualities that may be perturbing as well as oceanic. But in addition to strong practical reasons for real change in the human species, truth requires an imaginative insight into the interdependence of all species.

Using the term 'nomadic' to describe a theoretical that spreads beyond static limits, Rosi Braidotti remarks that it is, "framed by perceptions, concepts, and imaginings that cannot be reducd to human, rational consciousness." (19) Raia Prokhovnik reminds us that, "The idea of difference, one of the major achievements of second-wave feminist theorising, was always unsatisfactory when still tied to the mind/body dichotomy because that dualism could not take body (or subjectivity or gendered or emotion) seriously." (20) The familiar opposition of woman as nature (body) to man as reason (mind) automatically results in the doctrine of man's inherent right to rule and to shape and master woman. However, the situation changes when the opposition and polarity of dichotomous thinking are replaced by concern for relationship and connection with others. Relationship "places the either/or position, which implies dominance/ subordination and self/other relationships, in the wider context of a both-and position. ... While the dominant term of a dichotomous pair perpetually asserts independence, the relational mode of thinking involves the invitation to acknowledge interdependence." (21)

The elision of the personal and the political by many feminists in the seventies at once springs to mind. Irigaray rejects the dividing of problems related to "sexuate difference and the problem of difference of race, of culture, of generation etc., [because they] affirm that the first concerns intimate life and the second the political world ... cultures and traditions are, in great part, constructed starting from sexual and sexuate difference , at the level of genealogies or marriages and alliances." (22) These remarks unite the personal and the political at a fundamental level. Third-wave feminist theory is likewise concerned with releasing the emotional/relational aspects of human understanding from repression and implacable preconception, and restoring it to the fullness of its natural origins.

Changing Aims and Styles

Elsewhere, younger feminists have busied themselves with reconciling the past and present of feminism. A political shift has visibly altered the aims and consequent style of some third-wave American feminists. Leslie Heywood and Jennifer Drake have thrown themselves unreservedly into an all-inclusive project, which is clearly directed to readers outside the middle class and academia. These feminists describe themselves as "hybrid. In addressing a broad and comprehensive audience, they prefer to assert their declassed position in popular and demotic language that at times evokes the work of Solanas. They strongly repudiate the conflation of third-wave feminism and post-feminist: ".. 3rd wave by no means defines our feminism as a groovier alternative to an over-and-done with feminist movement .. post-feminist characterises a group of young, conservative women who explicitly define themselves against and criticise feminists of the 2nd wave." (23) The procedure whereby they found the sort of contributors they were hoping for is highly illuminating: "We wanted, needed … a kind of writing that was intellectually rigorous and heartfelt and unpretentious at once … critical analysis without jargon, lived personal experience that was tied to the social scene." (24) The inclusiveness they were seeking was achieved by advertising on a nationwide scale . *3rd Wave Agenda* moves fluently between chapters that apply practical solutions to material problems and chapters that discuss the needs and nature of feminism in comparatively abstract terms. Both make use of a mixture of formal and informal language and gladly take on popular culture and politics of every shade. Of one of their contributors, they remark that she,"critically engages the Camille Paglia, Katie Roiphe, Naomi Wolf representations of third wave feminism … [she] argues for the value of feminist history and the need to make that history a more vital present part of contemporary culture." (25) This same contributor comments that, "academic feminists must intensify efforts to speak to the overall feminist community." (26) The book goes a long way towards fulfilling these aims and does not fear rejection or criticism resulting from taking explicit political positions. "Whereas second wave feminists strove for equality with men, third wave feminists cannot reasonably expect equality from capitalism." (27) And,"writers in 3rd Wave Agenda believe that living in a world that preserves the status quo of free market competition and upward mobility is not enough to maintain our sanity if it is even possible."(28) This political position perceives cooperation rather than competition as the foundation of rich relationships in a sane society.

Angela McRobbie, is a British third-wave feminist and sociologist who also succeeds in drawing in a wide audience . Using materials taken from both popular and high culture, she examines how feminist politics is currently pitting itself against right-wing, capitalist politics and its manipulations of the general public through the media. She does not represent this as a losing battle. Feminism is, she tells us, "a self-organised politics, taking place from the ground up, a kind of disputatious and contentious force.. [which] nevertheless has had enormous potential to create disruption and to bring about change." (29) One wonders if it is precisely this "self-organised" and quite often openly homemade quality of feminism that makes it such a slippery adversary. " .. what feminism actually means varies literally from one self-declared feminist to the next." She speaks about the unease experienced by governments that want to retain the status quo and yet represent themselves as gender aware, but she does not underestimate the techniques used to make feminism seem "monstrous, dogmatic and authoritarian." She notes how a subtle right wing dismissal of political correctness made in the name of commonsense "sews the seeds of doubt about various forms of radicalism. It devalues the women's movement and the anti-racist movement as sites of extremism , attractive only to angry and dangerous kinds of people." (30)

Women may not, of course, wish to avoid appearing angry and dangerous. A large number of young feminists now declare their anger. The politics of anger perhaps first surfaced in the ladette. A direct descendant of punk, she appeared early on this scene and became a widespread model for young women who resented the social restrictions imposed on their sex. She threw herself into in a boyish pursuit of pleasure in a theatrical and inverse variant of masquerade that redefined or even suspended her sex. The pseudo-male persona that gave her entry into male groups in fact supports Irigaray's claim that the controlling force in patriarchal cultures is male homosexuality. Though the media portrayed her as an unprecedented social disaster - irrational, aggressive, violent and 'unfeminine' - the ladette often only represented a carefree interlude in which the young woman smashed through barriers that had excluded her from male social preserves and activities. In an ironic awareness of masculine prejudices, some young activists have also parodied themselves as "sluts". However, the model of the angry young woman as the totality of today's feminist does not express the frequency with which this anger will later channel itself into more complex strategies for outmanoeuvering the narrow constraints of mainstream society.

Loose Connections, Odds and Ends

The effects of repressing the mother and of the destruction of maternal cultures have echoed through many of the chapters of this book. They have done so throughout the history of East and West, and from Ancient Greece to the London of Mary Wollestoncraft and on into the twentieth and twenty-first centuries. Freud's influence in re-establishing the virtual excision of a meaningful mother from the modern era has helped to construct a psychological orphanage in which loss of the mother does damage to boys and devastates girls. When Irigaray discusses what it means to be a girl-child in a phallocentric culture, she is keenly aware that the social conditioning the child receives will be utterly ruthless - woman "has to renounce her mother and her auto-eroticism in order not to love herself anymore. In order to love man alone." (31) The effects of this loss are painfully familiar. Women are forced into a self-negation and inward-turning hatred that can take on dramatic form in activities such as the self-harming common in women's prisons.

In certain respects, Irigaray's descriptions run parallel to those used by Deleuze and Guttari. Claire Colebrook shows how these two philosophers counter Freud's ideas on sexuality: ".. a true politics needs to think sexual flow, becoming and difference, *anti-oedipally*: against the idea of the child who represses its desire for its mother and becomes just like its father." (32) We are indoctrinated to believe that, if we are to enter into society and be part of human history, we must abandon our first love for our mother. This book has noted the deep sense of loss that follows from forsaking our maternal origins and perceptions such as that described by Bachofen, who saw the mother's love for her infant as the sole illuminating feature of the dark pre-historic era. In the Deleuzian view, "Politics begins from the image of 'man' as other than woman, as the being capable of renouncing biological life for cultural ends. 'Man' is therefore produced through the repression and prohibition of woman. The prohibition produces the law and bodies regulated by the law." (33) We have also seen how law (primarily the Law of the Father) occupies the immediate foreground, as fatherright displaces motherright in more than one classical Greek tragedy and men become dominant by suppressing feminine expressions of human culture. Freud's interpretation of the story of Oedipus as the primary example of human desire excludes its possible reference to the destruction of an earlier society that valued women and the meaning of the mother. It also elevates the fate of the individual above the fate of the collective, a move that reinstalls hierarchy and individualism as if no more communal alternative should or could exist. Colebrook describes the philosophical framework of two third-wave feminists who argue for "the central role of the imagination in sexual politics," and work from the premise that, "One's identity is not one's own but is formed through our perception of others and of the political whole." Either one imagines ".. a political whole or culture capable of creating and affirming difference " or "the white male body of reason becomes *the* norm for the political body." (34) The psychological interpretations promoted in Freudian doctrines show up Freud"s own politically motivated agenda with floodlit clarity.

Questions of desire are inevitably political. Deleuze and Guttari renounce a system that bases desire on the repression of its origin . They contest a desire that is reduced to an individual ego that ignores its primary social and political sources. They see desire as "a flow of connection, production and ever more complex differentiation," and the Freudian story about incest as a means of prohibition that "*produces the mother* as a denied object and creates a law that ... turns the power of life against life." (35) 'Becoming-woman ' is an anti-oedipal, revolutionary antidote to this negation of life. Deleuze and Guttari turn towards a collective whole in which hierarchy, dichotomy and division have no place. They seek not only to dethrone man as the overlord of woman but mankind as the overlord of all non-human species. This not only shatters man's customary assumption of control, it flings him into a common space where he has no special destiny. The fact that man's right to rule is purely a product of his imagination does not give comfort to the chronically paranoid institutions of the status quo. And there is also the vexed question of women's relation to the spiritual. The exclusion of woman from spiritual matters troubled Luce Irigaray and several other second-wave feminists, but third-wave feminism is more preoccupied with a universe where man exists on an equal footing with other, non-abstract, living things. Deleuze is anything but an essentialist. He sees the full collective of being as made up of a continuing stream of events rather than of solid, readily identifiable blocs. Traditional perceptions of god and the individual both become redundant in the encounter with the Deleuzian life force, which he construes as desire. The incomprehensible vastness of this full collective cuts the ground from beneath the religious patriarchy.

The feminist may note that the male who seeks to privilege himself and subordinate women is himself usually being subordinated by other wealthy and power wielding males at the top of a pyramidal structure. Conflicts between males are ubiquitous and legendary. They spill over with heroism, ideology, revolution and bloodshed. From time to time some of these struggles will procure improvements in the lives of less privileged women and men, but in most cases a dethroned leader or regime will rapidly be replaced by some other self-privileging, dominant male or regime and bloody seizures of power have usually led to further bloodshed. The revolution of 'becoming woman' is different in kind. 'Becoming woman' transforms the meaning of being human and replants meaning in a ground that cannot be secured as the exclusive property of single individuals, groups, genders or species.

Resonances both of the 'being nothing' that Cordelia and Sor Juana preferred over a false identity and of the less deliberately self-annihilating 'not being one' of Irigaray haunt the comment that, for Deleuze, woman "is never done with becoming imperceptible, that is with going back through a kind of zero degree that makes possible mutations and new becomings" …

which also includes "the becoming feminist of women *and* men. Women and their (virtual) bodies exist only in contexts from which they continue to turn away." (36) Restoring the body along with the mother, a theme extensively developed in the work of Elizabeth Grosz, is another important aspect of third-wave feminist theory. And more unexpectedly and somewhat obliquely, Valerie Solanas also prefigures the Deluzian 'becoming woman' who is not confined to any gender. In her *erasure* of sex, she proposes that a woman may be a man and vice versa. In *Scum Manifesto*, the sex of the individual is defined less by biological difference than by her/his philosophical and political stance. And Angela Carter breaks away from traditional woman with Sade's male-identifying female in order to reveal the intensely misogynistic despair of Sade and every other libertine and to reinstate a non-masochistic, feminine erotic that expresses another aspect of 'becoming woman'.

Finally, discussions of feminine language, silence and writing here have said very little about *style*. Deleuze once again fills this gap with his descriptions of feminine forms, termed the "free indirect" style, and makes special reference to Virginia Woolf's *The Waves*. Deleuze and Guttari speak of "a collective assemblage" that does not take on a "transcendent position outside life" or "a higher moralism". (37) Ursula Le Guin's unusual anthropological fantasy, *Always Coming Home,* also exemplifies feminine style. With no protagonist and the proliferation of multitude of small incidents, the collective accumulates more importance than the individual. (38)

The third volume of the *Native Tongue* trilogy, *Earthsong*, also bypasses the usual ways of representing the individual and sets going a huge chorus of different voices, belonging to both the living and the dead, the past and the present. In many ways, this volume spans the gap between past and present feminisms. When we take "second- and third-wave feminist histories together: the resulting juxtaposition of feminist visions both enriches and challenges us." (39)

In her novel, *Lolly Willowes,* (40) Sylvia Townsend Warner likens middle-aged women without male consorts to blackberries: "I seem to see all over England, all over Europe, women living and growing old, as common as blackberries, and as unregarded." The simile of a stock that escapes control and extends through subterranean connections prefigures the metaphor, "rhizomatic thinking" which Rosi Braidotti uses to describe how feminism travels underground and emerges in many other locations. She speaks of "a self that, not being One, functions as a relay point for many sets of intensive intersections and encounters with multiple others. Moreover, not being burdened with being One, such a subject can envisage forms of resistance and political agency that are multi-layered and complex." (41) This framework undermines the rigid structures prescribed by logic and jettisons the requirement that all parts of an idea should be visibly and rationally interconnected. Braidotti describes feminism as "passionate, humourous, and politically rigorous" and "disrespectful of dominant norms." She comments, "the collective endeavour of the women's movement is one of the most successful political experiments of the twentieth century."(42) The expression of values that are feminine in either small or large form has been suppressed by a masculinism existing on both natural and supernatural levels, but one glance at the history of women shows how far woman has travelled in a gruelling and often belittled journey to reach a new 'becoming'. To become free in a social order where for millenia one sex has been subjected to the will of another is difficult enough. But the liberation of women is also a quest to find freedom from a history of constraint coming from their own thoughts and perceptions. As Genevieve Lloyd writes, "The life of freedom is the life in which it becomes possible to gain insight into the fictions that are current and replace them with better fictions." (43) Lloyd is construing freedom of thought as the raw material out of which all other forms of freedom must be made.

So what freedoms lie ahead for feminism and where will the rising surge of its "fourth wave" take us? So far, this wave is youthful, vigorous and wide-ranging enough to extend from deeply serious initiatives, as in campaigns against female genital mutilation or domestic violence, to more localised and sunnier appearances where, simply by their unprecedented numbers or even in semi-comic demonstrations, women are ripping apart codes relating to their conduct and comportment. It is too early to predict what this new resurgence will bring . But it is already clear that feminism is no longer a minority movement and is at last recognising its own potential scale and the power of its rapidly evolving diversity. With luck, it will not only dissolve traditional female stereotypes but also abolish the idea that there must be a given prototype or single model to which women should conform. To give unalterable meaning to *woman* or even to *feminine* is to participate in the patriarchal myth.

Footnotes

1) It is tempting to speculate on whether feminism was among the causes that swarmed together to produce the collapse of the traditions of morality that underpinned the patriarchal order.

2) Prokhovnik, Raia. *RationalWoman:A FeministCritique of Dichotomy.* p.186 Manchester University Prtess 1999.

3) The term used by the philosopher, Gilles Deleuze,

4) I came upon the philosophy of Gilles Deleuze and Felix Guttari comparatively lately and so have mainly relied on Claire Colebrook's lucid expositions of their thinking and relevance to feminism rather than trusting myself with imperfectly digested primary sources.

5) Colebrook, Claire. *Deleuze and Feminist Theory.* p 11. Ed. Ian Buchan and Claire Colebrook. Edinburgh University Press. 2000. in reference to Deleuze and Guttari's 1987 work, *A Thousand Plateaus: Capitalism and Schizophrenia.*

6) Grosz, Elizabeth. 'Deleuze's Bergson: Duration, the Virtual and a Politics of the Future.' *Deleuze and Feminist. Theory..* p.216.

7) ibid. p. 217

8) Saunders, Lise Shapiro. *Third Wave Feminism: a critical exploration.* p.6. Edited by Stacy Gillis, Gillian Howie, Rebecca Mumford. Palgrave Macmillan. 2007.

9) Le Doeuff, Michèle. *The Philosophical Imaginary* p.55 Continuum.2002. (First published 1980)

10) ibid. p. 54.

11) Lloyd, Genevieve. *No One's Land: Australia and the Philosophical Imagination.* Hypatia 2000 p.38.

12) de Beauvoir, Simone. *The Second Sex* p.772 Vintage 2011.

13) "The Anglo-American distinction between biological sex and socially constructed gender identity rules out the possibility of thinking the primariily psychoanalytical concept of 'sexualite'." French terms are not "physiological or psychical, but made up of fantasies and desires." Stella Sandford. p. 23-30. Radical Philosophy. 165.

14) *Third Wave Feminism: a critical exploration.* p.285.

15) ibid. p. 287.

16) Colebrook, Claire. *Deleuze & Feminist Theory.* p.4. edit Ian Buchanan &Claire Colebrook. Edinburgh University Press. 2000.

17) Braidotti, Rosi. *Nomadic Theory.* p.34.. Columbia University Press. 2011

18) Colebrook. *Deleuze and Feminist Theory.* p.2

19) Braidotti. *Nomadic Theory.* p.3

20) Prokhovnik, Raia. *Rational Woman: A Feminist Critique of Dichotomy.* p.170 Manchester University Prtess. 1999.

21) Prokhovnik ibid. p.50. I do not propose to discuss questions such as sex/gender and other dichotomies that Prokhovnik subjects to analysis.

22) As cited in *Third Wave Feminism: a critical exploration* p.290

23). Heywood, Leslie and Jennifer Drake. *3rd Wave Agenda* p.1.

24) ibid. p.1.

25) ibid. p.14

26) Soriso,Carolyn. ibid p.16

27) Sadler, Michelle. Ibid. p 22

28) ibid p. 17

29) McRobbie, Angela. *The Aftermath of Feminism: Gender,Culture and Social Change.* p.2. Sage 2008.

30) ibid. p.37.

31) As quoted in chapter 3, *Sixteen Takes on a Self Invented Woman*

32) Colebrook, Claire. *Deleuze*. p143. Routledge 2002.

33) ibid. p.143.

34) ibid p 149 The reference is to Moira Gatens and Genevieve Lloyd

35) ibid p. 143.

36) Conley,Verena Andermatt. *Deleuze & Feminist Theory*. edited Ian Buchanan and Claire Colebrook p.29. Edinburgh University Press. 2000.

37) Colebrook. *Deleuze* p113. In literary criticism, the term for this style is "free indirect".

38) . Le Guin's preferred title for *Always Coming Home* (Bantam Books. 1986) was *The Meandering Water Tribe* because" a feminist revolution – the only one that has any chance of succeeding – would have to meander towards its goal. Patriarchal revolutions (which always fail) go in a straight line, in a hurry…" She praises water as a metaphor for feminist force because it "wears away resistance gently but inexorably, over time, and is almost impossible to withstand."

39) Afterword by Susan M. Squier & Julie Vedder in Elgin, Suzette Hayden. *Earthsong,*. p267. Feminist Press 2000. (First published 1994)

40) Townsend Warner, Sylvia *Lolly Willowes,* p.234. The Women's Press. I978 (first published1926)

41) Braidotti. op cit pps 283-4

42) Braidotti. op cit p 276.

43) Lloyd, Genevieve. The Power of Spinoza: Feminist Conjunctions. Susan James interviews Genevieve Lloyd and Moira Gatens. Hypatia 2000. p. 55-56

Bibliography

A

Allende, Isabelle. Eva Luna, pps 3&21. Penguin. 1989.

Apuleius, Lucius. The Golden Asse. 2nd century. translated by William Adlington (1566). Collier Books, N.Y. 1967.

Aretino, Pietro. The School of Whoredom. Hesperus Press Ltd., London, 2003.

Jane Arthurs, Revolting Women: The Body in Comic Performance. ed Jane Arthurs and Jean Grimshaw. Cassell, London, 1999.

B

J.J. Bachofen, *Mother Right,* An Investigation of the Religious and Juridical Character

Matriarchy in the Ancient World, 1926. *Myth, Religion and Mother Right, Selected writings of J.J. Bachofen*. Routledge & Kegan Paul, London, 1967.

Bateson. Mind and Nature. Wildwood House, London, 1979.

Bateson, Gregory. Naven. Cambridge Univ. Press. 1936

Beauvoir, Simone de. *The Second Sex*. . Translated by Constance Borde & Sheila Malovany-Chevalier. Vintage.2011

Beauvoir, Simone de. *Must We Burn de Sade?* Grove Press. 1966.

Beauvoir, Simone de, interview with Marx and Courtivron. ed. New French Feminisms Harvester Press, UK 1981.

Berneri, Marie Louise. *Journey Through Utopia.* Freedom Press. London 1982. (first published 1950.)

Birnbaum, Lucia Chiavola. Liberazione della donna, feminism in Italy. Wesleyan University Press. USA. 1986.

Black Rose Anarcho-Feminists. *The Anarch-Feminist Manfesto.* Siren: A Journal of Anarcho Feminism. Volume 1, No 1. Chicago.

Bloom, Harold. Omens of the Millenium, Fourth Estate. London. 1996.

Braidotti, Rosi. *Nomadic Theory: the Portable Rosi Braidotti.* Columbia University Press. 2011.

Braund, S.H. 'A Woman's Voice? Laronia's role in Juvenal's Satire 2'. Women in Antiquity. ed Richard Hawley & Barbara Levick. Routledge. London. 1995.

Briffault, Robert.. The Mothers. Allen & Unwin. 1959. (first published 1927)

Brown, N.O.. *Love's Body.*

Buchanan, Ian & Colebrook, Claire. Deleuze and Feminist Theory. Edinburgh University Press. UK 2000.

C

Roberto Calasso, *The Marriage of Cadmus and Harmony*, Jonathan Cape, 1988.

Carter, Angela. *Nights at the Circus.* Picadoe, 1984.

Carter, Angela. The Magic Toyshop. Heinemann. 1967.

Carter, Angela. *The Sadeian Woman.* Virago. London 1979.

Carter, Angela, Alison's Giggle. Shaking a Leg. Vintage. 1998.

Chaudhiri, Shohini. *Feminist film theorists - Laura Mulvey,*

Kaja Silverman, Theresa de Laurentis. Taylor & Francis 2006

Cixous, Hélene & Clément, Catherine. The Newly-Born Woman. Theory and History of Literature, Vol 24. Manchester University Press. 1986.

Clément, Catherine.. *Bildoungue Roman. Une Vie de Freud?* Christian Bourgois Editeur, Paris, 1978.Clément, Catherine. Jesus au Bucher. Editions du Seuil.2000.

Clément Catherine. Enclave Esclave. *French Feminisms* (L'arc no 61, 1975)

Clément, Catherine. New French Feminisms, ed. Elaine Marks & Isabelle de Courtivron.. Harvester Press, U.K. 1981.

Clément, Catherine. *The Weary Sons of Freud*. Verso. 1987.

Colebrook, Claire. *Gilles Deleuze* . Routledge Critical Thinkers. 2002.

Coleman, E.A.M.. *The Dramatic Use of Bawdy in Shakespeare*. Longman. London. 1974.

Conley, Verena Andermatt. *Deleuze & Feminist Theory*. edited Ian Buchanan and Claire Colebrook p.29. Edinburgh University Press. 2000.

D

Daly, Mary. *Gyn/Ecology*. The Women's Press. London. 1979.

Delphy, Christine. *The Invention of French Feminism: An Essential Move*. Yale French Studies. No 87

Deren, Maya. The Voodoo Gods. Paladin, 1975, UK.

Derrida, Jacques. Choreographies, p69. Diacritics, Summer 1982.

Derrida, Jacques. *Of Grammatology*. John Hopkins Univ Press. 1976.

Derrida, Jacques. *Spurs/ Eperons*. University of Chicago Press.

Dinensen, Isak. Last Tales. The Blank Page

le Doeuff, Michele. The Philosophical Imaginary Continuum, London & N.Y. 2002. Dodderidge, Esme. *The New Gulliver*. The Women's Press. 1988.

Donne, John. Collected Works.

Douglas, Mary. Implicit Meanings. Routledge & Kegan Paul. 1975

Douglas, Mary. Purity and Danger. Routledge & Kegan Paul. 1966

Duras, Marguerite. New French Feminisms. Signs. Winter 1975.

Dworkin, Andrea, *Pornography*. The Women's Press, London, 1981.

E

Easton, Susan. 'Hegel and Feminism', Radical Philosophy no 38, Summer 1984, UK.

Elgin, Suzette Haden. Native Tongue, The Women's Press 1985

Elgin, Suzette Haden The Judas Rose, The Women's Press, 1988,

Elgin, Suzette Haden Earth Song, Feminist Press, City University of N.Y. 2002.

Eliade, Mircea. *Techniques of Yoga.*

F

Figes, Eva. Patriarchal Attitudes.

Fox Keller, Evelyn. Reflections on Gender and Science, Yale University, 1985.

Freud, Sigmund & Jung, C.G. The Freud/ Jung Letters (Hogarth Press & Routledge Kegan Paul. 1974)

BIBLIOGRAPHY

Freud Sigmund. Volume 7 On Sexuality. Taboo of Virginity

G

Gallop, Jane Feminism and Psychoanalysis . Macmillan, London, 1982.

Gallop, Jane., *Reading Lacan*, Cornell University Press, 1985.

Gautier, Xaviere, Is there Such a Thing as Women's Writing? New French Feminisms, ed. Elaine Marks & Isabelle de Courtivron, p.63-4. Harvester Press ltd 1981.

Ghandi, Mahatma. All Men Are Brothers. Life and Thoughts of Mahatma Gandhi as told In His Own Words. Navajivan Publishing House. Ahmedabad. 1960.

Gilligan, Carol. In a Different Voice: Psychological Theory and Women's Development, Harvard University Press. Cambridge, Mass and London. 1982.

Ginzburg, Carlo. Ecstasies, Deciphering the Witches' Sabbath, Hutchinson Radius, London. 1990.

Goodman, Lizbeth 'Gender and Humour and Comic Subversions.' Imagining Women: Cultural Representations and Gender, Polity Press, 1992.

Griffin, Susan. *Pornography and Silence*. Harper Row. 1981.

Groddeck, Georg. *Exploring the Unconscious: Unconscious Symbolism in Language and Art. 1927.* Vision Press. London. 1949.

Gross, Elisabeth. Leftwright,, Intervention Publications 20, 1986, Australia

Grosz, Elizabeth.. 'Deleuze's Bergson: Duration, the Virtual and a Politics of the Future.' *Deleuze and Feminist. Theory.*

Grosz, Elizabeth. Sexual Subversions. Allen & Unwin. Australia. 1989.

361

Gubar, Susan. The Blank Page: Issues of Female Creativity. Writing and Sexual Difference, ed E. Abel, Harvester Press. 1982.

Guzzani, Sabina. Revolution is Possible. Italian television series, terminated after Episode 1.

H

Harding, James M. *Cutting Performances: Collage Events, Feminist Artists & the American Avant-Garde.* University of Michigan Press. 2010.

Harding, James M. The Simplest Surrealist Act: Valerie Solanas and the (re)Assertion of Avantgarde Priorities. The Drama Review 45. Winter 2001.

Harrison, Jane, Prolegomena to the study of Greek Religion (1903), Meridian Books, USA, 1966

Heath, Stephen , Notes on Suture, *Screen*, vol 19.

Heller, Dana. Shooting Solanas. Feminist Studies, Vol 27. Issue 1, 2001.

Heywood, Leslie & Drake,Jennifer. *3rd Wave Agenda*

hooks, bell. Feminisms. Oxford Reader. O.U.P. Oxford - New York. 1997.

Hrdy, Sarah Blaffer. Mother Nature, Vintage, 2000.

I

Irigaray, Luce. An Ethics of Sexual Difference, The Athlone Press, London, 1993.

Irigaray, Luce. *Between East and West, from Singularity to Community.* Columbia University Press. 2002.

Irigaray, Luce. Elemental Passions. The Athlone Press. London. 1992.

Irigaray, Luce, Democracy Begins Between Two. The Athlone Press, London 2000.

Irigaray, Luce. Meres et filles vue par Luce Irigary. Libération. 1979.

Irigaray, Luce. The Other: Woman. Feminisms. Oxford Reader. O.U.P. 1997.

Irigaray, Luce. Sexes & Genealogies, from. p.203. Columbia University Press.USA. 1993

Irigaray. Speculum of the Other Woman. Cornell University Press.. 1985.

Irigaray, Luce. The Question of the Other. Yale French Studies 87. Yale University. 1995.

Irigaray, Luce. *The Way of Love. Continuum.* 2002

Irigaray, Luce. When the goods get together. New French Feminisms, ed Elaine Marks and Isabelle de Courtivron. The Harvester Press. 1984

J

Jones, Ann Rosalind. Editor's Introduction to Catherine Clemént's *The Weary Sons of Freud*. Verso 1987

K

Kahn, Coppelia."Excavating those Dim Minoan Regions: Maternal Subtexts in Patriarchal Literature." *Diacritics* Summer 1982.

Kappeler, Susanne. *The Pornography of Representation*. Polity Press, 1986.

Katz, Marilyn A. Ideology and 'the status of women' in ancient Greece, Women in Antiquity ed Richard Hawley & Barbara Levick, Routledge, 1995.

Keller, Evelyn Fox.*Reflections on Gender and Science.*

Kelly, Mary. ,Imaging Desire, Massachusetts Institute of Technology. 1996.

Kornegger, Peggy. Anarchism: The Feminist Connection. Quiet Rumours: an Anarcha-Feminist anthology. Dark Star, London. (Second Wave. Fall, 1975.)

Kramer, Heinrich & Sprenger, James. Malleus Maleficarum, (1486) Arrow Books, London, 1971.

Kristeva, Julia. *About Chinese Women*, Marion Boyars,

London, 1977

L

Lacan,Jacques. Ecrits, A Selection. Tavistock Publications Ltd. 1977

Le Doeuff, Michele. The Philosophical Imaginary. Continuum, London & N.Y. 2002.

Lee, Tanith. *Madame Two Swords*. Donald M. Grant. West Press. 1988.

Lefanu, Sarah. In the Chinks of the World Machine, The Women's Press. 1988.

Le Guin, Ursula. Always Coming Home.   Also, see correspondence with Tiptree in Julie Phillips biography.

Leon, Celine T, *Feminist Interpretations of Simone de Beauvoir..* ed Simons, Margaret A. Penn State Press. 1995.

Lewis, CS. *The Allegory of Love.* (1936) Galaxy Book. 1958.

Lispector, Clarice, *The Hour of the Star.* (Brazilian ed. 1977) Carcenet Press. Manchester. 1992.

Lloyd, Genevieve. *No One's Land: Australia and the Philosophical Imagination*. Hypatia. 2000.

Lloyd, Genevieve. The Power of Spinoza: Feminist Conjunctions. Susan James interviews Genevieve Lloyd and Moira Gatens. Hypatia 2000.

Lubac, Henri de, S.J. The Eternal Feminine, A Study on the Poem by Teilhard de Chardin. Collins. London. 1971.

M

MacKinnon, Catharine, *Feminism Unmodified*, Harvard. 1987.

Mahoney, Maureen A. The Problem of Silence in Feminist Psychology. Feminist Studies, Fall 1996.

Malinowski, The Sexual Life of Savages in North-Western Melanesia.

Maraini, Dacia. *Bagheria.* Peter Owen. 1994.

Maraini, Dacia. The Silent Duchess (translated Dick Kitto and Elspeth Spottiswood) Peter Owen, London, 1992.

Marai, Sandor. *Embers.* Penguin. 2003.

Marie de Champagne (and André Capellanus). Treatise on Love and the Remedies of Love, (12th century)

Masson, Jeffrey. The Assault on Truth: Freud's Suppression of the Seduction Theory .   Farar, Straus & Giroux. 1984

McRobbie, Angela, *The Aftermath of Feminism: Gender, Culture and Social Change.* Sage 2008.

Meade, Marion. *Eleanor of Acquitaine.* EP Dutton 1977, Orion Books 2001.

Mernissi., Fatima.   *Beyond the Veil: Male-Female Dynamics in Muslim Society.* revised .. Al Saqui Books. London. 1985.

Michelet, Jules. *La Sorciere*, Garnier Flammarion, Paris.

Millett, Kate. Sexual Politics. Abacus, London, 1972.

Millot, Catherine, The Feminine Superego, from The Woman in Question, ed Parveen Adams & Elizabeth Cowie, Verso, London, 1990

Mills, Sara; Pearce, Lynne; Spaull, Sue; Millard, Elaine.Feminist Readings/ Feminists Reading. Harvester. UK 1989.

Mills, Patricia Jagentowicz, 'Hegel's Antigone', Feminist Interpretations of G.W.F. Hegel, ed Patricia Jagentowicz Mills. Penn State University, 1996.

Minow, Martha. Adjudicating Differences. *Conflicts in Feminism.* ed. Hirsch , Marianne &. Fox Keller, Evelyn. Routledge 1990.

Mitchell, Juliet & Jacqueline Rose. Feminine Sexuality: Jacques Lacan & the Ecole Freudienne. Macmillan Press. London. 1982.

Mitchell, Juliet. *Psychoanalysis and Feminism*. Allen&Lane and Random House. 1974. Vintage Books. 1975.

Moi, Toril. *What is a Woman?* OUP 1999.

Montrelay, Michèle. Inquiry into Femininity. m/f 1. 1978.

Morris, Meaghan. The Pirate's Fiancée. Verso. 1988

.Morrow, James. The Last Witchfinder, Weidenfeld & Nicholson, London, 2006.

O

Oakley, Ann.. What is a Housewife? *British Feminist Thought, ed Terry Lovell.* Basil Blackwell, 1990.

The Orestia, translation by Ted Hughes. Faber & Faber, London, 1999.

P

Paz, Octavio. *The Monkey Grammarian..* Peter Owen Publishers. London 1989

Phillips, Julie. James Tiptree, Jr. The Double Life of Alice B. Sheldon. St.Martin's Press, N.Y. 2006.

Pollet , Katha, on Dworkin in The Nation, May 2, 2005.

Prokhovnik, Raia. *Rational Woman A feminist critique of dichotomy.* Manchester University Press.2002.

R

Ranke-Heinemann, Uta. Eunuchs for the Kingdom of Heaven. Penguin, 1991.

Réage, Pauline. *L'histoire d'O.*

Reed, Evelyn. Woman's Evolution. Pathfinder. USA. 1974.

Riding, Laura. The Mask. Selected Poems.

Riviere, Joan. *Womanliness as Masquerade*. IJP X, 1929

Ronell, Avita. Introduction to SCUM Manifesto, Verso 2004.

Rougement, Denis de. , Passion and Society, Faber & Faber, London, 1962.

Rowe, Kathleen. The Unruly Woman: Gender and the Genres of Laughter. University of Texas. 1995

Russ, Joanna, The Female Man. The Women's Press. U.K. 1985.

Russ, Joanna, 'The Subjunctivity of Science Fiction', Extrapolation, 15.

Russo, Mary. The Female Grotesque: Risk, Excess and Modernity. Routledge. 1994

S

Sadler, Michelle, *3rd Wave Agenda.* Leslie Heywood and Jennifer Drake

Stella Sandford. Radical Philosophy. 165.

Saunders,Lise Shapiro. *Third Wave Feminism: a critical exploration.* Edited by Stacy Gillis, Gillian Howie, Rebecca Mumford. Palgrave Macmillan. 2007.

Shrage, Laurie. The fallacies of anti-porn feminism. Feminist Theory, Volume 6, Number 1.

Sen, K.M.. Hinduism. Penguin. 1961.

Shorter, Edward. A History of Women's Bodies. Pelican Books. U>K> 1984.

Showalter, Elaine. The Female Malady. Pantheon Books. 198

Showalter, Elaine. Sexual Anarchy.. Penguin 1990.

Simons, Margaret A. Introduction to *Feminist Interpretations of Simone de Beauvoir*, ed. Margaret A. Simons. Penn State Press. 1995.

Snitow, Ann, A Gender Diary. Conflicts in Feminism ed Marianne Hirsch & Evelyn Fox Keller. Routledge, N.Y. & London. 1990.

Solanas, Valerie. *Scum Manifesto*: 1) Verso. 2004

(introduction by Avita Ronell); 2) Olympia Press. 1983 (introduction by Maurice Girodias); 3) Matriarchy Study Group.1983; 4) Mille et Une Nuits (introduced by Michèl Houellebecq) 1998.

Sophocles, Antigone,. translation by Robert Fagles. Penguin Classics. U.K. 1984

Soriso, Carolyn. 3rd *Wave Agenda.* Leslie Heywood and Jennifer Drake

Stallybrass, Peter and White, Allon . The Poetics and Politics of Transgression. Metheun. London. 1986.

Stendhal, Love. Paul Elek, London 1959.

Stendhal. *Le Rouge et le Noir.*

Swift, Jonathan. *A Vindication of the Beggars' Opera.* See also *A Modest Proposal.*

W

Warner, Sylvia Townsend. Lolly Willowes, The Women's Press, London 1978 (first ed1926

Warner, Sylvia Townsend.The Mother Tongue, One Thing Leading to Another (p.135) Virago Press, 1990.

Weedon, Chris.   *Feminist Practice & Poststructuralist Practice.* Basil Blackwell. 1987

Wilson, Leslie.   Malefice, Picador, Pan Books, London. 1992..

Winnicott, D.W, Home Is Where We Start From,. Penguin Books, London, 1986.

Winnicott, D.W. *Playing and Reality.* Penguin Books. 1974.

Women's Report Collective: Pornography. *No Turning Back*, Ed. Feminist Anthology Collective. The Women's Press, London, 1981.

Wood, Sharon. Italian Women's Writing - 1860 - 1994 Athlone. London & Atlantic Highlands. 1995.

Wood, Sharon. "The Language of the Body and Dacia Maraini's Marianna Ucria." Journal of Gender Studies, Nov 1993.

Z

Zoline, Pamela. The Heat Death of the Universe. *Busy About the Tree of Life*. The Women's Press. London. 1988.

Index

INDEX